MW00581511

Cuneiform Texts from the Folios of W. G. Lambert, Part One

Mesopotamian Civilizations

Cuneiform Texts *from the* Folios *of* W. G. Lambert, Part One

PREPARED FOR PUBLICATION AND EDITED BY
A. R. GEORGE AND JUNKO TANIGUCHI

EISENBRAUNS | University Park, Pennsylvania

Library of Congress Cataloging-in-Publication Data

Names: George, A. R., editor. | Taniguchi, Junko, 1971–
    editor. | Lambert, W. G. (Wilfred G.)
Title: Cuneiform texts from the folios of W.G. Lambert,
    Part 1 / prepared for publication and edited by
    A.R. George and Junko Taniguchi.
Other titles: Mesopotamian civilizations ; 24.
Description: University Park, Pennsylvania : Eisenbrauns,
    [2019]– | Series: Mesopotamian civilizations ; 24 | Includes
    bibliographical references and index.
Summary: "A collection of drawings of 329 cuneiform
    tablets, found in the academic papers of W. G. Lambert,
    one of the foremost Assyriologists of the twentieth
    century. Texts range from historical inscriptions to literary
    and scholarly texts, written by Babylonian and Assyrian
    scribes"—Provided by publisher.
Identifiers: LCCN 2019026883 | ISBN 9781575067339 (v. 1 ;
    hardback)
Subjects: LCSH: Akkadian language—Texts—Catalogs. |
    Cuneiform inscriptions, Akkadian—Catalogs. | Sumerian
    language—Texts—Catalogs. | Cuneiform inscriptions,
    Sumerian—Catalogs.
Classification: LCC PJ3711 .C864 2019 | DDC 892/.1—dc23
LC record available at https://lccn.loc.gov/2019026883

CONTENTS

PREFACE AND ACKNOWLEDGMENTS

The late W. G. Lambert taught himself to copy cuneiform texts in the British Museum in the early 1950s and became a master of the art. He continued to make his distinctive pencil drawings until 2011, the year of his death. Many were published in his books, *Babylonian Wisdom Literature, Babylonian Literary Texts* (CT 46), *Atra-ḫasīs, Babylonian Oracle Questions*, and *Babylonian Creation Myths*, and in his very many journal articles, book chapters, and minor works. Lambert's achievement as a copyist is summed up in a biographical memoir commissioned by the British Academy (George 2015b: 338–39):

> [In 1951] he became a regular visitor to the Students' Room in the Department of Egyptian and Assyrian Antiquities at the British Museum. Here, under the initial guidance of the assistant keeper D. J. Wiseman (1918–2010), he taught himself to draw cuneiform texts from the original clay tablets. He had a very good eye for cuneiform signs but was not a born draughtsman and found it difficult at first to produce drawings with which he was satisfied. Quite soon, however, he had developed his own distinctive style. It was a compromise between the exact drawings of the kind produced by natural artists like Arno Poebel (which he admired enormously) and the freehand "copies" of prolific cuneiformists like R. Campbell Thompson (which he did not). In pursuit of clarity, he straightened slanting lines of text and introduced space between them. In pursuit of accuracy, he measured the horizontal distances between the vertical wedges of all the cuneiform signs on a given line of text and mapped them on to ruled paper, reproducing the signs as they were written, not in standardized form. He drew the whole at two, three or four times lifesize, having learned that publishers of illustrated books required artwork in magnified form, so as to give a neater effect when reduced in publication.

> In this way he produced beautifully clear cuneiform copies which made the text easier to read than the clay tablet from which it was taken, replicated the distinctive character of the ductus, and retained the exact proportions of the signs and any breaks in the surface. This latter point was essential, for Lambert insisted that a good Assyriologist should try to read what was damaged as well as what was clear, and to that end reproduction of the line of text in exact proportion, signs, damage and breaks, was paramount. What he did not do, in common with many others of that time, was attempt to represent a clay tablet as an archaeological object. Though he was certainly alive to the information that could be obtained from examining the physical object, especially the curvature of its surfaces and the place of its edges in relation to the inscription, he did not deem it necessary to include in his copies large expanses of broken clay. For him, a clay tablet was foremost a vehicle for cuneiform text, and it was the inscribed surface alone that he reproduced in drawing.

So prolific was Lambert's production of copies of cuneiform texts that he left on his death a very large number of sheets of drawings (folios), sorted by genre into folders and stored in a filing cabinet in his bedroom in Birmingham. In the months following the removal of Lambert's academic *Nachlass* to Buckhurst Hill, the sheets were numbered and indexed by the present editors. The individual sheets of cuneiform copies bear the folio numbers 1–92, 225, 405–91, 762–1031, 1064–2046, 4117, 4307, 4596, 6141–297, 6304, 6690–92, 6704, 7302–8, 8211–25, 29202. Many copies occupy several folios. Some drawings are copies that had been published and then returned to their maker (220+), and others are copies by other scholars (49+), but by far the majority of them are copies that Lambert made but did not see published. Three hundred and twenty-nine of these previously unpublished copies fill the present volume. The remaining portion will fill a second.

The texts collected in this volume are organized by genre: commemorative and votive inscriptions (nos. 1–8), late copies of royal inscriptions (nos. 9–18), other historical and historical-literary compositions (nos. 19–24), late copies of royal correspondence (nos. 25–31), Sumerian literary compositions (nos. 32–39), Akkadian-language compositions of mythological and "epic" content (nos. 40–55), Babylonian and Assyrian hymns, prayers, and praise poetry (nos. 56–166), incantations (nos. 167–251), wisdom literature (nos. 252–317), and fragments of unidentified literary compositions (nos. 318–29). Drawings of divination prayers (*ikrib*s), omen compendia, expository and scholarly texts, god-lists and lexical lists, will appear in the second volume in due course.

Most of the drawings are copies of cuneiform tablets and fragments in the British Museum, made in the 1950s and early 1960s during Lambert's summer vacations in London and later, after his move to Birmingham in 1964, during his weekly visits to the museum's Students' Room. This first volume contains 301 British Museum pieces, consisting of 438 numbered fragments and a few without numbers. Many of the pieces were joined by Lambert himself and bear witness to his remarkable talent for identifying broken fragments and reconstructing larger pieces from them. The volume is the largest publication of the British Museum's tablets to have appeared for a considerable time. The drawings of the other twenty-eight cuneiform texts published here were made at museums in Berlin, Birmingham, Cambridge (UK), Cambridge (Mass.), Durham, Istanbul, Manchester, Oxford, Philadelphia, and Sheffield. On Lambert's behalf, the editors acknowledge with gratitude the kind consent of the authorities of all these museums to the publication of his drawings of objects in their care.

Very few of the pencil copies had been inked in at the time of their creator's death, but they were all intended for eventual publication, because Lambert did not usually make rough copies and did not go to the trouble of making a drawing unless he intended to publish it. It is equally certain that Lambert would have collated each drawing against the original tablet before inking it. This exercise has probably been carried out for very few of the drawings, so that inevitably some corrections and alterations that he would have made have not been made. We did not think it appropriate as editors to tamper with the drawings ourselves and for that reason have not collated them, except in a handful of cases where we were in no doubt that Lambert would himself have made an alteration.

The pencil drawings have been finished by the editors using the technique of digital inking that was employed by Henry Buglass and Junko Taniguchi to complete the plates of Lambert's last book, *Babylonian Creation Myths* (2013). Some of Buglass's images were not used in that book and are published here. The credit for inking is as follows: by pen, Lambert: text nos. 2, 7, 10, 53, 71–72, 237, 241, 246, 250, 286, 292, 297, 316, 328; digitally, Buglass: nos. 47–50, 133, 245; Taniguchi: nos. 1, 3–4, 6, 9, 20–22, 26–31, 34, 42–46, 56–61, 63–70, 73, 75, 77–118, 120–21, 123–27, 167–214, 230–36, 239–40, 242–44, 247–49, 251, 258, 279, 314, 319–21, 326; George: nos. 5, 8, 11–19, 23–25, 32–33, 35–41, 51–52, 54–55, 62, 74, 76, 119, 122, 128–32, 134–66, 215–29, 238, 252–57, 259–78, 280–85, 287–91, 293–96, 298–313, 315, 317–18, 322–25, 327, 329.

Some of the cuneiform tablets drawn by Lambert have subsequently been copied and published by other scholars. Except in a few cases we have thought it useful to publish Lambert's drawing nevertheless. His rare combination of unmatched experience in reading cuneiform and excellence in draughtmanship always brings greater understanding of each tablet he copied. It is important for scholarship that this life's work of a master cuneiformist is publicly available for consultation.

A small number of individual tablets raised questions that could be answered only by their curators. For responses to our queries we are indebted to Jon Taylor (British Museum), Craig Barclay and Rachel Barclay (University of Durham Oriental Museum), Lucilla Burn (Fitzwilliam Museum, Cambridge), and Grant Frame

(University Museum, Philadelphia). Stefan Maul (University of Heidelberg) kindly identified tablets in Berlin that are already published or forthcoming in the series *Keilschrifttexte aus Assur literarischen Inhalts.* Christopher Walker, Enrique Jiménez, Mary Frazer, and Zsombor Földi volunteered information and made important identifications. To all these institutions and individuals go the editors' grateful thanks.

The drawings of cuneiform tablets are preceded by a catalogue and an index. The catalogue draws on annotations made by Lambert on his copies and in his notebooks, and sometimes quotes them, but it is not his work, and failings therein and in the index are the responsibility of the first-named editor.

ARG
JT
Buckhurst Hill, June 2018

ABBREVIATIONS

ABL	R. F. Harper, *Assyrian and Babylonian Letters Belonging to the Kouyunjik Collections of the British Museum*, 14 vols. (Chicago, 1892–1914)
ADD	C. H. W. Johns, *Assyrian Deeds and Documents ... in the Kouyunjik Collections of the British Museum*, 4 vols. (Cambridge, 1898–1923)
AH	Abu Habba; tablet signature, British Museum
AMT	R. C. Thompson, *Assyrian Medical Texts* (London, 1923)
ANE	object signature, Fitzwilliam Museum, Cambridge
BAM	*Babylonisch-assyrisches Medizin* (Berlin, 1963–)
BCM	object signature, Birmingham City Museums
BE	*The Babylonian Expedition of the University of Pennsylvania, Series A: Cuneiform Texts* 1 = H. V. Hilprecht, *Old Babylonian Inscriptions Chiefly from Nippur*, 2 vols. (Philadelphia, 1893, 1896)
BM	tablet signature, British Museum
BWL	W. G. Lambert, *Babylonian Wisdom Literature* (Oxford, 1960)
CBS	Collection of the Babylonian Section; tablet signature, University Museum, Philadelphia
CT	*Cuneiform Texts from Babylonian Tablets in the British Museum*
	12 = R. C. Thompson, *Cuneiform Texts* (London, 1901)
	14 = R. C. Thompson, *Cuneiform Texts* (London, 1902)
	44 = T. G. Pinches, *Miscellaneous Texts* (London, 1963)
	46 = W. G. Lambert and A. R. Millard, *Babylonian Literary Texts* (London, 1965)
	51 = C. B. F. Walker, *Miscellaneous Texts* (London, 1972)
DT	Daily Telegraph; tablet signature, British Museum
DUROM	object signature, University of Durham Oriental Museum
EAE	*Enūma Anu Ellil*
F	tablet signature, British Museum
HSM	object signature, Harvard Semitic Museum
JRL	tablet signature, John Rylands Library, Manchester
K	Kouyunjik; tablet signature, British Museum
KAL	*Keilschrifttexte aus Assur literarischen Inhalts* (Wiesbaden)
KAR	E. Ebeling, *Keilschrifttexte aus Assur religiösen Inhalts*, 2 vols. (Leipzig, 1919–23)
LKA	E. Ebeling and F. Köcher, *Literarische Keilschrifttexte aus Assur* (Berlin, 1953)
MSL	*Materials for the Sumerian Lexicon* (Rome)

N	Northumberland; object signature, University of Durham Oriental Museum
ND	Nimrud; field number, excavations at Nimrud
Ni	Nippur; tablet signature, Archaeological Museum, Istanbul
OECT	*Oxford Editions of Cuneiform Texts*
	XI = O. R. Gurney, *Literary and Miscellaneous Texts in the Ashmolean Museum* (Oxford, 1989)
PBS	*University Museum, Publications of the Babylonian Section*
	I/2 = H. F. Lutz, *Selected Sumerian and Babylonian Texts* (Philadelphia, 1919)
	X/2 = S. Langdon, *Sumerian Liturgical Texts* (Philadelphia, 1917)
R	H. C. Rawlinson, ed., *The Cuneiform Inscriptions of Western Asia*, 5 vols. (London, 1861–91)
RIM	Royal Inscriptions of Mesopotamia (Toronto)
RINAP	Royal Inscriptions of the Neo-Assyrian Period (Winona Lake, Ind.)
Rm	Rassam; tablet signature, British Museum
Si	Sippar; tablet signature, Archaeological Museums, Istanbul
Sm	Smith; tablet signature, British Museum
SP	Sumerian Proverb (collection)
STT	O. R. Gurney, J. J. Finkelstein, and P. Hulin, *The Sultantepe Tablets*, 2 vols. (London, 1957–64)
VAS	*Vorderasiatische Schriftdenkmäler*
	II = H. Zimmern, *Sumerische Kultlieder aus altbabylonischer Zeit* 1 (Leipzig, 1912)
	X = H. Zimmern, *Sumerische Kultlieder aus altbabylonischer Zeit* 2 (Leipzig, 1913)
	XXIV = J. van Dijk, *Literarische Texte aus Babylon* (Berlin, 1987)
VAT	Vorderasiatische Abteilung, Tontafel; tablet signature, Vorderasiatisches Museum, Berlin

Catalogue of Texts

All objects are clay tablets or tablet fragments, unless described otherwise.

Special abbreviations: cat. = catalogued, ed. = edited, // = duplicates

Citations in the catalogue of transliterations by folio number refer to the page numbers of Lambert's seven British Museum notebooks, which occupy the range folios 8897–10330. Scanned images of the notebooks are posted online at http://oracc.museum.upenn.edu /contrib/lambert/.

1–8. Commemorative and Votive Inscriptions

1. DUROM N2264, stone macehead. Content suggests a provenance in Girsu (Telloh). Dedication of Ur-Ninmar, *ensi* of Lagaš, to the god Šulšaga. Formerly in the collection of the Dukes of Northumberland, presumed acquired by Henry, Lord Warkworth, later Earl Percy (1871–1909), the eldest son of the seventh duke (Lambert 1979: 1). Loaned to the British Museum in 1939, purchased by the University of Durham in 1950, and now in the university's Oriental Museum.

2. BM 130829 (1949–11–12, 6), eye-stone. Dedicated to Šamaš by Hammurapi of Babylon. RIM E.4.3.6.2004, ed. Frayne 1990: 361–62. Formerly no. 2406 in the collection of the Dukes of Northumberland, loaned to the British Museum in 1939 and donated in 1949.

3. BM 56614 (82–7–14, 995A), shaft and head of a clay cone, excavated by Rassam at Sippar (Abu Habba). Inscription of Hammurapi of Babylon recording the construction of Sippar's wall. Exemplars 5–6 of RIM E.4.3.6.2 Sumerian version: ll. 1–46 (shaft), 36–40, 63 ff. (head), ed. Frayne 1990: 333–36.

4. Ni 10753, showing join to Ni 833 rev. (*BE* I/1 129), excavated at Nippur. Copy on clay tablet of bilingual inscription of Ammiṣaduqa, king of Babylon. Part of RIM E.4.3.10.1, ed. Frayne 1990: 425–27.

5. BCM 87′57 (ND 4319), stone duck weight, excavated by Mallowan at Nimrud. Property of Nergal-ilāya, officer of Adad-nārārī III, king of Assyria (810–783 BC). Photograph and edition in George 1979: 134, no. 47, and pl. 17.

6. DUROM N2266, stone macehead. Dedicated to the god Nabû by Nabû-mukīn-apli, a governor of Babylon in the early first millennium BC. Photograph and translation in Ball 1899: 216–17; see further Brinkman 1968: 171 n. 1034 (may be "seventh century"); Finkel 1987, copy from cast. RIM B.6.0.2001, ed. Frame 1995: 271–72. Collection history is the same as no. 1.

7. Sm 1197, from Nineveh. Fragment of an inscription of Esarhaddon, king of Assyria (680–669), similar to RINAP Esarhaddon 48: 82–84, ed. Leichty 2011: 108. Transliteration folio 10108.

8. Sheffield Museum J98.92, clay cylinder fragment. Content suggests a provenance at Dilbat (Tell

ed-Dulaim, Dailem). Part of a building inscription of an unidentified Assyrian king, "governor
of Babylon," recording work on E-ibbi-Anum, the
temple of Uraš at Dilbat.

9–18. Late Copies of Royal Inscriptions

9. BM 77438 (84-2-11, 178), purchased from Spartali & Co. and probably from Babylon. Obv.: Late
Babylonian copy of an inscription of Gaddaš,
king of Babylon. See further Brinkman 1976:
127–28; Stein 2000: 149–50.

10. K 11536, from Nineveh. Neo-Babylonian copy of
an inscription of, or text about, a Kassite-period
king. Another copy: Brinkman 1976: pl. 5, ed.
p. 385, no. 10.

11. Rm II 405, from Nineveh. Neo-Assyrian copy
of a bilingual commemorative inscription of
Burnaburiaš, king of Babylon, cat. Brinkman
1976: 117 E.3.9. Very probably the same composition as nos. 12–15 (Borger apud Brinkman 1985:
249 n. 2). Ed. Bartelmus 2016: 502 MS F, copy
p. 501.

12. K 4807+Sm 977+79-7-8, 80+314, from Nineveh.
Neo-Assyrian copy of a bilingual composition
commemorating the dedication of a chariot to
Enlil by a king of Babylon, probably Burnaburiaš.
Old copy of K 4807 in IV R^1 12, composite copy
of K 4807+Sm 977 with nos. 14 and 15 in IV R^2
12, ed. Zimmern 1906: 153–56; Stein 2000: 170–76
(Akk. only). On this composition, see further
Lambert 1973: 277; Borger 1975: 228 sub IV R^2
t12; Brinkman 1976: 141–42. J.5.1; Brinkman 1985:
249 (see no. 11). New ed. Bartelmus 2016: 502–10,
MS A, copy pp. 498–99.

13. Sm 699, from Nineveh. Duplicate of no. 12, q.v.
Another copy: Brinkman 1985: 252. Probably part
of no. 14. Ed. Bartelmus 2016: 504–5, MS D, copy
p. 501.

14. K 1832+5072+5249+DT 5, from Nineveh. Duplicate of no. 12, q.v., text incorporated in IV R^2 12.
Only reverse surface is preserved, but obverse
fragments may be no. 13 and, from the bottom of
the obverse, almost certainly K 6727 (so Borger

1975: 228 "Schluss Vs."; copy Lambert 1973: 274).
Ed. Bartelmus 2016: 506–10, MS B, copy p. 500.

15. K 8269, from Nineveh. Duplicate of no. 12, q.v.
Old copy: Delitzsch 1887: 56–57, text incorporated
in IV R^2 12. Ed. Bartelmus 2016: 503–5, 507–9,
MS C, copy p. 501.

16. Sm 2030+81-7-27, 231, from Nineveh. Identified
as a further source for the composition repre-
sented by nos. 12–15 by Borger (apud Brinkman
1985: 249 n. 2) and Lambert (folio 9972: "dup."
of K 6727). Transliteration folio 9972.

17. BM 98846 (Th 1905-4-9, 352), excavated at Nineveh by Thompson in 1905, probably in the temple
of Nabû. Identified by Lambert as related to nos.
12–15 (folio 2265). Transliteration folio 9887.

18. K 18603, from Nineveh. Perhaps from the same
tablet as no. 17 (so Lambert folio 2265). RIM
B.2.0.1001, ed. Frame 1995: 68.

19–24. Other Historical and Historical-Literary Compositions

19. BM 96260 (1902-4-12, 372), purchased from
Géjou, probably from Borsippa. Fragment of a
Late Babylonian chronicle about [. . .]-Sîn, king
of Ur.

20. K 3992, from Nineveh. Fragment mentioning
Agum and the "daughters of Babylon." See Brinkman 1976: 96, Dᵃ.5.1; Stein 2000: 177–78.

21. 81-7-27, 117, from Nineveh. Dynastic Chronicle,
exemplar C. Old copy: *ADD* 888 (Johns),
ed. Grayson 1975: 144.

22. Rm 957, from Nineveh, joins Rm 142 (Lambert
1957: pl. 4; photograph of joined fragments: CDLI
P426359.). Neo-Assyrian copy of the Tukultī-
Ninurta epic.

23. K 5191, from Nineveh. Neo-Assyrian copy of the
bilingual composition commemorating Nebu-
chadnezzar I's return of the statue of Marduk to
Babylon. RIM B.2.4.9 ex. 3, ed. Frame 1995: 29.

24. BM 35000 (Sp II 524), purchased from Spartali &
Co., probably from Babylon. Late Babylonian
copy of the same text as no. 23, q.v. RIM B.2.4.9
ex. 4, ed. Frame 1995: 29.

25–31. Late Copies of Royal Correspondence

25. BM 55628 (82–7–4, 229), purchased from Spartali & Co., probably from Babylon. Late Babylonian school-exercise tablet (Gesche 2000: 711), narrow columns, only one side copied. Excerpt from the royal letter known as the "Weidner Chronicle" (M. Frazer).

26. BM 141832 (2005–12–22, 1). Late Babylonian copy of a letter to Nazimaruttaš, king of Babylon.

27. K 3045, from Nineveh. Neo-Assyrian copy of a letter of Adad-šuma-uṣur, king of Babylon, to Aššur-nārārī III of Assyria and Nabû-dayyānī. Old copy: *ABL* 924 (Harper), ed. Weidner 1959: 48, no. 42. See also no. 28.

28. K 19350, from Nineveh. Fragment of same text as no. 27, but in Neo-Babylonian script. Lambert (1992a: 34) suspected K 19037 as a fragment of the same tablet, but no copy of it is present in the *Nachlass*.

29. BM 35496 (Sp III 2), purchased from Spartali & Co., probably from Babylon. Late Babylonian copy of a royal letter ("Kedorlaomer"). Old copy: Pinches 1897: 82–83. Edition forthcoming from J. Taylor.

30. BM 35404 (Sp II 987), purchased from Spartali & Co., probably from Babylon. "Thin tablet: not much lost top and bottom, one wide col. a side." Late Babylonian copy of a royal letter ("Kedorlaomer"). Old copy of obv.: Pinches 1897: 84–85. Edition forthcoming from J. Taylor.

31. K 4930, from Nineveh. Annotated "same tablet as K 8486," which L. identified as a late "copy of an Old Babylonian letter . . . from a king to a general about a siege" (Lambert 2007: 145–46).

32–39. Sumerian Literary Compositions

32. K 7171, from Nineveh. Neo-Assyrian copy of the bilingual version of King Sîn-iddinam's Appeal to Utu, ed. Hallo 1982, MS G. Joined since copying to K 4615+ (Borger 1991: 60–61, 77, and pls.; photograph of joined fragments CDLI P357096).

33. K 8937, from Nineveh. Neo-Assyrian copy of the same composition as no. 32, ed. Hallo 1982, MS F. Old copy: Meek 1913: 74, no. 3.

34. Fitzwilliam ANE.87.1904. Old Babylonian copy of a composition about King Šulgi ("Šulgi K," see Klein 1981: 40 n. 73a). Photograph CDLI P448621.

35. BCM 206′78. Old Babylonian copy of a *balag*-composition, cat. George 1979: 122, no. 41; dupl. BM 86535, ed. Kramer 1985. Edition forthcoming from A. Cavigneaux.

36. BCM A.1851–1982, should join VAT 1334+ (*VAS* II 12) (+) CBS 497 (*PBS* X/2 12). Old Babylonian copy of a *balag*-composition. Edition forthcoming from A. Cavigneaux.

37. BCM A.1850–1982. Old Babylonian copy of a *balag*-composition. Parallel Cohen 1988: 266, rev. iv. Edition forthcoming from A. Cavigneaux.

38. BCM A.1849–1982. Old Babylonian copy of *balag*-composition. Partial duplicate of *VAS* X 123. Edition forthcoming from A. Cavigneaux.

39. BM 39670 (80–11–12, 1557), from Babylon or Borsippa. Late Babylonian copy of a *balag*-composition or other liturgical text; cf. Cohen 1988: 48–49, ll. 3–9.

40–55. Akkadian-Language Compositions of Mythological and "Epic" Content

40. K 21072, from Nineveh. Neo-Babylonian copy of Anzû II 47–55 (obv.), 120–28 (rev.). Same tablet as K 3008 etc. (*CT* 46 38; Lambert 1980: 82; 1992a: 57).

41. BM 36708 (80–6–17, 440), from Babylon or Borsippa. Fragment from the right side of probably a two-column tablet, near the top edge. Narrative poetry concerning Ninšubur (obv.? 9′: [ᵈ*nin-šub*] *ur an-nit* [*i-na še-me-šú*]) and the harnessing of Anzû (rev.? 12′).

42. BM 36974 (80–6–17, 718), from Babylon or Borsippa. Late Babylonian copy of Erra I 134–41.

43. BM 39336+39457 (80–11–12, 1222+1343), from Babylon or Borsippa. Late Babylonian copy of Erra IV in four columns: ll. 4–18 (i), 43–45 (ii), 112–16 (iii).

44. BM 37779 (80–6–17, 1536), from Babylon or Borsippa. Late Babylonian copy of Erra V 26–33.

45. BM 36734 (80–6–17, 467), from Babylon or Borsippa. Late Babylonian copy of Erra V 1–9 (obv.), 31–49 (rev.).

46. BM 32462 (76–11–17, 2199), purchased by George Smith, probably from Babylon. Very Late Babylonian copy of a mythological narrative in which an unidentified deity begs Marduk for mercy; probably Enmešarra occurs (col. a 12′: . . .]-šár-ra).

47. BM 76746 (AH 83–1–18, 2118), from Sippar. Late Babylonian exercise tablet: obv. an expository text featuring mythology of Ninurta; rev. lexical, not copied. Transliteration of obv. folio 10022.

48. F 216, probably from Babylon. Late Babylonian copy of a mythological narrative featuring Dagan (5′: [ᵈ*d*]*a-gan an-ni-ta ina še-me-e-š*[*u*]) and his father, Alala. Perhaps part of BM 33483+ (Murder of Anšar: Lambert 2013: 316–20).

49. BM 51205+51606 (82–3–23, 2201+2640), probably from Sippar. Neo-Babylonian copy of mythological narrative in which the Tablet of Destinies was returned to Enlil (obv. 7′). Since L. made his copy the fragment has been joined to BM 52093.

50. BM 35865 (Sp III 397), purchased from Spartali & Co., written in Babylon. Part of a large tablet of at least two columns a side. Late Babylonian copy of mythological narrative featuring primeval deities, Enki, Anšar, and Laḫmu (obv. 7), and thus reminiscent of the Murder of Anšar (Lambert 2013: 316–20). However, it goes on to mention probably wheat (14) and certainly chick-pea (15), and may be a previously unattested Dispute poem. Arsacid colophon, 78 BC at the earliest.

51. Sm 866, from Nineveh. Neo-Assyrian copy of Gilgameš V; fragment from the bottom of MS H col. iii, overlapping with the end of MS dd col. i. Transliteration folio 9666.

52. K 1850b, from Nineveh. Neo-Assyrian copy, passage of epic-style dialogue about a forest and something "clad in death." Probably Gilgameš IV, but lacking a link to the extant text.

53. BM 32755 (76–11–17, 2525), purchased by George Smith, probably from Babylon. Very Late Babylonian copy of an unidentified composition, content perhaps mythological.

54. K 21117, from Nineveh. Neo-Assyrian copy, passage of epic-style dialogue.

55. BM 66640 (82–9–18, 6633), probably from Sippar. Late Babylonian school-exercise tablet: obv. (a) mythological passage featuring Anšar; (b) lexical or explanatory list; rev. lexical excerpts, not copied. Another copy: Gesche 2000: 523.

56–166. Babylonian and Assyrian Hymns, Prayers, and Praise Poetry

56. 80–7–19, 152+81–2–4, 188, from Nineveh. Neo-Assyrian copy of Ashurnaṣirpal I's Prayer to Ištar, colophon of Ashurbanipal, ed. von Soden 1974–77: 38–45, with photographs; see also Lambert 1980: 71 n. 2. Old copy: Brünnow 1890: 79–80 (81–2–4, 188 only).

57. 83–1–18, 430, from Nineveh. Neo-Assyrian copy of Bullussa-rabi's Hymn to Gula (Lambert 1967) 70–83 (obv.), 158–66 (rev.).

58. BM 62744 (AH 82–9–18, 2713), from Sippar. Late Babylonian copy of Bullussa-rabi's Hymn to Gula in two columns: ll. 3–43 (i), 54–100 (ii).

59. K 17508, from Nineveh, joins K 9258 (Lambert 1967: pl. 16). Neo-Assyrian copy of Bullussa-rabi's Hymn to Gula 180–83.

60. BM 54801 (82–5–22, 1130), probably from Sippar. Late Babylonian copy of Bullussa-rabi's Hymn to Gula in two columns: ll. 11–15 (i), 59–67 (ii).

61. K 10065, from Nineveh. Neo-Assyrian copy of Bullussa-rabi's Hymn to Gula 166–73.

62. BM 99811 (83–1–21, 2173), probably from Sippar. Late Babylonian school-exercise tablet: (a) Bullussa-rabi's Hymn to Gula 58–62; (b) *Ludlul bēl nēmeqi* III 9–13 (ed. Oshima 2014: 413–14, MS III.i), remainder unidentified.

63. K 232+3371+13776, from Nineveh (or Nimrud?). Neo-Assyrian copy of a syncretistic hymn to the goddess Gula, continued by text on nos. 64–68 // *KAR* 109+343 (obv.: ll. 60′–95′, rev.: 1″–15″). Edition of the whole in preparation by E. Bennett. Old copies (K 232 only): Craig 1897: 16–18; Martin

1900: 145 (rev. only); ed. Martin 1900: 104–10; Mullo Weir 1929: 9–18.

64. BM 75974 (AH 83-1-18, 1334), from Sippar. Neo-Babylonian copy of the same composition as no. 63: ll. 49′–95′ (obv.), 97′–139′ (rev.) // *KAR* 109+343.

65. BM 76319 (AH 83-1-18, 1687), from Sippar. Neo-Babylonian copy of the same composition as nos. 63–64: ll. 62′–76′.

66. BM 68611 (82-9-18, 8610), probably from Sippar. Late Babylonian copy of the same composition as nos. 63–64: ll. 78′–102′ (obv.), 103′–26′ (rev.).

67. BM 37616 (80-6-17, 1373), from Babylon or Borsippa. Late Babylonian copy of the same composition as nos. 63–64: ll. 10″–20″ (obv.), 1‴–15‴+ (rev.).

68. BM 36333 (80-6-17, 59), from Babylon or Borsippa. Late Babylonian school-exercise tablet: obv.(?) (a) *Udug-ḫul* XIII–XV 60–62 (ed. Geller 2016b: 451, MS k); (b) same composition as nos. 63–64, ll. 87′–91′; rev.(?), not copied, excerpts from *Ea* VI–VIII, see Gesche 2000: 239–40. Another copy: *CT* 12 30 (Thompson).

69. 80-7-19, 115, from Nineveh. Neo-Assyrian copy of hymn in praise of Ninisinna, in two columns // no. 70. Transliteration folio 8933.

70. K 9221+11328, from Nineveh. Neo-Assyrian copy of the same composition as no. 69, in two columns. Transliteration folios 8933, 9579.

71. K 15067, from Nineveh. Neo-Assyrian copy of a composition in praise of a goddess. Transliteration folio 8967.

72. Sm 1810, from Nineveh. Neo-Assyrian copy of a composition in praise of a goddess. Transliteration folio 8935.

73. K 13975, from Nineveh. Neo-Assyrian copy of a composition addressed to a goddess or woman.

74. K 2523, from Nineveh. Neo-Assyrian copy of a composition in praise of Marduk. Catchline, colophon of Ashurbanipal. Transliteration folios 8973–74.

75. 81-2-4, 471, from Nineveh. Neo-Assyrian copy of *šuilla* Nabû 6, ed. Mayer 1990: 461–62, MS D, copy p. 479. Transliteration folio 9051.

76. Rm 401, from Nineveh. Neo-Assyrian copy of a composition in praise of a god. Transliteration folio 8967.

77. Sm 85, from Nineveh. Neo-Assyrian copy of a composition in praise of a goddess(?), l. 6 quoted in Lambert 2013: 470. Transliteration folio 9052.

78. K 6928+Sm 1896, from Nineveh. Neo-Assyrian copy of an incantation prayer to a goddess. Obv. 19′–20′ cited in George 2015a: 89. Dupl. K 15210 (folios 9352, 9849).

79. K 14094, from Nineveh. Neo-Assyrian copy of a composition including hymn or prayer to a goddess, dupl. VAT 9898 (forthcoming in *KAL*; unfinished copy by Lambert, folios 1208–10). Transliteration folio 9055.

80. CBS 1702, probably from Sippar via the dealer Khabaza. Neo-Babylonian copy of *šuilla* Zarpanītum 1, dupl. *LKA* 48a rev. (ed. Ebeling 1953a: 70–71).

81. BM 78278 (Bu 88-5-12, 134), probably from Sippar. Old Babylonian copy of Marduk Prayer no. 1 in four columns: ll. 7–30 (i), 64–85 (ii). Ed. Oshima 2011: 142–49, MS D. Old copy: *CT* 44 21 (Pinches).

82. BM 72181 (82-9-18, 12186), probably from Sippar. Late Babylonian copy of Marduk Prayer no. 1, probably in four columns: ll. 39–47 (obv.), 155–57 (rev.).

83. BM 74250 (82-9-18, 14272), probably from Sippar. Late Babylonian copy of Marduk Prayer no. 1, 160–66. Joined since Lambert made his copy, now +66652 (no. 87)+72231+72273+72714 (E. Jiménez).

84. BM 76492 (AH 83-1-18, 1862), from Sippar. Late Babylonian copy of Marduk Prayer no. 1 in four columns: ll. 3–27 (i), 58–82 (ii), 134–60 (iii), 188–207, colophon (iv). Ed. Oshima 2011: 142–57, MS F, copy pls. 1–2.

85. BM 34366 (Sp I 483) (+) 45746 (SH 81-7-6, 159), purchased from Spartali & Co. and J. M. Shemtob, respectively, written in Babylon. Late Babylonian copy of Marduk Prayer no. 1 in four columns: ll. 1–13 (i), 69–77 (ii), 155–70 (iii), 205–7, colophon (iv). Ed. Oshima 2011: 142–57, MS I, copy pls. 6–7 (BM 45746 only). Arsacid colophon, 35 BC (see Strassmaier 1892: 204; correct Oshima 2003: 111 n. 25).

86. BM 45618 (SH 81-7-6, 11), purchased from J. M. Shemtob, probably from Babylon. Late

Babylonian copy of Marduk Prayer no. 1 in four columns: ll. 3–31 (i), 51–86 (ii), 149–56 (iii), 201–7, colophon (iv). Ed. Oshima 2011: 142–57, MS H, copy pls. 4–5.

87. BM 66652 (82-9-18, 6645), probably from Sippar. Late Babylonian copy of Marduk Prayer no. 1, 172–84. Ed. Oshima 2011: 155–56, MS G, copy pl. 3. Joined since Lambert made his copy, now + 72231+72273+72714 +74250 (no. 83) (E. Jiménez).

88. BM 34218+34334 (Sp I 324+448), purchased from Spartali & Co., probably from Babylon. Late Babylonian copy of Marduk Prayer no. 1, probably in four columns: ll. 49–61 (i), 101–16 (ii). Ed. Oshima 2011: 146–51, MS J, copy pl. 3.

89. BM 38343 (80-11-12, 225), from Babylon or Borsippa. Neo-Babylonian copy of Marduk Prayer no. 1, probably in four columns: ll. ? (iii), 165–81 (iv).

90. VAT 14642, excavated at Babylon by Koldewey (Pedersén 2005: 278, N18, no. 5). Late Babylonian school-exercise tablet: (a) Marduk Prayer no. 1, 12–15; (b) *aluzinnu*-composition, dupl. II *R* 60 i 22–25; (c)–(g) not copied (see Borger 1967: 330, sub *LTBA* 1: 68). Ed. Oshima 2011: 143, MS k. Old copy: Matouš 1933, no. 68.

91. BM 36437 (80-6-17, 164), from Babylon or Borsippa. Late Babylonian school-exercise tablet: (a) unidentified Sumerian; (b) Marduk Prayer no. 1, 12–16, remainder lexical, not copied. Ed. Oshima 2011: 143, MS n. Another copy: Gesche 2000: 258.

92. BM 33716 (Rm IV 274), probably from Babylon. Late Babylonian school-exercise tablet: (a) Marduk Prayer no. 1, 61–65; rev. lexical, not copied. Ed. Oshima 2011: 147–48, MS l, copy pl. 8.

93. BM 54980 (82-5-22, 1311), probably from Sippar. Late Babylonian school-exercise tablet: (a) Marduk Prayer no. 1, 71–77; rev. lexical, not copied.

94. BM 38025 (80-6-17, 1854), from Babylon or Borsippa. Late Babylonian school-exercise tablet: (a) unidentified incantation, transliteration folio 9911; (b) Marduk Prayer no. 1, 76–78; rev. unidentified.

95. BM 36656 (80-6-17, 388), from Babylon or Borsippa. Late Babylonian school-exercise tablet: (a) unidentified; (b) Marduk Prayer no. 1, 105–8.

96. BM 37571+37931 (80-6-17, 1328+1760), from Babylon or Borsippa. Late Babylonian school-exercise tablet: (a) *Udug-ḫul* X 55–57 (Geller 2016b: 334, MS w); (b) Marduk Prayer no. 1, 127–32; remainder lexical, not copied. Ed. Oshima 2011: 151–52, MS o. Another copy: Gesche 2000: 299.

97. BM 61649+61672+62689+62816 (82-9-18, 1620+1643+2658+2785) +82987+82988 (83-1-21, 150+151)+F 9, probably from Sippar. Late Babylonian copy of Marduk Prayer no. 2 in four columns: ll. 5–24 (i), 53–75 (ii), 6′–33′ (iii), 22″–47″ (iv). Ed. Oshima 2011: 222–39, MS H, copy pls. 10–15.

98. BM 136878 (82-5-22, 1784), probably from Sippar. Late Babylonian copy of Marduk Prayer no. 2, 17–21. Ed. Oshima 2011: 223–24, MS J, copy pl. 19.

99. BM 61635 (82-9-18, 1607)+76511+76845 (AH 83-1-18, 1881+2217)+F 8+64, from Sippar. Late Babylonian copy of Marduk Prayer no. 2 in four columns: ll. 19–49 (i), 70–104 (ii), 8′, 12′–31′, 33′–40′ (iii), 7″–end, colophon (iv). Ed. Oshima 2011: 232–39, MS I, copy pl. 17 (rev. only).

100. Si 857, probably from Sippar. Late Babylonian copy of Marduk Prayer no. 2 in four columns: ll. 10–18 (i), 57–76 (ii), 20′–33′ (iii), 32″–end (iv). Ed. Oshima 2011: 222–39, MS K (Si "851").

101. VAT 11152+11170, excavated at Aššur by Andrae. Neo-Assyrian copy of Marduk Prayer no. 2, 32–57. Ed. Oshima 2011: 225–27, MS D. Other copies: Ebeling, *KAR* 351 and 344, and Köcher *apud* Lambert 1959–60b: pl. 23 (unjoined). Another fragment of this tablet, VAT 10313 (ll. 8–18), will be published in *KAL*. L.'s copy: folio 1449.

102. BM 66558 (82-9-18, 6551), probably from Sippar. Late Babylonian copy of Marduk Prayer no. 2 in four columns: ll. 18–30 (i), 25″–37″ (iv). Ed. Oshima 2011: 222–39, MS L, copy pl. 18.

103. BM 41295 (81-4-28, 843), probably from Babylon. Late Babylonian copy of Marduk Prayer no. 2 in four columns: ll. 17–34 (i), 78–110 (ii), 15′–41′ (iii), 28″–44″ (iv).

104. K 9917+17647, from Nineveh. Neo-Assyrian copy of Marduk Prayer no. 2 in four columns: ll. 21–34 (i), 74–93 (ii), 13′–24′ (iii), 27″–37″ (iv). Ed. Oshima 2011: 222–39, MS C. Other copies: Lambert 1959–60b: pls. 19–20 (K 9917 only);

Oshima 2011: pl. 9 (K 17647 only). Another copy of col. i is on folio 1433.

105. K 17797, from Nineveh. Neo-Assyrian copy of Marduk Prayer no. 2, 17–24. Fragment of the same tablet as no. 104. Ed. Oshima 2011: 223–24, MS F, copy pl. 9.

106. HSM 6836 (1909.5.272), probably from Babylon. Neo-Babylonian copy of Marduk Prayer no. 2 in four columns: ll. 44–48 (i), 88–95 (ii), 96–106 (iii).

107. F 4, probably from Sippar. Late Babylonian copy of Marduk Prayer no. 2, 11–13.

108. F 5, probably from Sippar. Late Babylonian copy of Marduk Prayer no. 2, 13–16.

109. BM 35285 (Sp II 854), purchased from Spartali & Co., probably from Babylon. Late Babylonian copy of Marduk Prayer no. 2, 74–79.

110. BM 37659 (80–6–17, 1416), from Babylon or Borsippa. Late Babylonian copy of Marduk Prayer no. 2, 95–100.

111. BM 37354 (80–6–17, 1111), from Babylon or Borsippa. Late Babylonian copy of Marduk Prayer no. 2, 95–97 (E. Jiménez). Rev. blank.

112. Sm 1732, from Nineveh, joins K 3183+ (Lambert 1959–60b: pl. 18). Neo-Assyrian copy of Marduk Prayer no. 2, 92–99. Ed. Oshima 2011: 230–31, MS A2, copy pl. 9. The cuneiform of K 16922, another fragment that joins K 3183+ (Lambert 1992a: 2; Oshima 2011: pl. 9) is not recorded in the Lambert folios.

113. K 18397, from Nineveh. Neo-Assyrian copy of Marduk Prayer no. 2, 32″–34″. Ed. Oshima 2011: 237–38, MS G, copy pl. 19.

114. Sm 1751, from Nineveh. Identified on folio 1405 as "Marduk [Prayer no.] II?, to [MS] A," i.e., another piece of K 3183+ etc. (see no. 112).

115. BM 54644 (82–5–22, 964)+66895 (82–9–18, 6889), probably from Sippar. Late Babylonian copy of a commentary on Marduk Prayer no. 2.

116. BM 54203 (82–5–22, 353), probably from Sippar. Late Babylonian school-exercise tablet: (a) bilingual incantation; (b) Marduk Prayer no. 2, 29–33; remainder lexical, not copied. Copy and transliteration of whole: Gesche 2000: 387–90. Ed. Oshima 2011: 224–25, MS u.

117. BM 66609 (82–9–18, 6602), probably from Sippar. Late Babylonian school-exercise tablet: (a) Marduk Prayer no. 2, 55–58; (b) *Urra* IV 341–49; remainder not copied. Copy and transliteration of whole: Gesche 2000: 518–19. Ed. Oshima 2011: 227, MS q.

118. BM 55300 (82–5–22, 1632), probably from Sippar. Late Babylonian school-exercise tablet: (a) unidentified; (b) Marduk Prayer no. 2, 79–82; rev. unidentified.

119. BM 36726 (80–6–17, 459), from Babylon or Borsippa. Late Babylonian school-exercise tablet: (c) Marduk Prayer no. 2, 1′–5′, remainder not copied. Copy and transliteration of whole: Gesche 2000: 278–82. Ed. Oshima 2011: 231–32, MS t, copy of (c) pl. 21.

120. BM 87226 (1900–10–13, 6), purchased from Djemi and Adbulkarim. Late Babylonian school-exercise tablet: obv. (a) unidentified; (b) Marduk Prayer no. 2, 3′–15′; rev. *Urra* IV 87–97, not copied. Ed. Oshima 2011: 232, MS s, copy of whole pl. 20.

121. BM 37392 (80–6–17, 1149), from Babylon or Borsippa. Late Babylonian school-exercise tablet: (a) unidentified; (b) Marduk Prayer no. 2, 17′–20′.

122. VAT 10174, excavated at Aššur by Andrae. Neo-Assyrian school-exercise tablet: (a) excerpt from a composition in praise of Babylon (ll. 6–7, quoted in Lambert 1992b: 143), not copied; (b) Šamaš Hymn 143–54 (Lambert 1960: 134, MS g, copy pl. 36), not copied; (c) Marduk Prayer no. 2, 24′–35′ (Oshima 2011: 233–35, MS o); (d) Erra and Išum I 121–31 (Cagni 1969: 70, MS D), not copied. Copy of whole: *KAR* 321 (Ebeling).

123. BM 33811 (Rm IV 371), probably from Babylon. Late Babylonian school-exercise tablet: (a) Marduk Prayer no. 2, 32′–33′; (b) unidentified; rev. lexical, not copied.

124. BM 37959+38018 (80–6–17, 1788+1847), from Babylon or Borsippa. Late Babylonian school-exercise tablet: obv. (a) *Udug-ḫul* X 14 (Geller 2016b: 327, MS o); (b) Marduk Prayer no. 2, 14″–18″; (c) unidentified; rev. lexical, not copied. Copy and transliteration of whole: Gesche 2000: 313–14. Ed. Oshima 2011: 236, MS v.

125. BM 37692 (80–6–17, 1449), from Babylon or Borsippa. Late Babylonian school-exercise tablet: (a) Marduk Prayer no. 2, 36″–38″; (b) lexical.

126. BM 55408 (82–5–22, 1741), probably from Sippar. Late Babylonian school-exercise tablet: obv.

incantations, not copied; rev. (a) unidentified; (b) Marduk Prayer no. 2, 36″–40″.

127. BM 37937+38060 (80–6–17, 1766+1889), from Babylon or Borsippa. Late Babylonian school-exercise tablet: (a) *Enūma eliš* I 90–95 (Lambert 2013: 54, MS t); (b) Marduk Prayer no. 2, 40″–47″; (c) star-list. Old copy (38060 only): Lambert 2013: pl. 8.

128. BM 65472 (82–9–18, 5459)+76294 (83–1–18, 1662)+82985 (83–1–21, 148), probably from Sippar. Neo-Babylonian copy of the Šamaš Hymn in four columns: ll. 33–39 (i), 81–98 (ii), 99–117 (iii).

129. BM 74197 (82–9–18, 14216), probably from Sippar. Late Babylonian copy of the Šamaš Hymn in four columns: ll. 31–34 (i), 169–79 (iv).

130. Si 832, probably from Sippar. Neo-Babylonian copy of the Šamaš Hymn 84–92 (obv.), 93–105 (rev.).

131. BM 134517 (1932–12–12, 512), excavated at Nineveh by Thompson. Neo-Assyrian copy of the Šamaš Hymn 118–126 (obv.), 127–30 (rev.).

132. K 20637, from Nineveh. Neo-Assyrian copy of the Šamaš Hymn 173–82.

133. BM 42652 (81–7–1, 413), probably from Babylon. Late Babylonian copy of the Šamaš Hymn 157–63.

134. BM 40080 (81–2–1, 44), probably from Babylon. Late Babylonian school-exercise tablet: obv. (a) bilingual incantation // Cooper 1971: 11–22, no. 7, not copied; (b) Šamaš Hymn 1–4; rev. (c) *Urra* VII B (*MSL* VI 117–20 MS S₁), not copied.

135. BM 36296+38070 (80–6–17, 22+1899), from Babylon or Borsippa. Late Babylonian school-exercise tablet: obv. (a) *Udug-ḫul* XIII–XV 102–3 (Geller 2016b: 463, MS ff); (b) Šamaš Hymn 1–7; rev. (c) *Urra* XV (*MSL* IX 10 MS S₈), not copied. Other copies (36296 obv. only): Geller 1980: 47; 2016b: 689.

136. BM 37122 (80–6–17, 871), from Babylon or Borsippa. Late Babylonian school-exercise tablet: obv. Šamaš Hymn 58–62; rev. lexical, not copied.

137. BM 33514+33517+33531+33719+33738+33744+33766 (Rm IV 62+72+87+277+296+302+324+unnumbered fragment)+48918 (81–10–8, 1629), probably from Babylon. Late Babylonian school-exercise tablet: obv. (a) *Muššu'u* VII 7–9, ed. Lambert 2013: 157, MS g; (b) Šamaš Hymn 69–80; rev. (c) lexical (giš), not copied.

138. BM 35077 (Sp II 613), purchased from Spartali & Co., probably from Babylon. Late Babylonian school-exercise tablet(?): Šamaš Hymn 70?–79.

139. BM 37502 (80–6–17, 1259), from Babylon or Borsippa. Late Babylonian school-exercise tablet: (a) Šamaš Hymn 102–6; (b) unidentified.

140. BM 101558 (83–1–26, 3219). Late Babylonian school-exercise tablet: (a) *Udug-ḫul* X; (b) Šamaš Hymn 116–21; (c) unidentified. Another copy: Gesche 2000: 665.

141. BM 65461 (82–9–18, 5448+AH 83–1–18, 2116)+ unnumbered fragment, from Sippar. Neo-Babylonian school-exercise tablet: obv. (a) Šamaš Hymn 163–71; (b) *Enūma eliš* III 64–72 (Lambert 2013: 78, MS k); rev. *Urra* XIX (*MSL* X 131–32 MS S₈), not copied. Other copies (65461 excerpt a only): Lambert 1960: pl. 75; (excerpt b only): King 1902: pl. 34; Lambert 2013: pl. 16.

142. VAT 17553, excavated at Babylon by Koldewey (Pedersén 2005: 254, N15, no. 4). Late Babylonian school-exercise tablet: obv. (a) unidentified bilingual; (b) Šamaš Hymn 166–71; rev. not copied, lexical? Another copy: *VAS* XXIV 115 (van Dijk).

143. 79–7–8, 225, from Nineveh. Neo-Assyrian copy of *Ludlul bēl nēmeqi* I 25–30 (obv.), 97–100 (rev.). Ed. Oshima 2014: 383, 392–93, MS I.L, copy pl. 5.

144. K 1757+18963, from Nineveh. Neo-Assyrian copy of *Ludlul bēl nēmeqi* I 51–55. Ed. Oshima 2014: 386–87, MS I.H, copy pl. 5.

145. BM 66345 (82–9–18, 6338), probably from Sippar. Late Babylonian copy of *Ludlul bēl nēmeqi* I 6–21. Ed. Oshima 2014: 380–82, MS I.C, copy pl. 4. Part of the same tablet as no. 146.

146. BM 73592 (82–9–18, 13603), probably from Sippar. Late Babylonian copy of *Ludlul bēl nēmeqi* I 20–39 (obv.), 85–101 (rev.). Ed. Oshima 2014: 382–84, 391–93, MS I.E, copy pl. 4. Part of the same tablet as no. 145.

147. BM 37695 (80–6–17, 1452), from Babylon or Borsippa. Late Babylonian copy of *Ludlul bēl nēmeqi* I 12–22 (obv.), 104–13 (rev.). Ed. Oshima 2014: 381–82, 393–94, MS I.B, copy pl. 3.

148. BM 68444 (82–9–18, 8442), probably from Sippar. Late Babylonian copy of *Ludlul bēl nēmeqi* I 38–53. Ed. Oshima 2014: 384–86 MS I.D, copy pl. 3.

149. BM 32208+32214+32371+32378+32449+32659+ 32694+fragments (S† 76–11–17, 1936+1941+ 2103+2110+2186+2427+2463+2478), purchased by George Smith, probably from Babylon. Late Babylonian copy of *Ludlul bēl nēmeqi* in six (or eight?) columns: I 48–62 (i), I 117–20, II 1–40 (ii), II 84–86? (iii), IV/V 25–53 (i′), IV/V 108–19 (ii′). Ed. Lenzi and Annus 2011; Oshima 2014: 377–78, MS A, copy pls. 1–2, photographs, ibid.: pls. 35–36. Other copies: Lambert 1960: pl. 4 (32214 and 32694 only).

150. BM 65956+67872 (82–9–18, 5948+7870)+93047 (83–1–21, 1783), probably from Sippar. Neo-Babylonian copy of *Ludlul bēl nēmeqi* II 1–23 (obv.), 94–120 (rev.). Ed. Oshima 2014: 396–99, 408–12, MS II.D, copy pl. 10.

151. BM 82957 (83–1–21, 120), probably from Sippar. Late Babylonian copy of *Ludlul bēl nēmeqi* II 16–25 (obv.), 103–9 (rev.). Ed. Oshima 2014: 398–99, 409–10, MS II.E, copy pl. 8.

152. BM 38067 (80–6–17, 1896), from Babylon or Borsippa. Late Babylonian copy of *Ludlul bēl nēmeqi* II 31–48. Ed. Oshima 2014: 400–403, MS II.B, copy pl. 8.

153. BM 54794 (82–5–22, 1123), probably from Sippar. Late Babylonian copy of *Ludlul bēl nēmeqi* II 49–59 (obv.), 60–71 (rev.). Ed. Oshima 2014: 403–5, MS II.C, copy pl. 9.

154. BM 37576 (80–6–17, 1333), from Babylon or Borsippa. Late Babylonian school-exercise tablet: obv. (a) unidentified; (b) *Ludlul bēl nēmeqi* II 25–30; rev. not copied. Ed. Oshima 2014: 400, MS II.p, copy of whole pl. 9.

155. BM 33861 (Rm IV 422+423), probably from Babylon. Late Babylonian school-exercise tablet: lower obv. *Ludlul bēl nēmeqi* II 34–39; rev. *Urra* XXII MS S₂, XXIII MS S₆, XXIV MS S₃ (*MSL* XI 22, 68, 78), not copied. Ed. Oshima 2014: 401–2, MS II.Q.

156. BM 55481 (82–7–4, 54), purchased from Spartali & Co., probably from Babylon. Neo-Babylonian copy of *Ludlul bēl nēmeqi* III 8–28 (obv.), 90–108 (rev.). Ed. Oshima 2014: 413–15, 420–22, MS III.C, copy pl. 11.

157. BM 77093 (AH 83–1–18, 2472), from Sippar. Neo-Babylonian copy of *Ludlul bēl nēmeqi* III 42–62. Ed. Oshima 2014: 416–18, MS III.H.

158. BM 68435 (82–9–18, 8433), probably from Sippar. Late Babylonian school-exercise tablet: obv. (a) unidentified trace; (b) *Ludlul bēl nēmeqi* III 67–78; rev. (c) *An = Anum* 1–5. Ed. Oshima 2014: 418–19, MS III.g, copy pl. 11. Another copy: Gesche 2000: 558.

159. Si 728, probably from Sippar. Neo-Babylonian copy of *Ludlul bēl nēmeqi* III/IV. Ed. Oshima 2014: 426–27, MS IVB.

160. BM 123392 (Th 1932–12–10, 335), excavated at Nineveh, "palace of Ashurnaṣirpal," by Thompson. Neo-Assyrian copy of *Ludlul bēl nēmeqi* III/IV. Ed. Oshima 2014: 428, photograph, pl. 48. Another copy: *CT* 51 219 (Thompson).

161. BM 38002 (80–6–17, 1831), from Babylon or Borsippa. Late Babylonian school-exercise tablet: obv. (a) unidentified; (b) *Ludlul bēl nēmeqi* IV/V 16–22. Ed. Oshima 2014: 430–31, MS V.m.

162. BM 74201 (82–9–18, 14220), probably from Sippar. Late Babylonian school-exercise tablet: obv. (a) trace; (b) *Ludlul bēl nēmeqi* IV/V; rev. lexical, not copied. Ed. Oshima 2014: 433–34, MS V.i, copy pl. 12. Copy of whole: Gesche 2000: 614.

163. BM 34650 (Sp II 133), purchased from Spartali & Co., probably from Babylon. Late Babylonian copy of *Ludlul bēl nēmeqi* IV/V 1–22 (obv.), 107–20, colophon (rev.). Ed. Oshima 2014: 429–30, 437–38, MS V.B, copy pl. 12.

164. BM 77253 (SH 83–9–28, 4), purchased from Shemtob, probably from Babylon. Late Babylonian copy of *Ludlul bēl nēmeqi* IV/V in four or more columns, rev. only: ll. 8–27 (i′), 1′–19′ (ii′). Ed. Oshima 2014: 429–31, 435–37, MS V.C, copy pl. 13.

165. K 8576, from Nineveh. Neo-Assyrian copy of *Ludlul bēl nēmeqi* IV/V(?), Ashurbanipal colophon. Ed. Oshima 2014: 438, MS V.L.

166. K 8306, from Nineveh. Annotated "dupl. VAT 10650 (K 8576)," which indicates that L. considered it a duplicate of VAT 10650 (*Ludlul bēl*

nēmeqi IV/V, part of Oshima's MS V.F), and speculated that it was part of the same tablet as K 8576 (no. 163).

N.B. Other excerpts of *Ludlul bēl nēmeqi* on school-exercise tablets copied by Lambert and published since *BWL*:

BM 61433 (c) I 88–92 (Lambert 2013: pl. 19; ed. Oshima 2014: 391–92, MS I.u, copy pl. 7);

BM 71949 (b) I 78–84 (here pl. 109, no. 207, q.v.);

BM 93079 (c) I 55–59 (Lambert 2013: pl. 8; ed. Oshima 2014: 387, MS I.v, copy pl. 7);

BM 99811 (b) III 9–13 (here pl. 33, no. 62, q.v.).

167–251. Incantations

167. BM 54656 (82–5–22, 977)+59925 (82–7–14, 4335)+61552+64515+66907+66914+74091 (82–9–18, 1524+4495+6901+6908+14102) (+) 55415 (82–5–22, 1748) (+) 59211 (82–7–14, 3620), probably from Sippar. Late Babylonian copy of Marduk's Address to the Demons in four columns: ll. 1–57 (i), 58–83 (ii), 25′–65′ (iii), 66′–71′, 96′–127′, catchline = *Udug-ḫul* XII 1, Seleucid colophon (iv). Ed. Geller 2016b: 342–58, 370–92, MS b.

168. K 6666, from Nineveh. Neo-Assyrian copy of Marduk's Address to the Demons in four columns: ll. 1–19 (i), unplaced (ii), 25′ (iii). Ed. Geller 2016b: 342–45, MS M.

169. K 8961, from Nineveh. Neo-Assyrian copy of Marduk's Address to the Demons 10–22 (i). Ed. Geller 2016b: 343–36, MS A.

170. BM 72748 (82–9–18, 12756), probably from Sippar. Late Babylonian copy of Marduk's Address to the Demons in four columns: ll. 16–59 (i), 77–119 (ii), 8′–44′ (iii), 70′–109′ (iv). Ed. Geller 2016b: 344–87, MS a.

171. K 13768+Sm 164, from Nineveh. Neo-Assyrian copy of Marduk's Address to the Demons 42–58. Ed. Geller 2016b: 349–53, MS B. Another copy: Lambert 1956: pl. 15 (13768 only).

172. BM 66922+68471 (82–9–18, 6916+8469), probably from Sippar. Late Babylonian copy of Marduk's Address to the Demons 52–70 (obv.), 8′–13′ (rev.). Ed. Geller 2016b: 352–56, 366–67, MS d.

173. BM 45377+45402 (81–7–1, 3138+3163)+46369+46375+46383+46434+46435+46437+46454 (81–7–28, 94+101+109+160+161+163+180)+unnumbered fragment, probably from Babylon. Late Babylonian copy of Marduk's Address to the Demons 1–33 (obv.), 1′–8′, catchline(?), colophon (rev.). Ed. Geller 2016b: 342–48, 365–66, MSS n+ee.

174. K 14694, from Nineveh, joins K 3275+ obv. i (copy Lambert 1956: pl. 13). Neo-Assyrian copy of Marduk's Address to the Demons 33–40. Ed. Geller 2016b: 348–49, MS K.

175. BM 76237 (AH 83–1–18, 1604), from Sippar. Late Babylonian copy of Marduk's Address to the Demons 51–62. Ed. Geller 2016b: 351–54, MS e.

176. BM 45403(81–7–1, 3164)+unnumbered fragment, probably from Babylon. Late Babylonian copy of Marduk's Address to the Demons 42–56, 85–103. Ed. Geller 2016b: 349–53, 359–62, MS o.

177. BM 45372 (81–7–1, 3133)+46401 (81–7–28, 127), probably from Babylon. Late Babylonian copy of Marduk's Address to the Demons 62–72 (obv.), 73–85 (rev.). Ed. Geller 2016b: 354–59, MS p.

178. BM 46499 (81–7–28, 225), probably from Babylon. Late Babylonian copy of Marduk's Address to the Demons 80–85. Ed. Geller 2016b: 358–59, MS q.

179. BM 46442 (81–7–28, 168), probably from Babylon. Late Babylonian copy of Marduk's Address to the Demons 100–10. Ed. Geller 2016b: 362–64, MS r.

180. BM 46501 (81–7–28, 227), probably from Babylon. Late Babylonian copy of Marduk's Address to the Demons 111–22. Ed. Geller 2016b: 364–65, MS s.

181. BM unnumbered (81–7–28, unnumbered), probably from Babylon. Annotated "to 46501," so suspected by L. to be part of the same tablet as no. 180.

182. K 17113+18488, from Nineveh, joins K 3349+ obv. (copy Lambert 1959–60a: pl. 25). Neo-Assyrian copy of Marduk's Address to the Demons 81–93. Ed. Geller 2016b: 358–60, 376–89, MS D.

183. K 10857, from Nineveh. Neo-Assyrian copy of Marduk's Address to the Demons 95–100. Ed. Geller 2016b: 361–62, MS E.

184. K 9595+10943+11586, from Nineveh. Neo-Assyrian copy of Marduk's Address to the Demons 97–111 (obv.), 47′–55′, 64′–70′ (rev.). Ed. Geller 2016b: 361–64, 376–89, MS I.

185. VAT 10820a (+) 10820b, excavated at Aššur by Andrae. Neo-Assyrian copy of Marduk's Address to the Demons 87–108 (obv.), 9′, 26′–34′ (rev.). Ed. Geller 2016b: 359–72, MS S. Another copy: *KAL* IX 35, ed. Jakob 2018: 75–77.

186. K 18617, from Nineveh. Neo-Assyrian copy of Marduk's Address to the Demons 13′–24′. Ed. Geller 2016b: 367–69, MS O.

187. BM 36783 (80-6-17, 521), from Babylon or Borsippa. Late Babylonian copy of Marduk's Address to the Demons 3′–29′. Ed. Geller 2016b: 365–70, MS dd.

188. K 21293, from Nineveh. Neo-Assyrian copy of Marduk's Address to the Demons 19′–23′. Ed. Geller 2016b: 368–69, MS II.

189. BM 46421+46485+46492+46510 (81-7-28, 147+ 211+218+236) (+) 46429 (81-7-28, 155) (+) unnumbered fragments, probably from Babylon. Late Babylonian copy of Marduk's Address to the Demons 9′–26′ (obv.), 122′–27′, Alexander colophon (rev.). Ed. Geller 2016b: 366–70, 390–92, MS t. The unnumbered fragment at the top left of pl. 100 has now been given the number BM 46421a (Geller 2016a).

190. BM 54638+54639+54957 (82-5-22, 958+959+ 1287), probably from Sippar. Late Babylonian copy of Marduk's Address to the Demons 22′–51′ (obv.), 52′–96′ (rev.). Ed. Geller 2016b: 369–85, MS ff (from l. 84′ misidentified as MS t).

191. BM 45382 (81-7-1, 3143)+46332+46393+46423+ 46440+46461+46497 (81-7-28, 57+119+149+166+ 187+223), probably from Babylon. Late Babylonian copy of Marduk's Address to the Demons 24′–47′ (obv.), 106′–22′ (rev.). Ed. Geller 2016b: 369–76, 387–90, MS v.

192. BM 136877 (82-5-22, 1783), probably from Sippar. Late Babylonian copy of Marduk's Address to the Demons 35′–40′. Ed. Geller 2016b: 372–74, MS f.

193. K 21405, from Nineveh. Neo-Assyrian copy of Marduk's Address to the Demons, somewhere in ll. 6′–99′. Annotated "(+) K 9595+10943+11586?," so perhaps part of no. 184, q.v.

194. K 13857+18834, from Nineveh. Neo-Assyrian copy of Marduk's Address to the Demons 78′–92′. Ed. Geller 2016b: 381–84, MS Q.

195. BM 43790 (81-7-1, 1551), probably from Babylon. Late Babylonian copy of Marduk's Address to the Demons 110′–21′. Ed. Geller 2016b: 388–90, MS x.

196. BM 45373 (81-7-1, 3134)+46318+46323+46368+ 46484 (81-7-28, 43+48+93+210)+unnumbered fragment, probably from Babylon. Late Babylonian copy of Marduk's Address to the Demons 48′–77′ (obv.), 78′–105′ (rev.). Ed. Geller 2016b: 376–87, MS w.

197. K 9400, from Nineveh. Neo-Assyrian copy of Marduk's Address to the Demons 123′–28′, catchline(?). Ed. Geller 2016b: 390–91, MS I (but J on p. 340).

198. BM 37866 (80-6-17, 1623), from Babylon or Borsippa. Late Babylonian copy of Marduk's Address to the Demons 126′–27′, catchline = *Udug-ḫul* XII 1, colophon. Ed. Geller 2016b: 391–92, MS jj; cf. Wiggermann 1992: 114.

199. K 6726, from Nineveh, joins K (3307+)+7035 (copy Lambert 1959–60a: pl. 24). Neo-Assyrian copy of Marduk's Address to the Demons 41′–59′. Ed. Geller 2016b: 374–78, MS C.

200. K 11362+12229, from Nineveh. Neo-Assyrian copy of Marduk's Address to the Demons 58′–73′. Ed. Geller 2016b: 378–80, MS F. Another copy: Lambert 1956: pl. 16 (12229 only).

201. BM 46558 (81-8-30, 24), probably from Babylon. Late Babylonian copy of Marduk's Address to the Demons 73′–80′ (obv.), 81′–90′ (rev.). Ed. Geller 2016b: 380–84, MS hh.

202. K 5784, from Nineveh. Neo-Assyrian copy of Marduk's Address to the Demons 117′–22′. Ed. Geller 2016b: 389–90, MS R.

203. BM 68429 (82-9-18, 8427), probably from Sippar. Late Babylonian school-exercise tablet: (a) Marduk's Address to the Demons 18–23, ed. Geller 2016b: 345–46, MS g; (b) *Tintir* II 17–19.

204. BM 54661+55311 (82-5-22, 982+1643), probably from Sippar. Late Babylonian school-exercise tablet: obv. (a) unidentified bilingual; (b) Marduk's Address to the Demons 22–28, ed. Geller 2016b: 346–47, MS h; (c) Akkadian religious text; rev. lexical, not copied.

205. BM 55305 (82-5-22, 1637), probably from Sippar. Late Babylonian school-exercise tablet: obv. (a) Marduk's Address to the Demons 25–31,

ed. Geller 2016b: 346–48, MS i; (b) *aluzinnu* composition // II *R* 60 no. 1(?); (c) menological lore, ᴅɪš iti.bára.sag.sag // BM 66141+; rev. lexical, not copied. Copy of whole: Gesche 2000: 423.

206. BM 71975 (82-9-18, 11979), probably from Sippar. Late Babylonian school-exercise tablet: obv. (a) unidentified trace; (b) Marduk's Address to the Demons 50–55, ed. Geller 2016b: 351–52, MS j; (c) unidentified Akkadian; rev. lexical, not copied. Copy of whole: Gesche 2000: 586; of obv.: Oshima 2011: pl. 26. Transliteration folio 9999.

207. BM 71949 (82-9-18, 11952), probably from Sippar. Late Babylonian school-exercise tablet: obv. (a) Marduk's Address to the Demons 75–79, ed. Geller 2016b: 357, MS l; (b) *Ludlul bēl nēmeqi* I 78–84; (c) traces; rev. (a) *An = Anum* I 26–31; (b) *An = Anum* III 1–7.

208. BM 36646 (80-6-17, 378), from Babylon or Borsippa. Late Babylonian school-exercise tablet: obv. (a) Marduk's Address to the Demons 68′–70′, ed. Geller 2016b: 380, MS gg; remainder not copied; for details, see George 1992: 496. Copy of whole: ibid.: pl. 52, no. 46.

209. BM 68038+68385 (82-9-18, 8036+8383), probably from Sippar. Neo-Babylonian school-exercise tablet: obv. lexical, not copied; rev. (a) Marduk's Address to the Demons 25′–38′, ed. Geller 2016b: 370–73, MS m; (b) hemerology ᴅɪš iti.bára.sag. sag // BM 66141+; (c) menological lore, ᴅɪš iti. du₆.kù *lullubê* // BM 66141+ catchline; (d) traces.

210. BM 64676 (82-9-18, 4657), probably from Sippar. Late Babylonian school-exercise tablet: obv. (a) bilingual incantation; (b) Marduk's Address to the Demons 12′–17′, ed. Geller 2016b: 367–68, MS bb; (c) bilingual text; rev. lexical, not copied.

211. K 8804, from Nineveh; top left-hand corner of the same tablet as no. 212. Neo-Assyrian copy of a commentary on Marduk's Address to the Demons. Ed. Lambert *apud* Geller 2016b: 397–98, MS TT.

212. K 9478, from Nineveh; bottom left-hand corner of the same tablet as no. 211. Neo-Assyrian copy of a commentary on Marduk's Address to the Demons. Ed. Lambert *apud* Geller 2016b: 397–98, MS TT.

213. JRL 1053, from Aššur. Neo-Assyrian copy of a commentary on Marduk's Address to the Demons; colophon of Kiṣir-Nabû. Ed. Geller 2016b: 393, MS V. Another copy: Al-Rawi 2000: 48.

214. BM 47529+47685 (81-10-8, 234+390), probably from Babylon. Late Babylonian copy of a commentary on Marduk's Address to the Demons. Ed. Geller 2016b: 396–97; Wee 2016.

215. BM 48883 (81-10-8, 1594), written in Babylon (dim.kur.kur.ra^ki). Late Babylonian copy of zi—pàd incantations, "Gattung I": obv. // Ebeling 1953b: 361, ll. 1–15; rev. Seleucid colophon.

216. BM 37402 (80-6-17, 1159), from Babylon or Borsippa. Late Babylonian school-exercise tablet: obv. zi—pàd incantation similar to "Gattung I" 8–12; rev. *Urra* XXIV (*MSL* XI 78 MS S₁₀), not copied.

217. BM 46736 (81-8-30, 202), probably from Babylon. Neo-Babylonian school-exercise tablet: obv. (a) "Gattung II" // *PBS* I/2 115 ii 91–93; (b) *Udug-ḫul* XVI 178′–79′, ed. Geller 2016b: 553, MS l; (c) "Gattung I" // Ebeling 1953b: 364, ii 1–6; rev. lexical (gi), not copied. Another copy: Geller 2016b: 697; cf. ibid.: 499.

218. BM 38367 (80-11-12, 249), from Babylon or Borsippa. Late Babylonian copy of zi—pàd incantations in four columns, "Gattung I": iii // Ebeling 1953b: 364–67, iv // ibid.: 371–72.

219. K 2893+3011+Sm 1258+1346, from Nineveh. Neo-Babylonian copy of zi—pàd incantations in four columns, "Gattung II," ed. Ebeling 1953b: 381–93. K 22037 belongs to the same tablet (Lambert 1992a: 70), but no copy of it was found in the *Nachlass*.

220. K 3179+3381+4914+13484+Sm 1861+1912, from Nineveh. Neo-Assyrian copy of zi—pàd incantations in six columns, "Gattung II," ed. Ebeling 1953b: 379–93 (K 3179+3381+Sm 1861 only).

221. K 9359, from Nineveh. Part of the same tablet as no. 220.

222. DT 91, from Nineveh. Neo-Assyrian copy of zi—pàd incantations, "Gattung II": rev. // Ebeling 1953b: 387.

223. BM 44216 (81-7-1, 1977), probably from Babylon. Late Babylonian copy of zi—pàd incantations,

"Gattung II": rev. i′ // Ebeling 1953b: 385, ii′ //
Ebeling 1953b: 391.

224. BM 40805 (81–4–28, 351), probably from Babylon.
Neo-Babylonian copy of zi—pàd incantations,
"Gattung II": ii 3′ ff. // Ebeling 1953b: 381–82.
Since copying, BM 40805 has been joined to BM
40850 (folio 9488)+44195+44241.

225. BM 48168 (81–10–8, 878), probably from Babylon.
Late Babylonian copy of zi—pàd incantations,
"Gattung II": obv. // Ebeling 1953b: 384.

226. BM 72015 (82–9–18, 12019), probably from Sippar.
Late Babylonian copy of zi—pàd incantations,
"Gattung II": obv.(?) // Ebeling 1953b: 388.

227. CBS 590, probably from Sippar via the dealer
Khabaza. Late Old (or Middle?) Babylonian copy
of a zi—pàd incantation in three columns, "Gattung III," rubric ka-inim-ma! udug-ḫul-a-kam.
Old copy: *PBS* I/2 112 (Lutz). Ed. Ebeling 1953b:
395–403. For ll. 63–71, see Lambert 2002: 207.

228. K 14763, from Nineveh. Neo-Assyrian copy of a
bilingual text, original drawing (folio 1546) annotated "zi—pàd." Another copy: Ambos 2004: 248,
no. 10.

229. K 16753, from Nineveh. Neo-Babylonian copy of
bilingual text, perhaps an incantation, rev. blank.
L.: "Same scribe as K 2893+" = no. 219.

230. K 3514, from Nineveh. Neo-Assyrian copy of
incantations and rituals to appease an angry god,
ka-inim-ma dingir šà-dab-b[a gur-ru-da-kám].

231. K 3337, from Nineveh. Neo-Assyrian copy of
incantations and rituals to appease an angry god,
[ka-inim-ma] nam-érim-búr-da dingir šà-dab-ba
gur-ru-da-kám.

232. Rm 246, from Nineveh. Neo-Assyrian copy of
incantations and rituals to appease an angry god,
[ka-inim-ma dingir šà-dab-ba] gur-ru-da-[kám];
rev. blank.

233. K 15299, from Nineveh. Neo-Assyrian copy of an
unidentified composition. Transliterated on folio
9037, annotated "cf. šà.dib.ba."

234. K 11255, from Nineveh. Neo-Assyrian copy of
Ḫulbazizi // *STT* 215 iii 22–33; not *EAE* (Reiner
1998: 254).

235. K 4834, from Nineveh, joins col. iii of K 8152+
8979+9274+9838 (copy Lambert 1970: pl. 4)+5782;

see CDLI P395737 for the whole. Neo-Assyrian
copy of the compendium of fever incantations.

236. K 4861, from Nineveh. Neo-Assyrian copy of the
compendium of fever incantations, continues the
bilingual incantation begun in no. 235.

237. Rm 843, probably from Babylon. Late Babylonian
copy of *Maqlû* II 138–47, ed. Abusch 2016: 68–69,
MS v. Another copy: Schwemer 2017: pl. 37.

238. BM 128108 (1929–10–12, 764), excavated at
Nineveh, SW palace of Sennacherib, by Thompson. Neo-Assyrian copy of an anti-witchcraft
incantation, ed. Abusch and Schwemer 2016:
54–55, MS P.

239. K 6335, from Nineveh. Neo-Assyrian copy of
a compendium of incantations against various sicknesses // *KAR* 233 = *BAM* 338 // *STT*
138, on which see Köcher 1971: xii. See also nos.
240–42.

240. K 8104, from Nineveh. Part of the same tablet as
no. 239.

241. 82–5–22, 535, from Nineveh. Neo-Assyrian copy
of a compendium of incantations against various
sicknesses // no. 239, q.v.

242. Rm 595, from Nineveh. Neo-Assyrian copy of a
compendium of incantations against various sicknesses // no. 239, q.v.

243. K 10896, from Nineveh. Neo-Assyrian copy of an
incantation to expel sickness or demonic power:
rev. i′, cf. *BAM* 323 i 14–16 etc.; ii′ Ashurbanipal
colophon.

244. K 14713, from Nineveh. Neo-Assyrian copy of a
Sumerian incantation.

245. BM 37641 (80–6–17, 1398), from Babylon or Borsippa. Late Babylonian school-exercise tablet: obv.
(a) *Šurpu* II 94–99; (b) unidentified; rev. lexical,
not copied. Copy of whole with additional fragment: Gesche 2000: 301.

246. K 5416a+BM 98584+98589 (Th. 1905–4–9, 90+95),
from Nineveh. Neo-Assyrian copy in six columns
of a compendium of incantations to counter
stomachache, diarrhea, and other disorders. Old
copy: *AMT* 45 no. 5 (Thompson, K 5416a only).
Col. iv 3–33 ed. Böck 2014: 101–4.

247. K 13419, from Nineveh. Neo-Assyrian copy of a
Sumerian incantation, transliterated folio 9219; //

K 19590, cat. Lambert 1992a: 37, where are noted the following further duplicates: K 5036+ // 5127 (folios 9229–30) // 9336+ (folio 9215, copy Lambert *apud* Cooper 1978: pls. 8–9) // 10809 (folios 9243, 9268) // 10111 (no. 248) // Rm II 337 (folio 9924) // BM 121045+ etc. (Lambert and Millard 1968: 6). An excerpt of this composition is given on the Late Babylonian school-exercise tablet no. 119, obv. 1–6 (not copied by L. but see Gesche 2000: 279, BM 36726 a).

248. K 10111, from Nineveh. Neo-Assyrian copy of a Sumerian incantation // no. 247, q.v.

249. K 3416+9069, from Nineveh. Neo-Assyrian copy of incantation prayers: ll. 4′–9′ // *šuilla* Papsukkal no. 1 (Mayer 1976: 407).

250. K 9355, from Nineveh. Neo-Assyrian copy of *Udug-ḫul* VI 166′–68′, ed. Geller 2016b: 244–45, MS YY, copy pl. 47. Transliteration folio 9637.

251. K 11984, from Nineveh. Neo-Assyrian copy of a bilingual composition, perhaps an incantation.

252–317. Wisdom Literature

252. BM 68589 (82–9–18, 8588), probably from Sippar. Late Babylonian copy of the Babylonian Theodicy in four columns: ll. 47–66 (i), 224–41 (iv). Ed. Oshima 2014: 444–47, 457–59, MS F, copy pl. 14.

253. BM 47745 (81–11–3, 450), probably from Babylon. Late Babylonian copy of the Babylonian Theodicy in four columns: ll. 72–85 (ii), 203–20 (iii and edge). Ed. Oshima 2014: 447–49, 455–57, MS E, copy pl. 15.

254. BM 77255 (SH 83–9–28, 6), purchased from Shemtob, probably from Babylon. Late Babylonian copy of the Babylonian Theodicy in four columns: ll. 120–34 (ii); makes a bridging join between BM 40098 (cols. i–ii, iv, copy Lambert 1960: pls. 21, 23) and 40124 (col. iii, copy ibid.: pl. 20). Ed. Oshima 2014: 449–50, MS D, copy pl. 14.

255. BM 66882 (82–9–18, 6876+6960)+76009+76506+76832 (AH 83–1–18, 1372+1876+2204)+83044+83045+83046 (83–1–21, 207+208+209), from Sippar. Neo-Babylonian copy of a commentary on

the Babylonian Theodicy: obv. ll. 1–128, rev. ll. <189–297 and colophon; tablet owned or written by one Nabû-šuma-iddina son of Bēl-[…]. BM 6682+76506 ed. Lambert 1960: 70–76, 80–88, pl. 26. All ed. Oshima 2014: 440–49, 454–64, pls. 25–30 (copy), 60–61 (photograph).

256. BM 41931 (81–6–25, 552), purchased from Spartali & Co., probably from Babylon. Late Babylonian copy of the Counsels of Wisdom 2–16.

257. BM 76672 (AH 83–1–18, 2043), from Sippar, joins BM 33851 (copy Lambert 1960: pls. 27, 29). Late Babylonian copy of the Counsels of Wisdom in four columns: ll. 6–12 (i) and colophon (iv). The colophon attributes the tablet to Nabû-kuṣuršu in Artaxerxes 7, and is very similar to Hunger 1968: 50, no. 124.

258. BM 38097 (80–6–17, 1926), from Babylon or Borsippa. Late Babylonian copy of the Counsels of Wisdom 55–61.

259. BM 33463 (Rm IV 17) (+) 33496+33595+33819 (Rm IV 51+151+379), probably from Babylon. Late Babylonian copy of the Counsels of Wisdom in four columns: ll. 7–40 (i), 66–84 (ii), 85–100 (iii), 136–52 (iv).

260. BM 76666 (AH 83–1–18, 2037), from Sippar. Neo-Babylonian copy of the Counsels of Wisdom 23–36 (i).

261. BM 68401 (82–9–18, 8399), probably from Sippar. Neo-Babylonian school-exercise tablet: obv. (a) *Tintir* V 49–51; (b) Counsels of Wisdom 82–87; (c) unidentified; rev. *Urra* VIII, not copied. Copy and transliteration of whole: Gesche 2000: 554–56.

262. BM 38484+38488 (80–11–12, 368+372), from Babylon or Borsippa. Neo-Babylonian copy of the Counsels of Wisdom in four columns: ll. 33–43 (i), 135–49 (iv).

263. 82–5–22, 555, from Nineveh. Neo-Assyrian copy of the Counsels of Wisdom in four columns: ll. 86–95 (ii), 96–108 (iii). Bottom right-hand corner of K 7897+ (Lambert 1960: 98, MS A, pls. 27, 29).

264. BM 51070 (D 82–3–23, 2066), from Dilbat. Neo-Babylonian school-exercise tablet: obv. (a) unidentified; (b) Marduk prayer // Arnaud

2007: no. 33 etc. (E. Jiménez); (c) Counsels of Wisdom 15–18; (d) unidentified; rev. (a) *Urra* VI 182(?); (b) *Urra* VIIA 230–33, MSL VI 82 MS S2; (c) *Urra* VIII 74–77, MSL VII 5 MS S12, not copied. Copy of rev. CT 14 49 (Thompson).

265. BM 80065 (89-10-14, 612), purchased from Selim Homsy & Co., probably from Tell ed-Der. Old Babylonian wisdom dialogue. After Lambert made this copy he joined the fragment to BM 79111, but did not enlarge his drawing accordingly. The joined pieces have subsequently been published by Streck and Wasserman (2014), with a copy and photographs.

266. BM 50522+52767+52946 (82-3-23, 1513+3801+3980)+77468 (84-2-11, 208), probably from Sippar. Neo-Babylonian copy, preserving some older orthographies, of an Akkadian version of the Instructions of Šuruppak. Xerox of pencil draft on folios 1635–37 published by Alster 2005: pls. 13–15, ed. pp. 61–73, MS Akk2.

267. K 9471, from Nineveh. Fragment of a Neo-Assyrian copy of a Babylonian composition presenting admonitions against behavior taboo to various deities. Another manuscript is *STT* 120(+)121 (see Lambert 1960: 117). A variant version of the text is given on no. 268.

268. K 8954, from Nineveh. Fragment of a Neo-Assyrian copy of a variant version of no. 267.

269. F 224, from Babylonia. Fragment of a Late Babylonian copy of the Series of the Fox, ed. Jiménez 2017: 381–82, MS BabNB4.

270. BM 38535 (80-11-12, 419), from Babylon or Borsippa. Fragment of a Late Babylonian copy of the Series of the Fox in four columns, ed. Jiménez 2017: 378–80, MS BabNB3.

271. BM 68586 (82-9-18, 8585), probably from Sippar. Fragment of a Late Babylonian copy of the Series of the Fox, ed. Jiménez 2017: 393–95, MS SipSch1.

272. Ash. Mus. 1924–2050, excavated at Kiš by Mackay. Fragment of a Late Babylonian copy of (or excerpt from) the Series of the Fox, ed. Jiménez 2017: 392–93, MS KiSch1. Another copy: *OECT* XI 54 (Gurney).

273. K 13841, from Nineveh. Fragment of a Neo-Assyrian copy of a literary composition, probably the Series of the Fox; see Jiménez 2017: 386–87, MS NinNA7.

274. CBS 2266+2301+8803+8803a+11300+N 921, from Nippur. Neo-Babylonian school-exercise tablet in twelve columns, including one or more excerpts from the Series of the Fox (rev. iv); for full contents and discussion, see Jiménez 2017: 390–91, MS NipSch1. Obv. (*Urra* II) not copied; photograph at CDLI P259300. A copy of CBS 2301+8803 obv. is *PBS* V 132 (Poebel).

275. Rm 433, from Nineveh. Obverse fragment of an animal fable, probably the Series of the Fox, ed. Jiménez 2017: 383–85, MS NinNA8.

276. BM 34654 (Sp II 137), purchased from Spartali & Co., written in Babylon. Fragment of a Late Babylonian copy of the Fable of the Wren, and colophon. Written by Nabû-mušētiq-uddi, s. Bēl-[uballissu] of the Mušēzib family, dated to Arsaces 242 (69 BC). Ed. Jiménez 2017: 333–41, MS a, with collations on p. 332. Another copy: *CT* 51 93 (Pinches).

277. BM 35622 (Sp III 133), purchased from Spartali & Co., written in Babylon. Fragment of a Late Babylonian copy of the Fable of the Wren, and colophon. Written by a son of Marduk-šāpik-zēri. Ed. Jiménez 2017: 334, 338–41, MS b, with collation on p. 332.

278. BM 46735 (81-8-30, 201), probably from Babylon. Late Babylonian school-exercise tablet: obv.(?) a version of the Fable of the Wren, ed. Jiménez 2017: 334, 338, MS d, with collation on p. 332; rev. (?) a list of toponyms, ed. Jiménez 2017: 356.

279. VAT 17353, from Babylon. Middle Babylonian tablet of bilingual proverbs, ed. Lambert 1960: 263, 274 BE unnumbered. Another copy: *VAS* XXIV 113 (van Dijk).

280. K 16004, from Nineveh. Neo-Assyrian fragment of a collection of popular sayings // Lambert 1960: 218, iv 1–8, pl. 56; part of the same tablet as K 5797 (Lambert 1960: 215, pl. 55). Transliteration folio 9851. See also no. 322.

281. Rm II 379, from Nineveh. Fragment of a Neo-Assyrian copy of bilingual proverbs or sayings // VAT 10251 ii 7–12 (Lambert 1960: 226–27, pl. 58).

282. Rm II 311+80-7-19, 282, from Nineveh, joins 80-7-19, 289 (Lambert 1960: pl. 58).

Neo-Assyrian fragment of a collection of bilingual proverbs in four columns, part of the same tablet as K 8206 (Lambert 1960: pls. 58–59). Transliteration folio 9897 (80–7–19, 282 only).

283. K 14056, from Nineveh, joins K 8206 (Lambert 1960: pl. 59). Neo-Assyrian fragment of bilingual proverbs, "Assyrian Collection." Transliteration folio 9899.

284. K 13999, from Nineveh. Neo-Assyrian fragment of bilingual proverbs on the topic of the palace // K 4610+ (Lambert 1960: pl. 60) // no. 286 // VAT 10423+11077 (forthcoming in *KAL*).

285. K 14143, from Nineveh. Neo-Assyrian fragment, probably the same composition as no. 284.

286. 81–2–4, 376, from Nineveh. Neo-Assyrian fragment of bilingual proverbs, same composition as no. 284.

287. Sm 1784, from Nineveh. Neo-Assyrian fragment from the middle, ruled off in columns and sections, perhaps proverbs on the topic of the palace (L. "cf. K 14056" = no. 283).

288. K 6080, from Nineveh. Neo-Assyrian fragment of proverbs on the topic of the palace, probably the same composition as no. 284. Transliteration folio 9038, "dup. VAT 10423."

289. K 17246, from Nineveh, joins K 7654 (Lambert 1960: pl. 60; 1992a: 7). Neo-Assyrian fragment of bilingual proverbs.

290. K 11224, from Nineveh. Neo-Assyrian fragment of bilingual proverbs, part of the same tablet as K 4327+ (Lambert 1960: pl. 60). Transliteration folio 9723.

291. K 8888, from Nineveh. Neo-Assyrian fragment of bilingual proverbs, part of the same tablet as K 4207 (Lambert 1960: pl. 61) // BM 56607+ (see no. 299).

292. Ash. Mus. 1924–1945, excavated at Kiš by Mackay. Late Babylonian school-exercise tablet: (i) proverb // Lambert 1960: 235, ll. 19–20, pl. 61. Another copy: *OECT* XI 90 (Gurney).

293. BM 38274 (80–11–12, 156), from Babylon or Borsippa. Late Babylonian copy of a collection of bilingual proverbs // K 4347+ ii (Lambert 1960: 240, pl. 61), also "dup. MM(A) 86–11–109 rev. iv 19–24" (annotation by L. on folio 1527), but this

does not match the MMA tablet published under that accession number in *CTMMA* II 69 (Spar and Lambert 2005).

294. K 7645+8324, from Nineveh, joins K 9050+13457 (Lambert 1960: pl. 64). Neo-Assyrian fragment of a collection of bilingual proverbs. Old copy: Meek 1920: 154 (7645 only).

295. BM 66629 (82–9–18, 6622), probably from Sippar. Late Babylonian school-exercise tablet: (i′) Akkadian part of bilingual proverbs, cf. Lambert 1960: pl. 66, BM 38283 rev. 11–12, transliteration folio 10251; (ii′) *Urra* XXI 2: 9–11, not copied (Gesche 2000: 727).

296. BM 38554b (80–11–12, 438b), from Babylon or Borsippa. Fragment of a Late Babylonian copy of the bilingual version of Sumerian Proverb Collection 2: 66–69, and colophon. Probably part of the same tablet as BM 38283 (Lambert 1960: 262–63 and pl. 66), which it restores. Edition of the combined text forthcoming from E. Jiménez.

297. BM 121076 (Th 1929–10–12, 72), excavated at Nineveh by Thompson. Neo-Assyrian fragment of bilingual proverbs (Lambert and Millard 1968: 8) // BM 38539 (Lambert 1960: 266–67, pl. 67) // VAT 10810 rev. (ibid.: 261, pl. 68).

298. BM 66647 (82–9–18, 6640), probably from Sippar. Late Babylonian school-exercise tablet: obv. *Urra* I, not copied; rev. bilingual proverbs // BM 56607+68060+68590+76257 (no. 299). Another copy: Gesche 2000: 523.

299. BM (56607)+68060+68590 (82–9–18, 8058+8589)+76257 (AH 83–1–18, 1624)+82989 (83–1–21, 152), from Sippar. Neo-Babylonian copy of a bilingual proverb collection in six columns, joins BM 56607 (Lambert 1960: 270–71, pl. 70) // K 4207 (Lambert 1960: 234–35) (+) K 8888 obv. (no. 291) // BM 66647 rev. (no. 298).

300. BM 33885 (Rm IV 447), probably from Babylon. Late Babylonian school-exercise tablet: obv. *Urra* I (*MSL* IX 157), not copied; rev. lexical, proverb. Transliteration folio 10136.

301. K 4551, from Nineveh. Top left corner of a Neo-Assyrian copy of an unidentified bilingual composition, ruled off into columns and sections, perhaps proverbs.

302. K 7437, from Nineveh. Neo-Assyrian fragment from the middle of an unidentified composition, ruled off into columns and sections, perhaps bilingual proverbs.

303. K 10370, from Nineveh. Neo-Assyrian fragment from the middle of an unidentified composition, ruled off into columns and sections, perhaps bilingual proverbs. Transliteration folio 9670.

304. K 11237, from Nineveh. Neo-Assyrian fragment of an unidentified composition, lower left corner, ruled off into sections, perhaps bilingual proverbs. Transliteration folio 9721.

305. K 17544, from Nineveh. Neo-Assyrian fragment, top left corner, ruled off into sections, "bilingual proverbs?" (Lambert 1992a: 11), perhaps part of the same tablet as K 11237 (no. 304).

306. K 13341, from Nineveh. Neo-Assyrian fragment from the middle, ruled off into columns and sections, perhaps bilingual proverbs. Transliteration folio 9760.

307. K 14178, from Nineveh. Neo-Assyrian fragment from the middle, ruled off into columns and sections, perhaps proverbs.

308. K 17540, from Nineveh. Neo-Assyrian fragment from the right edge, ruled off into sections, perhaps bilingual proverbs with only Akkadian remaining.

309. K 18116, from Nineveh. Neo-Assyrian fragment from the middle, ruled off into columns and sections, "bilingual proverbs?" (Lambert 1992a: 18)

310. K 18210, from Nineveh. Neo-Assyrian fragment from the middle, ruled off into columns and sections, Sumerian proverbs (Lambert 1992a: 20).

311. K 21424, from Nineveh. Neo-Assyrian fragment from the middle, ruled off into sections, perhaps from a collection of bilingual proverbs with only Sumerian remaining.

312. K 16804, from Nineveh. Neo-Assyrian fragment of a multicolumn tablet, ruled off into columns, Akkadian proverbs or popular sayings.

313. Sm 222, from Nineveh. Neo-Assyrian fragment from the middle, ruled off into sections; perhaps proverbs (otherwise von Soden 1971: 45).

314. VAT 17359, excavated at Babylon by Koldewey (Pedersén 2005: 281, N19, no. 1). Late Babylonian fragment with only Akkadian remaining, ruled off into sections, probably proverbs or popular sayings. Another copy: *VAS* XXIV 114 (van Dijk).

315. K 2015+4563+5435a, from Nineveh. Neo-Assyrian copy of a bilingual wisdom composition in four columns. Old copy: Meek 1920: 121. Identified as a "Sumero-Akkadian bilingual precept collection" by Gordon 1960: 148.

316. 79–7–8, 209, from Nineveh. Neo-Assyrian copy of an Akkadian composition beginning with a second-person address, top left corner, annotated "wisdom" by L.; rev. uninscribed.

317. K 10715, from Nineveh. Neo-Assyrian fragment from the middle, perhaps a second-person address. Transliteration folio 9258, annotated "wisdom" by L.

318–329. Fragments of Unidentified Literary Compositions

318. K 1578, from Nineveh. Neo-Assyrian fragment from the middle. Another copy: Kinnier Wilson 1985: pl. 31.

319. K 5252, from Nineveh. Neo-Assyrian fragment from the right edge; the extant passage includes attributes of Ereškigal.

320. K 5911, from Nineveh. Neo-Assyrian fragment from the middle, ruled off into sections. Transliteration folio 9986.

321. K 9987, from Nineveh. Neo-Assyrian fragment from the middle of a multicolumn tablet.

322. K 10912, from Nineveh. Neo-Assyrian fragment from the right edge, ruled off into sections, annotated by L. "could be same tablet as K 16004" (no. 280). Transliteration folio 9715.

323. K 13442, from Nineveh. Neo-Assyrian fragment from the right corner, ruled off into sections, didactic address.

324. K 11411, from Nineveh. Neo-Assyrian fragment from the middle, mentioning Marduk and Babylon; copied by L. alongside 81–7–27, 106 (no. 325), with the comment, "two may be from same tablet".

325. 81–7–27, 106, from Nineveh. Neo-Assyrian fragment from the middle, mentioning Marduk and Zarpanītum.

326. K 13859, from Nineveh. Neo-Assyrian fragment from the middle, ruled off into sections. Another copy: Kinnier Wilson 1985: pl. 31.

327. Rm 221, from Nineveh. Neo-Assyrian fragment from the middle, ruled off into columns and sections, didactic address. Left col. // UM 55-21-29 rev. (CDLI P257289, E. Jiménez). Transliteration folios 9039–40.

328. Sm 1783, from Nineveh. Neo-Assyrian fragment from the middle, ruled off into sections, mentioning Ganzir, the gate of the netherworld.

329. BM 33842 (Rm IV 402), probably from Babylon. Neo-Babylonian copy of a composition constructed as a dialogue, ruled off into sections. Transliteration folios 9177–78.

Index of Museum Numbers

Museum Number	Text No.	Museum Number	Text No.
BM 33819	259	BM 37959+38018	124
BM 33842	329	BM 38002	161
BM 33851+76672	257	BM 38018	124
BM 33861	155	BM 38025	94
BM 33885	300	BM 38060	127
BM 34218+34334	88	BM 38067	152
BM 34334	88	BM 38070	135
BM 34366	85	BM 38097	258
BM 34650	163	BM 38274	293
BM 34654	276	BM 38343	89
BM 35000	24	BM 38367	218
BM 35077	138	BM 38484+38488	262
BM 35285	109	BM 38488	262
BM 35404	30	BM 38535	270
BM 35496	29	BM 38554b	296
BM 35622	277	BM 39336+39457	43
BM 35865	50	BM 39457	43
BM 36296+38070	135	BM 39670	39
BM 36333	68	BM 40080	134
BM 36437	91	BM 40098+40124+77255	254
BM 36646	208	BM 40805	224
BM 36656	95	BM 41295	103
BM 36708	41	BM 41931	256
BM 36726	119	BM 42652	133
BM 36734	45	BM 43790	195
BM 36783	187	BM 44216	223
BM 36974	42	BM 45372+46401	177
BM 37122	136	BM 45373+46318+46323+46368+46484+	196
BM 37354	111	BM 45377+45402+46369+46375+46383+	173
BM 37392	121	46434+46435+46437+46454+	
BM 37402	216	BM 45382+46332+46393+46423+46440+	191
BM 37502	139	46461+46497	
BM 37571+37931	96	BM 45402	173
BM 37576	154	BM 45403+	176
BM 37616	67	BM 45618	86
BM 37641	245	BM 45746	85
BM 37659	110	BM 46318	196
BM 37692	125	BM 46323	196
BM 37695	147	BM 46332	191
BM 37779	44	BM 46368	196
BM 37866	198	BM 46369	173
BM 37931	96	BM 46375	173
BM 37937+38060	127	BM 46383	173

Museum Number	Text No.	Museum Number	Text No.
BM 68429	203	BM 82989	299
BM 68435	158	BM 83044	255
BM 68444	148	BM 83045	255
BM 68471	172	BM 83046	255
BM 68586	271	BM 87226	120
BM 68589	252	BM 93047	150
BM 68590	299	BM 96260	19
BM 68611	66	BM 98584	246
BM 71949	207	BM 98589	246
BM 71975	206	BM 98846	17
BM 72015	226	BM 99811	62
BM 72181	82	BM 101558	140
BM 72748	170	BM 121076	297
BM 73592	146	BM 123392	160
BM 74091	167	BM 128108	238
BM 74197	129	BM 130829	2
BM 74201	162	BM 134517	131
BM 74250	83	BM 136877	192
BM 75974	64	BM 136878	98
BM 76009	255	BM 141832	26
BM 76237	175	DT 5	14
BM 76257	299	DT 91	222
BM 76294	128	F 4	107
BM 76319	65	F 5	108
BM 76492	84	F 8	99
BM 76506	255	F 9	97
BM 76511	99	F 64	99
BM 76666	260	F 216	48
BM 76672	257	F 224	269
BM 76746	47	K 232+3371+13776	63
BM 76832	255	K 1578	318
BM 76845	99	K 1757+18963	144
BM 77093	157	K 1832+5072+5249+DT 5	14
BM 77253	164	K 1850b	52
BM 77255	254	K 2015+4563+5435a	315
BM 77438	9	K 2523	74
BM 77468	266	K 2893+3011+Sm 1258+1346	219
BM 78278	81	K 3011	219
BM 80065	265	K 3045	27
BM 82957	151	K 3179+3381+4914+13484+Sm 1861+1912	220
BM 82985	128	K 3183+	112
BM 82987	97	K 3275+14694	174
BM 82988	97	K 3307+6726	199

Museum Number	Text No.	Museum Number	Text No.
K 14094	79	Rm II 405	11
K 14143	285	Sm 85	77
K 14178	307	Sm 164	171
K 14694	174	Sm 222	313
K 14713	244	Sm 699	13
K 14763	228	Sm 866	51
K 15067	71	Sm 977	12
K 15299	233	Sm 1197	7
K 16004	280	Sm 1258	219
K 16753	229	Sm 1346	219
K 16804	312	Sm 1732	112
K 17113+18488	182	Sm 1751	114
K 17246	289	Sm 1783	328
K 17508	59	Sm 1784	287
K 17540	308	Sm 1810	72
K 17544	305	Sm 1861	220
K 17647	104	Sm 1896	78
K 17797	105	Sm 1912	220
K 18116	309	Sm 2030+81–7–27, 231	16
K 18210	310		
K 18397	113	**Fitzwilliam Museum, Cambridge**	
K 18488	182	ANE.87.1904	34
K 18603	18		
K 18617	186	**Harvard Semitic Museum, Cambridge, Mass.**	
K 18834	194	HSM 6836	106
K 18963	144		
K 19350	28	**John Rylands Library, Manchester**	
K 20637	132	JRL 1053	213
K 21072	40		
K 21117	54	**Sheffield Museum**	
K 21293	188	J98.92	8
K 21405	193		
K 21424	311	**University of Durham Oriental Museum**	
Rm 142+957	22	DUROM N2264	1
Rm 221	327	DUROM N2266	6
Rm 246	232		
Rm 401	76	**University Museum, Philadelphia**	
Rm 433	275	CBS 590	227
Rm 595	242	CBS 1702	80
Rm 843	237	CBS 2266+2301+8803+8803a+11300+N 921	274
Rm 957	22	CBS 2301	274
Rm II 311+80–7–19, 282+289	282	CBS 8803	274
Rm II 379	281	CBS 8803a	274

Index of Texts

REFERENCES

Abusch, T. 2016. *The Magical Ceremony Maqlû.* Ancient Magic and Divination 10. Leiden.

Abusch, T., and D. Schwemer. 2016. *Corpus of Mesopotamian Anti-Witchcraft Rituals.* Vol. 2. Ancient Magic and Divination 8.2. Leiden.

Al-Rawi, F. N. H. 2000. Cuneiform inscriptions in the collections of the John Rylands Library, University of Manchester. *Iraq* 62: 21–63.

Alster, B. 2005. *Wisdom of Ancient Sumer.* Bethesda, Md.

Ambos, C. 2004. *Mesopotamische Baurituale aus dem 1. Jahrtausend v. Chr.* Dresden.

Arnaud, D. 2007. *Corpus des textes de bibliothèque de Ras Shamra-Ougarit (1936–2000).* Aula Orientalis Supplementa 23. Barcelona.

Ball, C. J. 1899. *Light from the East.* London.

Bartelmus, A. 2016. *Fragmente einer großen Sprache: Sumerisch im Kontext der Schreiberausbildung des kassitenzeitlichen Babylonien.* 2 vols. Berlin.

Böck, B. 2014. *The Healing Goddess Gula.* Leiden.

Borger, R. 1967. *Handbuch der Keilschriftliteratur.* Vol. 1. Berlin.

———. 1975. *Handbuch der Keilschriftliteratur.* Vol. 2. Berlin.

———. 1991. *Ein Brief Sîn-iddinams von Larsa an die Sonnengott sowie Bemerkungen über "Joins" und das "Joinen."* Nachrichten der Akademie der Wissenschaften in Göttingen I, Phil.-hist. Klasse 2. Göttingen.

Brinkman, J. A. 1968. *A Political History of Post-Kassite Babylonia, 1158–722 b.c.* Analecta Orientalia 43. Rome.

———. 1976. *Materials and Studies for Kassite History.* Vol. 1. Chicago.

———. 1985. Texts and fragments. *Journal of Cuneiform Studies* 37: 249–52.

Brünnow, R. E. 1890. Assyrian hymns. *Zeitschrift für Assyriologie* 5: 55–80.

Cagni, L. 1969. *L'epopea di Erra.* Studi semitici 34. Rome.

Cohen, M. E. 1988. *The Canonical Lamentations of Ancient Mesopotamia.* 2 vols. Potomac, Md.

Cooper, J. S. 1971. Bilinguals from Boghazköi I. *Zeitschrift für Assyriologie* 61: 1–22.

———. 1978. *The Return of Ninurta to Nippur.* Analecta Orientalia 52. Rome.

Craig, J. A. 1897. *Assyrian and Babylonian Religious Texts.* Vol. 2. Leipzig.

Delitzsch, F. 1887. *Assyrisches Wörterbuch.* Assyriologische Bibliothek 7. Leipzig.

Ebeling, E. 1953a. *Die akkadische Gebetsserie "Handerhebung."* Berlin.

———. 1953b. Sammlungen von Beschwörungsformeln. *Archív Orientální* 21: 357–423.

Finkel, I. L. 1987. On two inscribed mace-heads. *Revue d'Assyriologie* 81: 189.

Frame, G. 1995. *Rulers of Babylonia: From the Second Dynasty of Isin to the End of Assyrian Domination (1157–612 bc).* Royal Inscriptions of Mesopotamia: Babylonian Periods 2. Toronto.

Frayne, D. R. 1990. *Old Babylonian Period (2003–1595 bc).* Royal Inscriptions of Mesopotamia: Early Periods 4. Toronto.

Geller, M. J. 1980. A Middle Assyrian tablet of *Utukkû lemnūtu,* Tablet 12. *Iraq* 42: 23–51.

———. 2016a. Appeasing the ghost of W. G. Lambert. *Nouvelles assyriologiques brèves et utilitaires* 2016: 134–35, no. 80.

———. 2016b. *Healing Magic and Evil Demons: Canonical Udug-hul Incantations.* Die babylonische-assyrische Medizin in Texten und Untersuchungen 8. Berlin.

George, A. R. 1979. Cuneiform Texts in the Birmingham City Museum. *Iraq* 41: 121–40.

———. 1992. *Babylonian Topographical Texts.* Orientalia Lovaniensia Analecta 40. Leuven.

———. 2015a. On Babylonian lavatories and sewers. *Iraq* 77: 75–106. https://eprints.soas.ac.uk/21501/.

———. 2015b. Wilfred George Lambert (1926–2011). *Biographical Memoirs of Fellows of the British Academy* 14: 337–59. https://eprints.soas.ac.uk/21649/.

Gesche, P. 2000. *Schulunterricht in Babylonien im ersten Jahrtausend v. Chr.* Alter Orient und Altes Testament 275. Münster.

Gordon, E. I. 1960. A new look at the wisdom of Sumer and Akkad. *Bibliotheca Orientalis* 17: 122–52.

Grayson, A. K. 1975. *Assyrian and Babylonian Chronicles.* Texts from Cuneiform Sources 5. Locust Valley, N.Y.

Hallo, W. W. 1982. The royal correspondence of Larsa II: The Appeal to Utu. In G. van Driel et al., eds., *Zikir Šumim: Assyriological Studies Presented to F. R. Kraus,* 95–109. Leiden.

Hunger, H. 1968. *Babylonische und assyrische Kolophone.* Alter Orient und Altes Testament 2. Kevelaer.

Jakob, S. 2018. *Ritualbeschreibungen und Gebete,* III. Keilschrifttexte aus Assur literarischen Inhalts 9. Wiesbaden.

Jiménez, E. 2017. *The Babylonian Disputation Poems.* Leiden.

King, L. W. 1902. *The Seven Tablets of Creation.* 2 vols. London.

Kinnier Wilson, J. V. 1985. *The Legend of Etana: A New Edition.* Warminster.

Klein, J. 1981. *Three Šulgi Hymns.* Ramat Gan, Israel.

Köcher, F. 1971. *Die babylonisch-assyrische Medizin in Texten und Untersuchungen.* Vol. 4. *Keilschrifttexte aus Assur 4.* Berlin.

Kramer, S. N. 1985. BM 86535: A large extract of a diversified *balag*-composition. In J.-M. Durand and J.-R. Kupper, eds., *Miscellanea babylonica: Mélanges offerts à Maurice Birot,* 115–35. Paris.

Lambert, W. G. 1956. An Address of Marduk to the Demons. *Archiv für Orientforschung* 17: 310–21 and pls. 13–16.

——. 1957. Three unpublished fragments of the Tukulti-Ninurta Epic. *Archiv für Orientforschung* 18: 38–51 and pls. 1–4.

——. 1959–60a. An Address of Marduk to the Demons: New fragments. *Archiv für Orientforschung* 19: 114–19 and pls. 24–27.

——. 1959–60b. Three literary prayers of the Babylonians. *Archiv für Orientforschung* 19: 47–66 and pls. 8–23.

——. 1960. *Babylonian Wisdom Literature.* Oxford.

——. 1967. The Gula hymn of Bulluṭsa-rabi. *Orientalia* n.s. 36: 105–32 and pls. 8–23.

——. 1970. Fire incantations. *Archiv für Orientforschung* 23: 39–45 and pls. 1–11.

——. 1973. Antediluvian kings and Marduk's chariot. In M. A. Beek et al., eds., *Symbolae biblicae et mesopotamicae Francisco Mario Theodoro de Liagre Böhl dedicatae,* 271–80. Leiden.

——. 1978. Nabû hymns on cylinders. In B. Hruška and G. Komoróczy, eds., *Festschrift Lubor Matouš,* 2: 75–111. Budapest.

——. 1979. Near Eastern seals in the Gulbenkian Museum of Oriental Art, University of Durham. *Iraq* 41: 1–45.

——. 1980. New fragments of Babylonian epics. *Archiv für Orientforschung* 27: 71–82.

——. 1992a. *Catalogue of the Cuneiform Tablets in the Kouyunjik Collection of the British Museum, Third Supplement.* London.

——. 1992b. Prostitution. In V. Haas, ed., *Außenseiter und Randgruppen,* 127–57. Xenia 32. Konstanz.

——. 2002. A rare exorcistic fragment. In T. Abusch, ed., *Riches Hidden in Secret Places: Ancient Near Eastern Studies in Memory of Thorkild Jacobsen,* 203–10. Winona Lake, Ind.

——. 2007. *Babylonian Oracle Questions.* Mesopotamian Civilizations 13. Winona Lake, Ind.

——. 2013. *Babylonian Creation Myths.* Mesopotamian Civilizations 16. Winona Lake, Ind.

Lambert, W. G., and A. R. Millard. 1968. *Catalogue of the Cuneiform Tablets in the Kouyunjik Collection of the British Museum, Second Supplement.* London.

Leichty, E. 2011. *The Inscriptions of Esarhaddon, King of Assyria (680–669 BC).* Royal Inscriptions of the Neo-Assyrian Period 4. Winona Lake, Ind.

Lenzi, A., and A. Annus. 2011. A six-column tablet of *Ludlul bēl nēmeqi* and the reconstruction of Tablet IV. *Journal of Near Eastern Studies* 70: 181–205.

Martin, F. 1900. *Textes religieux assyriens et babyloniens.* Paris.

Matouš, L. 1933. *Die lexikalischen Tafelserien der Babylonier und Assyrer in den Berliner Museen.* Vol. 1. Berlin.

Mayer, W. R. 1976. *Untersuchungen zur Formensprache der babylonischen "Gebetsbeschwörungen."* Studia Pohl s.m. 5. Rome.

——. 1990. Sechs Šu-ila-Gebete. *Orientalia* 59: 449–90.

Meek, T. J. 1913. Cuneiform bilingual hymns, prayers, and penitential psalms. *Beiträge zur Assyriologie* 10.1: 1–127.

——. 1920. Some explanatory lists and grammatical texts. *Revue d'Assyriologie* 17: 117–206.

Mullo Weir, C. J. 1929. Four hymns to Gula. *Journal of the Royal Asiatic Society* 61: 1–18.

Oshima, T. 2003. Some comments on Prayer to Marduk, no. 1, lines 5/7. *Nouvelles assyriologiques brèves et utilitaires* 2003: 109–11, no. 99.

——. 2011. *Babylonian Prayers to Marduk.* Tübingen.

——. 2014. *Babylonian Poems of Pious Sufferers.* Tübingen.

Pedersén, O. 2005. *Archive und Bibliotheken in Babylon.* Abhandlungen der Deutschen Orient-Gesellschaft 25. Berlin.

Pinches, T. G. 1897. Certain inscriptions and records referring to Babylonia and Elam and their rulers, etc. *Journal of the Transactions of the Victoria Institute* 29: 43–90.

Reiner, E. 1998. Celestial omen tablets and fragments in the British Museum. In S. M. Maul, ed., *Festschrift für Rykle Borger zu seinem 65. Geburtstag am 24. Mai 1994,* 215–302. Cuneiform Monographs 10. Groningen.

Schwemer, D. 2017. *The Anti-Witchcraft Ritual Maqlû.* Wiesbaden.

Spar, I., and W. G. Lambert, eds. 2005. *Cuneiform Texts in the Metropolitan Museum of Art,* vol. 2, *Literary and Scholastic Texts of the First Millennium B.C.* New York.

Stein, P. 2000. *Die mittel- und neubabylonischen Königsinschriften bis zum Ende der Assyrerherrschaft.* Wiesbaden.

Strassmaier, J. N. 1892. Einige chronologische Daten aus astronomischen Rechnungen. *Zeitschrift für Assyriologie* 7: 197–204.

Streck, M. P., and N. Wasserman. 2014. Mankind's bitter fate: The wisdom dialog BM 79111+. *Journal of Cuneiform Studies* 66: 39–47.

von Soden, W. 1971. Der große Hymnus an Nabû. *Zeitschrift für Assyriologie* 61: 44–71.

——. 1974–77. Zwei Königsgebete an Ištar aus Assyrien. *Archiv für Orientforschung* 25: 37–49.

Wee, J. Z. 2016. A Late Babylonian astral commentary on Marduk's Address to the Demons. *Journal of Near Eastern Studies* 75: 127–67.

Weidner, E. 1959. *Die Inschriften Tukulti-Ninurtas I. und seiner Nachfolger.* Archiv für Orientforschung Beiheft 12. Graz.

Wiggermann, F. A. M. 1992. *Mesopotamian Protective Spirits: The Ritual Texts.* Cuneiform Monographs 1. Groningen.

Zimmern, H. 1906. *Zum babylonischen Neujahrsfest* [I]. Berichte … der sächsischen Gesellschaft der Wissenschaften, Phil.-hist. Klasse 58.3. Leipzig.

Cuneiform Texts

Plate 1 *Commemorative and Votive Inscriptions* 31

1 N2264

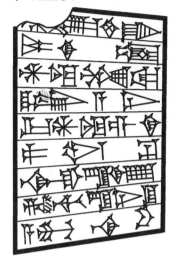

2 BM 130829

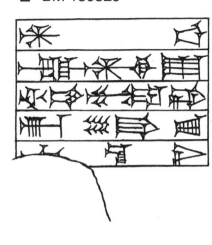

3 BM 56614

shaft

head

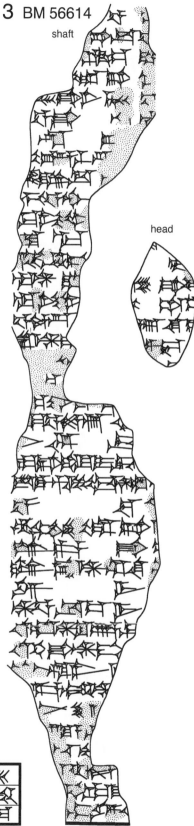

4 Ni 10753

rev.

obv.

Ni 833

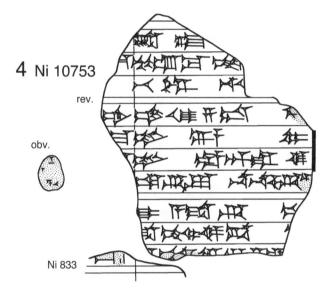

5 BCM 87'57

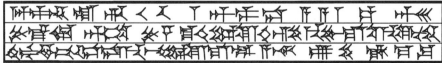

6 N2266

7 Sm 1197

8 J98.92

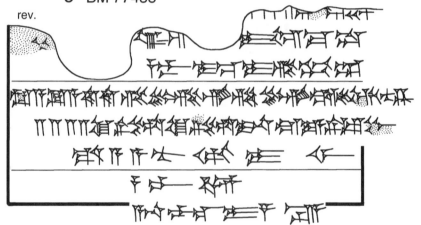

obv.

9 BM 77438

rev.

11 Rm II 405

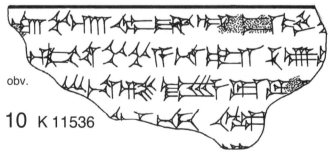

obv.

10 K 11536

rev.

Plate 3　　　　　*Late Copies of Royal Inscriptions*　　　　　33

12　K 4807+Sm 977+79-7-8, 80+314

upper obv.

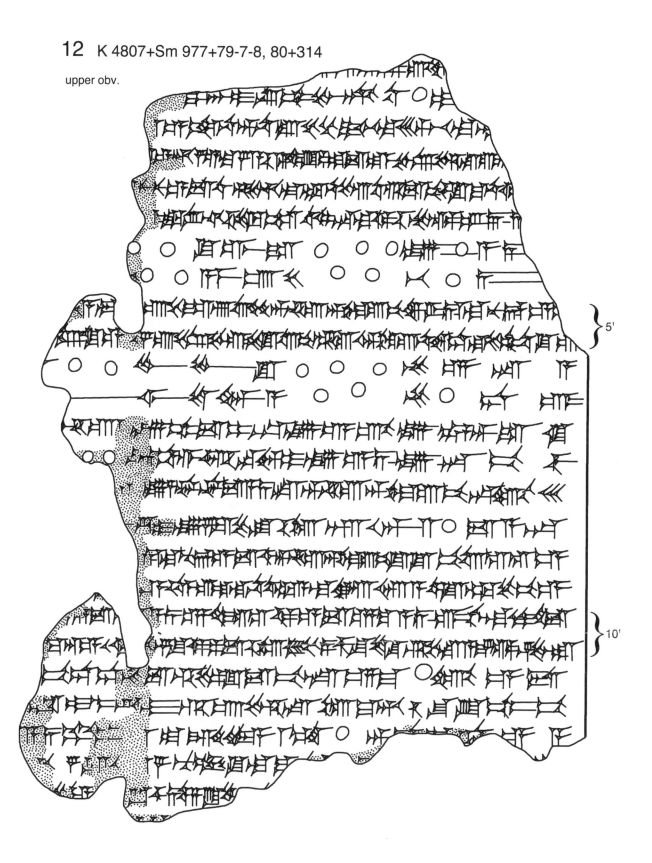

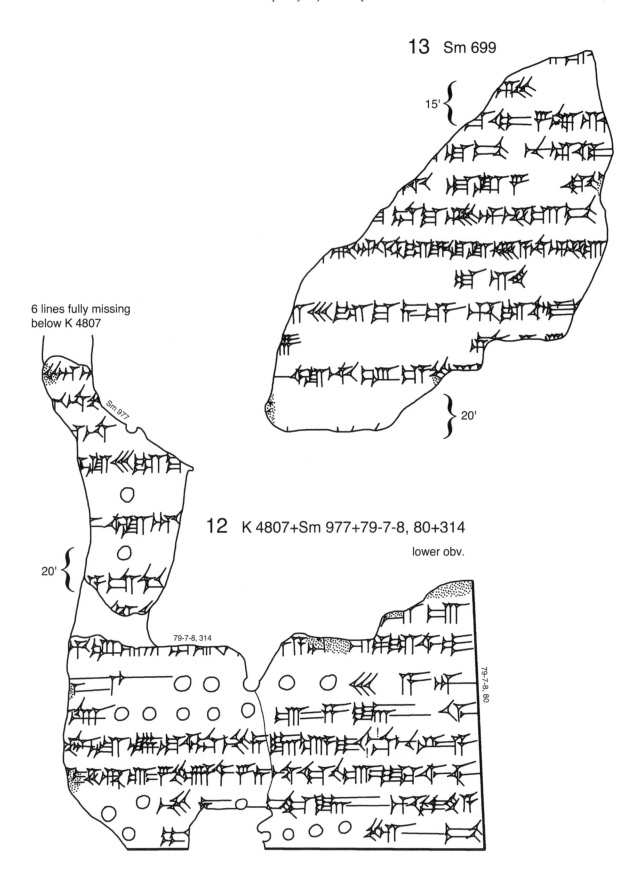

13   Sm 699

15'

20'

6 lines fully missing
below K 4807

Sm 977

20'

12   K 4807+Sm 977+79-7-8, 80+314

lower obv.

79-7-8, 314

79-7-8, 80

Plate 5　　　　　*Late Copies of Royal Inscriptions*　　　　　35

12　K 4807+Sm 977+79-7-8, 80+314

upper rev.

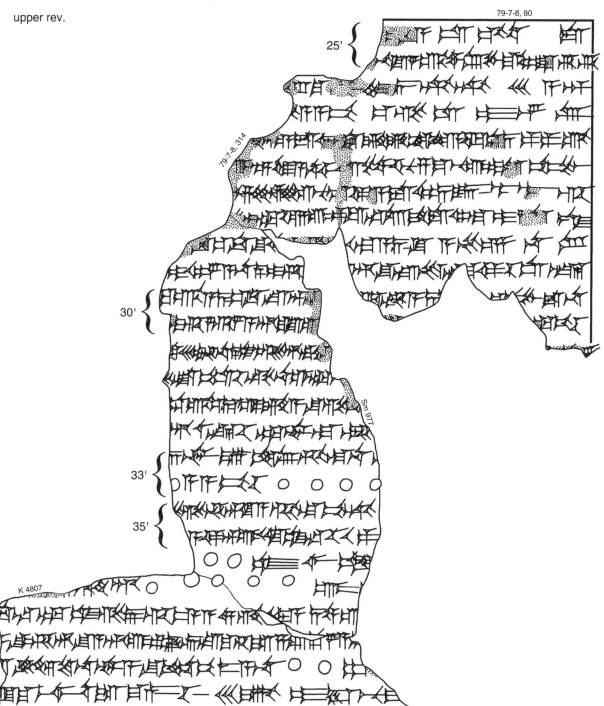

12   K 4807+Sm 977+79-7-8, 80+314
lower rev.

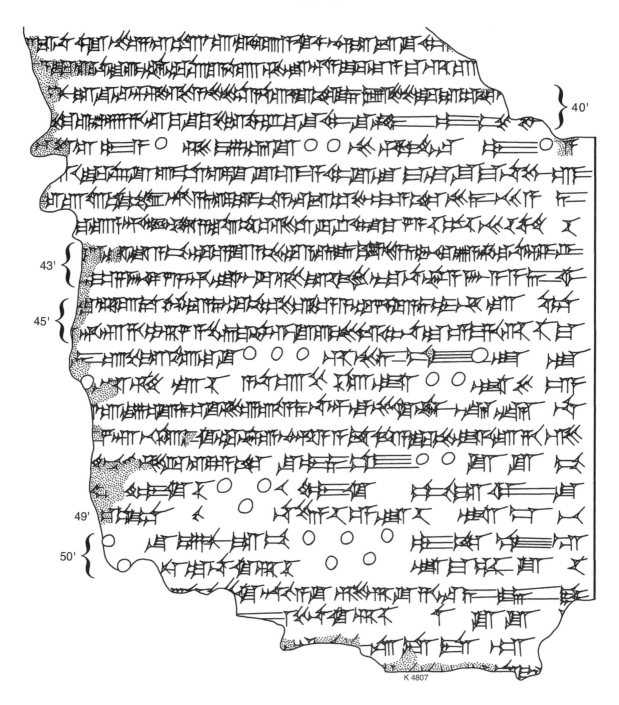

K 4807

14   K 1832+5072+5249+DT 5

upper rev.

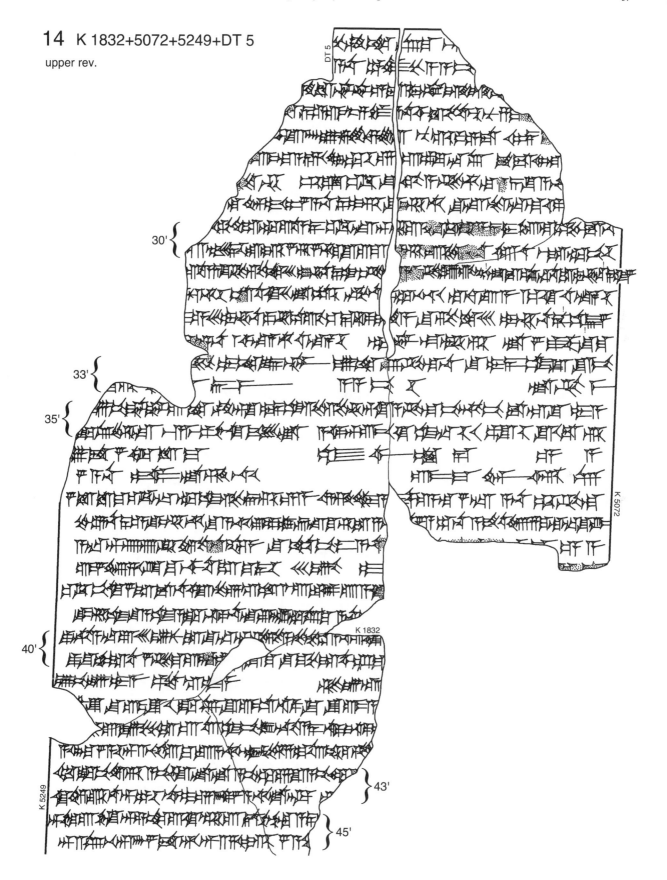

14   K 1832+5072+5249+DT 5

lower rev.

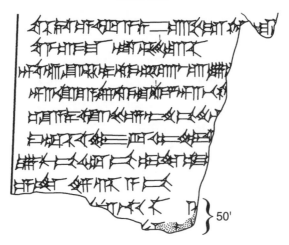

15   K 8269

Plate 9 *Late Copies of Royal Inscriptions* 39

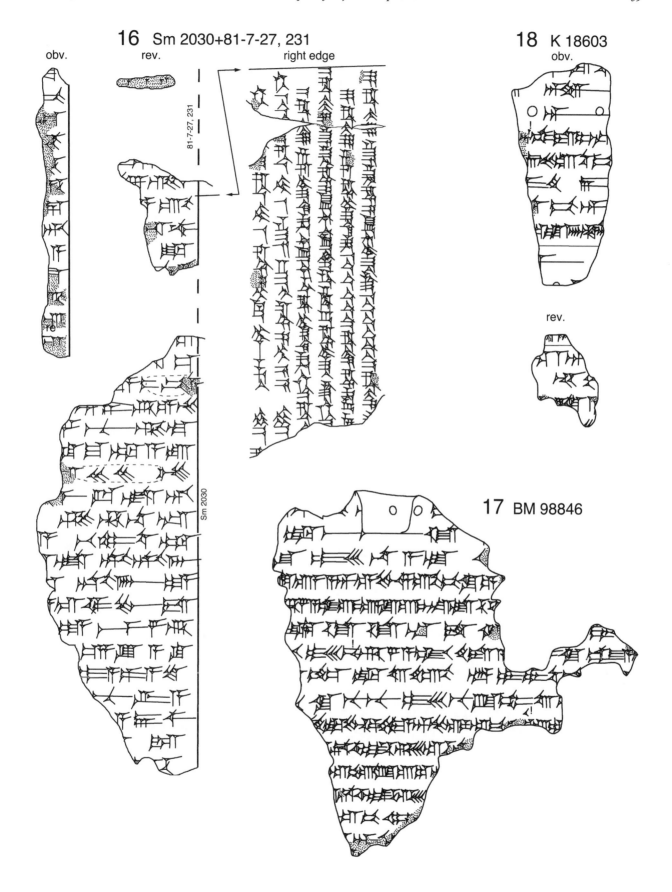

16 Sm 2030+81-7-27, 231

obv. rev. right edge

81-7-27, 231

Sm 2030

18 K 18603

obv.

rev.

17 BM 98846

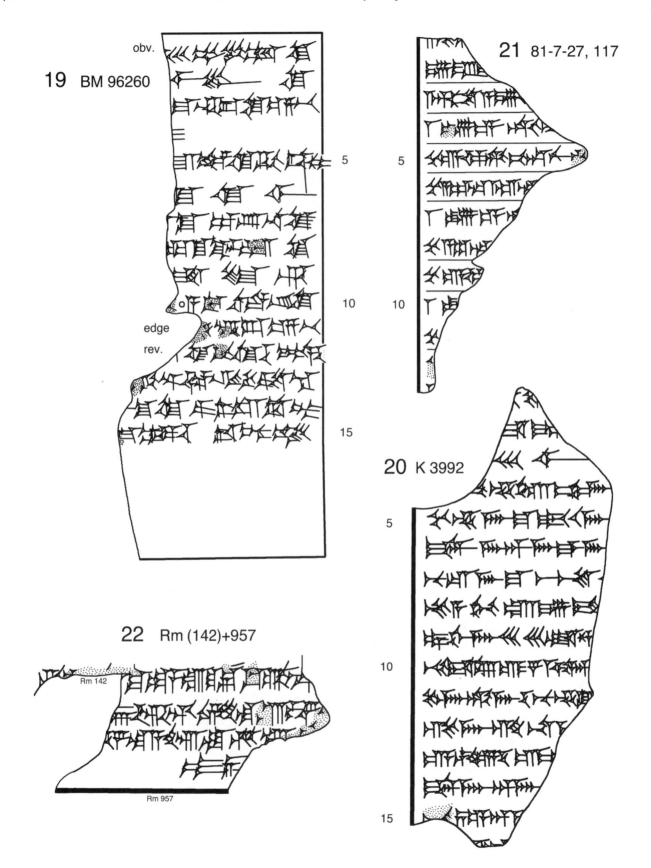

Plate 11   *Historical and Historical-Literary Compositions*   41

23 K 5191

25 BM 55628

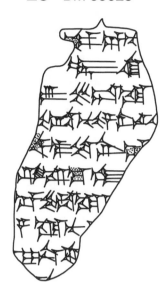

24 BM 35000

26   BM 141832

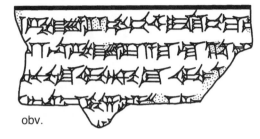

obv.

rev.

28   K 19350

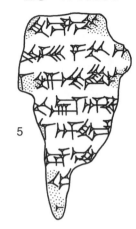

27   K 3045

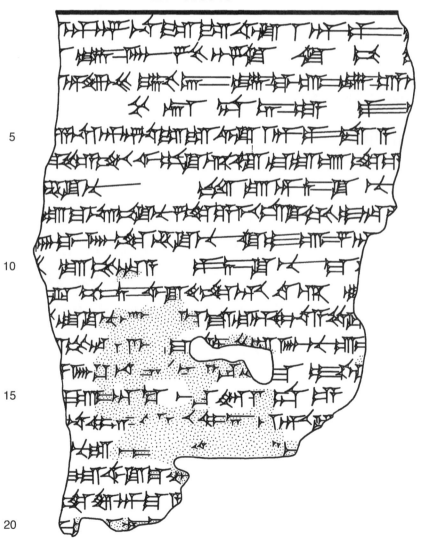

Plate 13 Late Copies of Royal Correspondence 43

29 BM 35496

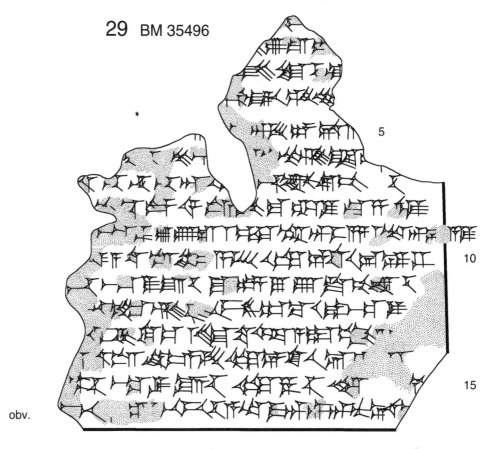

obv.

5

10

15

rev.

20

25

30 BM 35404

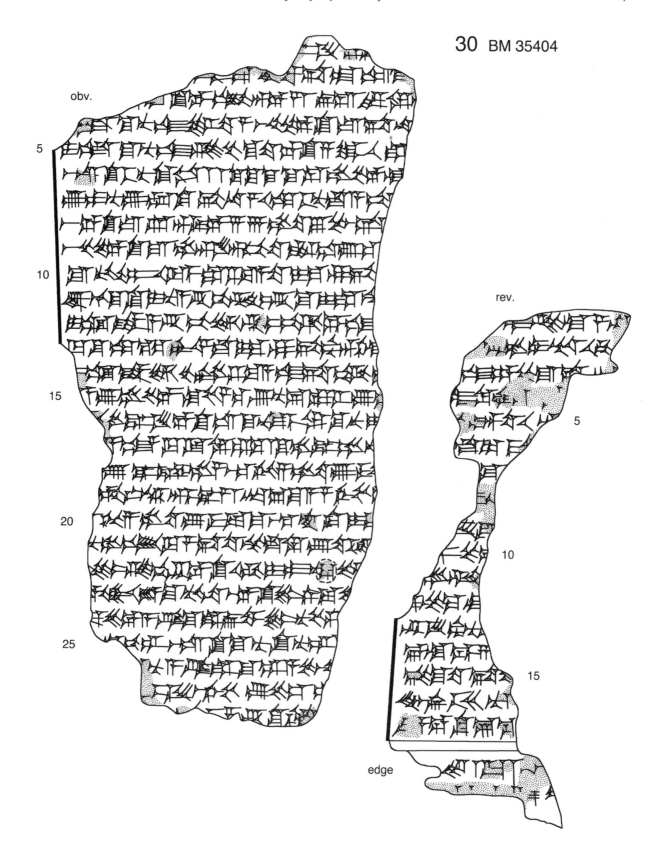

31 K 4930
obv. (rev. lost)

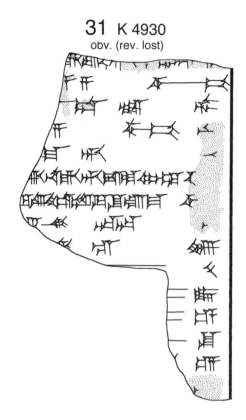

32 K 7171

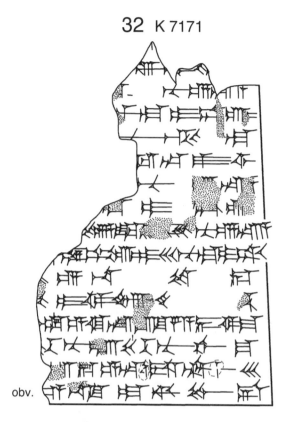

obv.

rev.

33 K 8937   obv. (rev. blank)

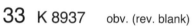
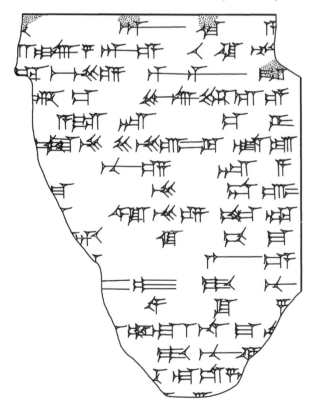

34 Fitzwilliam ANE.87.1904

upper obv.

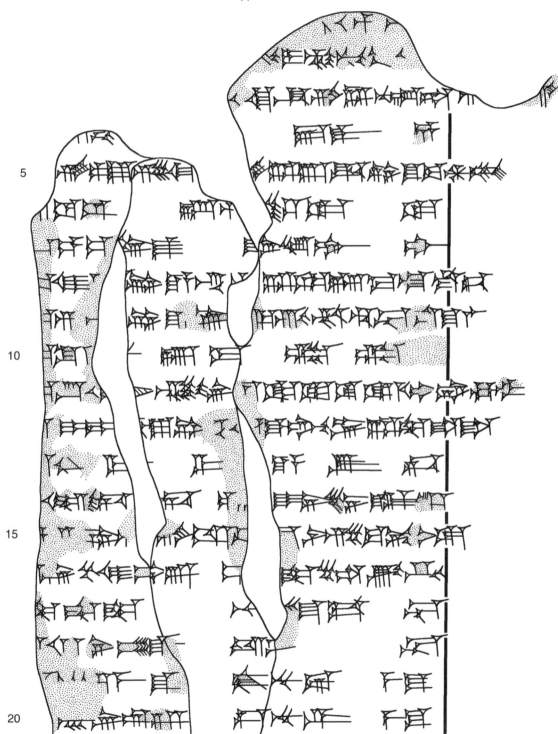

34   Fitzwilliam ANE.87.1904

lower obv.

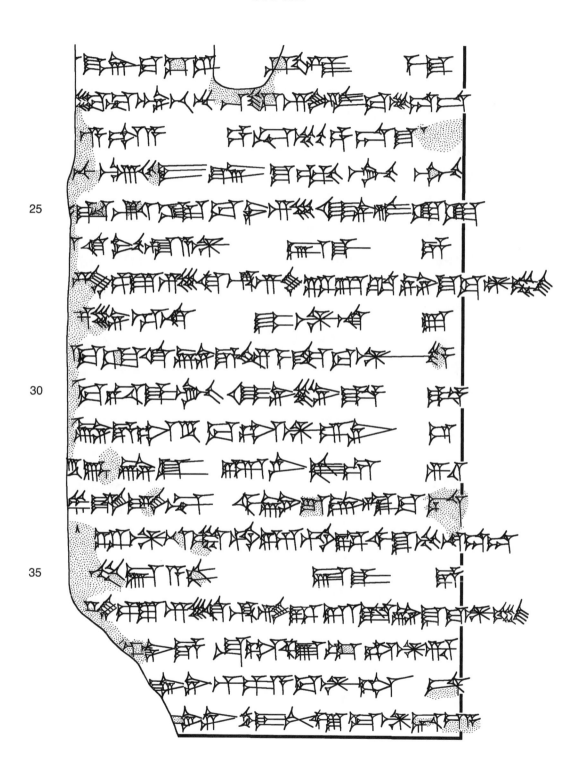

34   Fitzwilliam ANE.87.1904

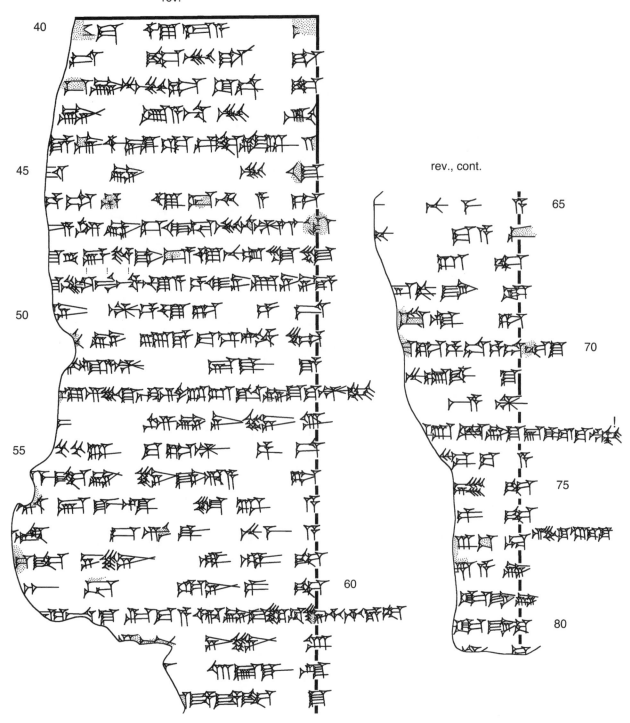

Plate 19   *Sumerian Literary Compositions*   49

35 BCM 206'78

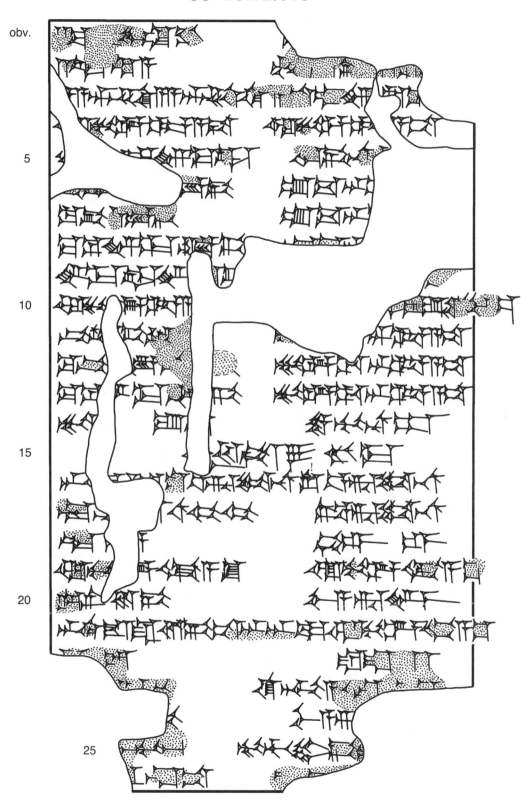

Plate 20

35 BCM 206'78

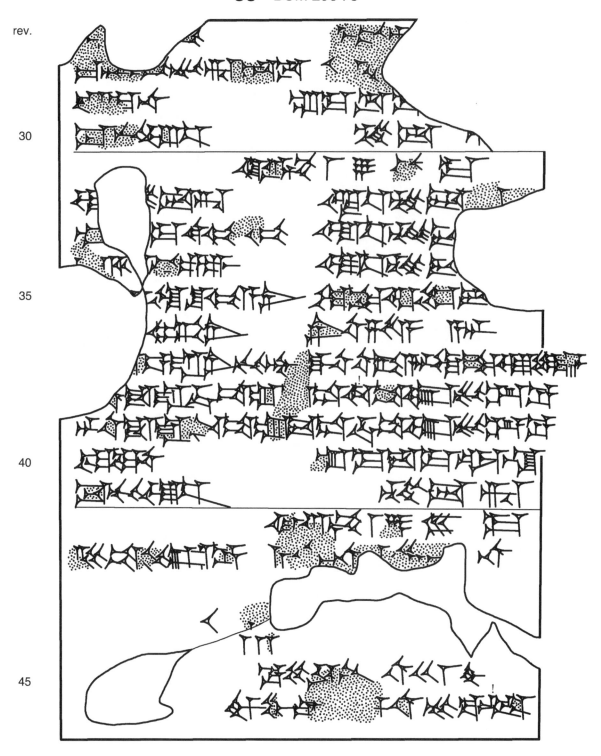

Plate 21   *Sumerian Literary Compositions*   51

36 BCM A.1851-1982   obv. iii   rev. iv

VAT 1334+
iv here

VAT 1334+ iii here

ii

37 BCM A.1850-1982

i

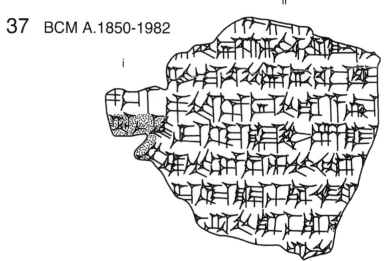

38   BCM A.1849-1982

obv.

rev.

Plate 23   *Sumerian Literary Compositions—Akkadian "Myth and Epic"*   53

39 BM 39670

40 K 21072

41 BM 36708

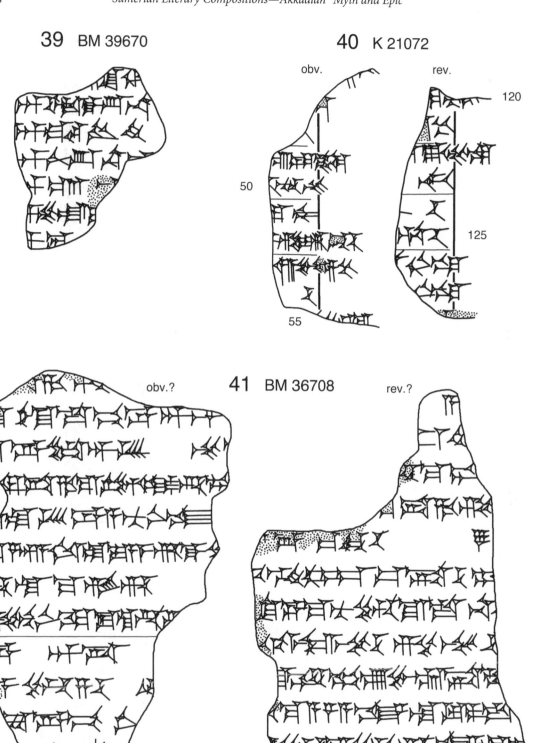

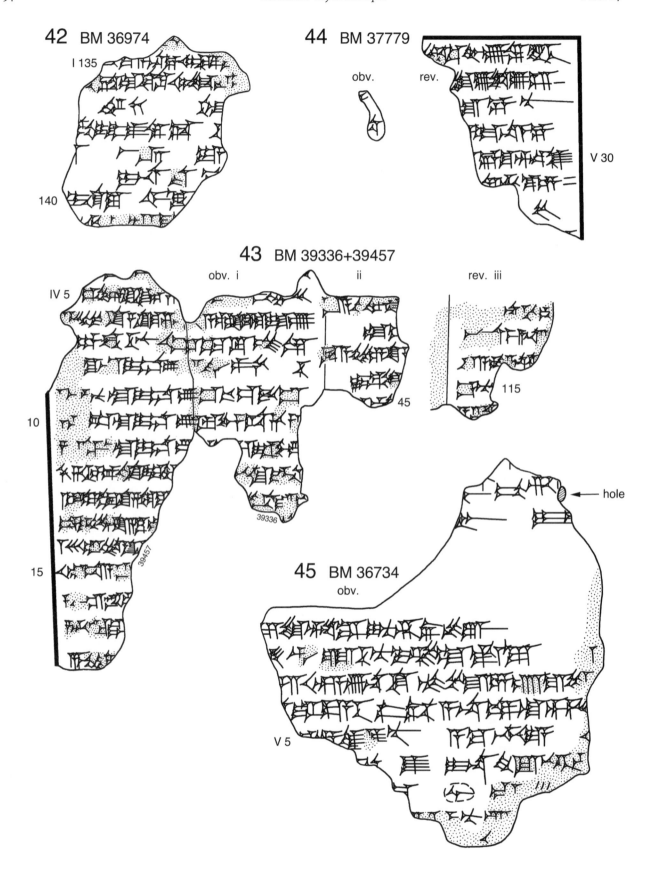

Plate 25   *Akkadian "Myth and Epic"*   55

45 BM 36734
rev.

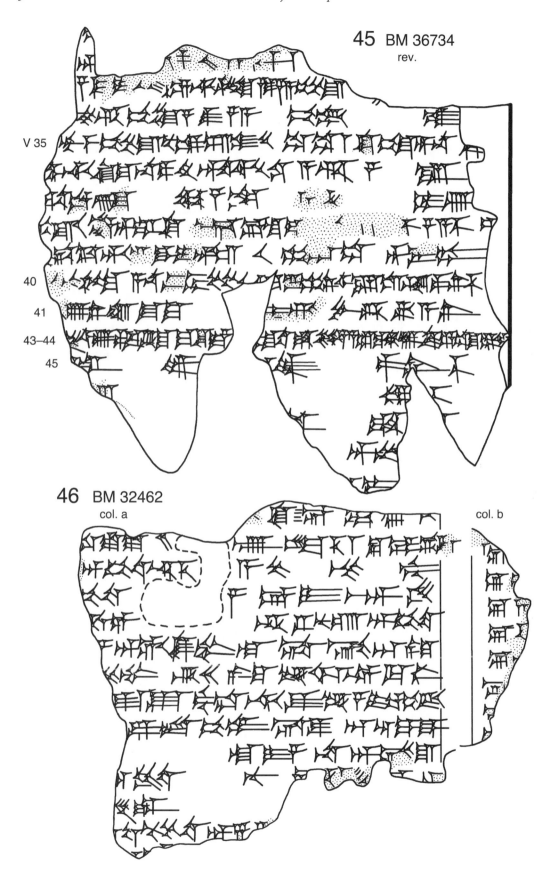

V 35

40

41

43–44

45

46 BM 32462

col. a   col. b

47 BM 76746
obv.

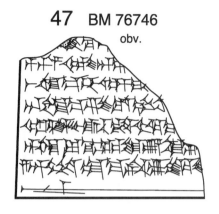

48 F 216

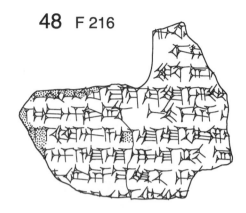

49 BM 51205+51606

obv.   rev.

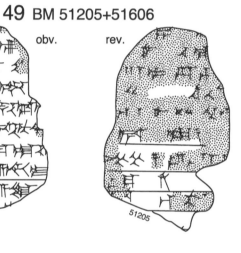

50 BM 35865

obv.   rev.

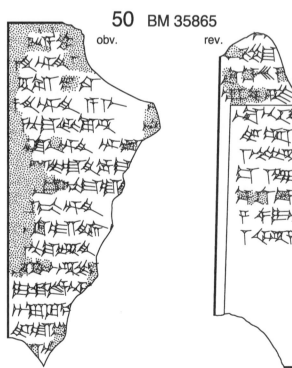

51   Sm 866

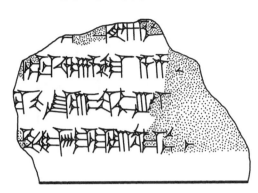

52   K 1850 b

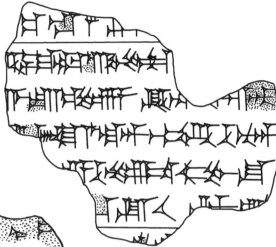

53
BM 32755

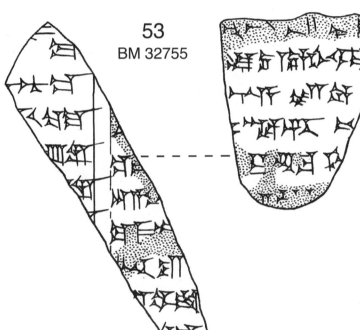

54   K 21117

55   BM 66640

obv.

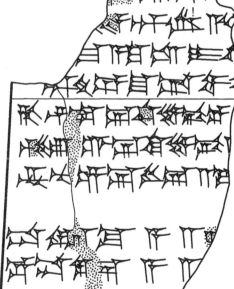

56   80-7-19, 152+81-2-4, 188
upper obv.

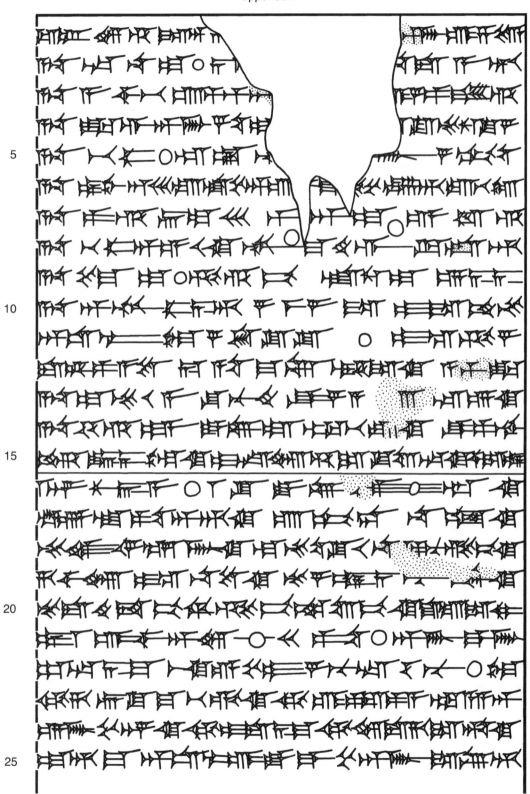

56   80-7-19, 152+81-2-4, 188

lower obv.

56   80-7-19, 152+81-2-4, 188
upper rev.

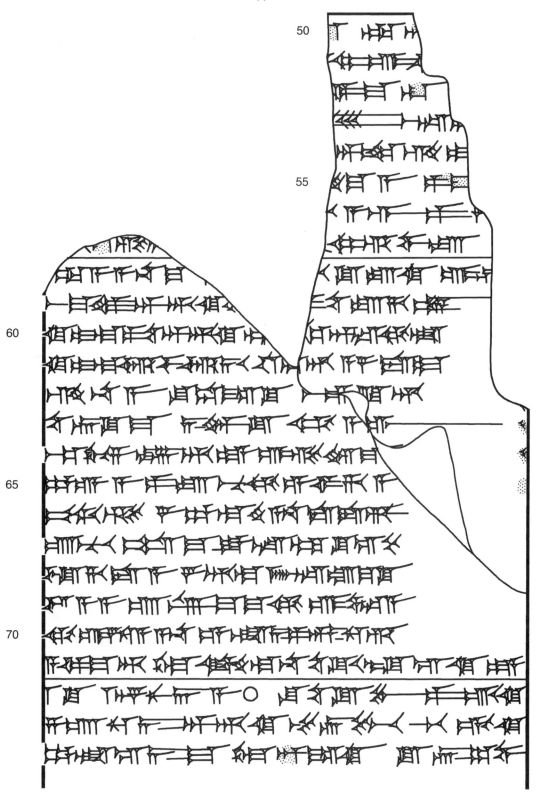

Plate 31   *Ashurnaṣirpal's Prayer—Hymns to Gula*   61

56   80-7-19, 152+81-2-4, 188
lower rev.

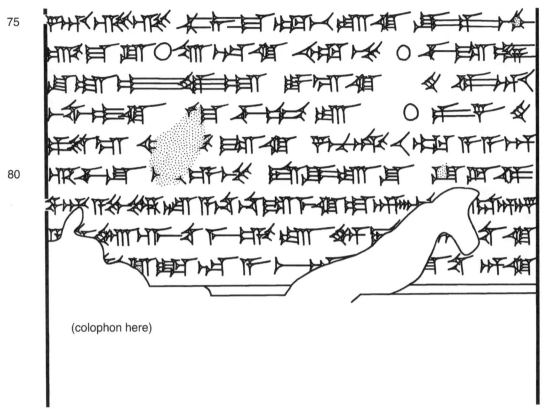

75

80

(colophon here)

57   83-1-18, 430

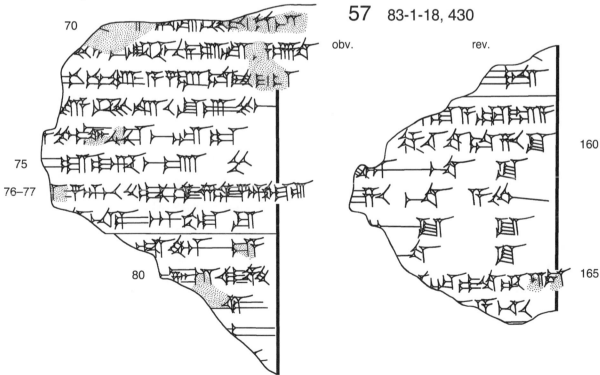

70

obv.   rev.

75

76–77

80

160

165

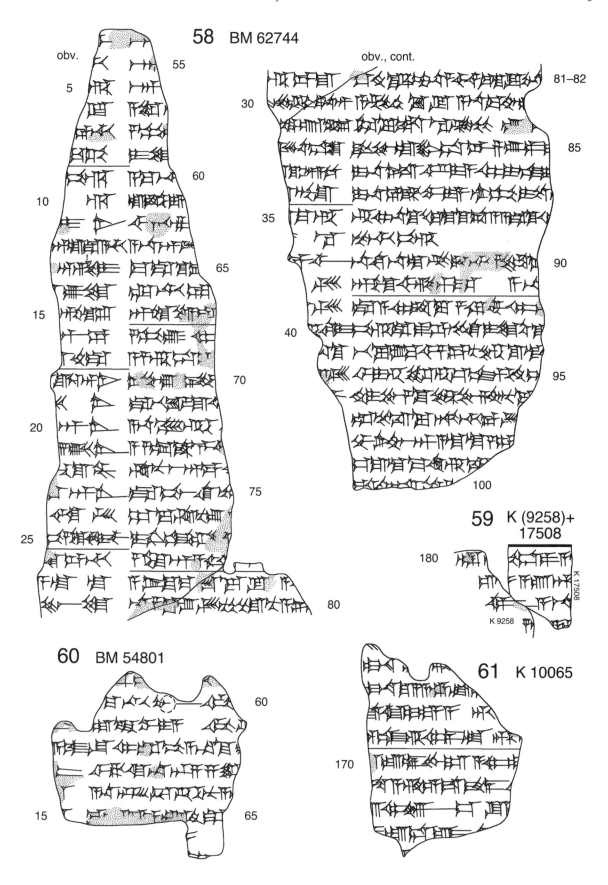

62   BM 99811

63   K 232+3371+13776

upper obv.

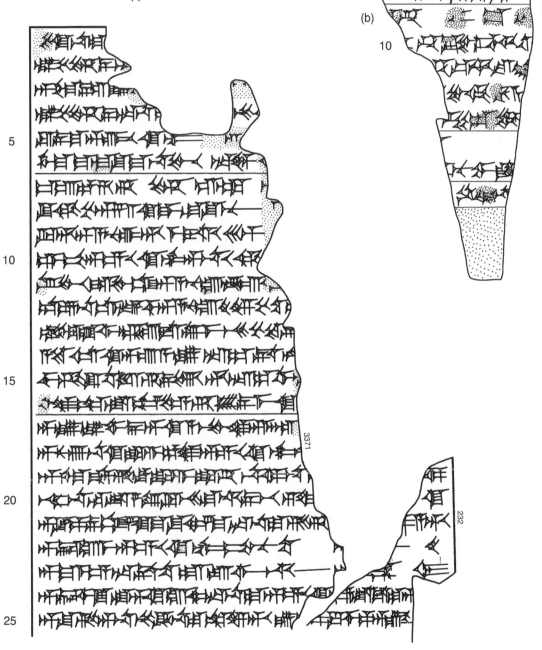

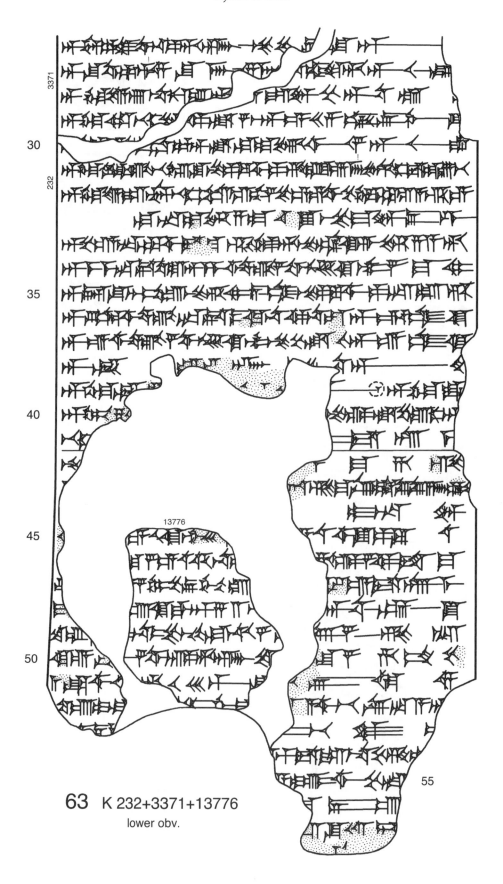

63 K 232+3371+13776

lower obv.

63   K 232+3371+13776

upper rev.

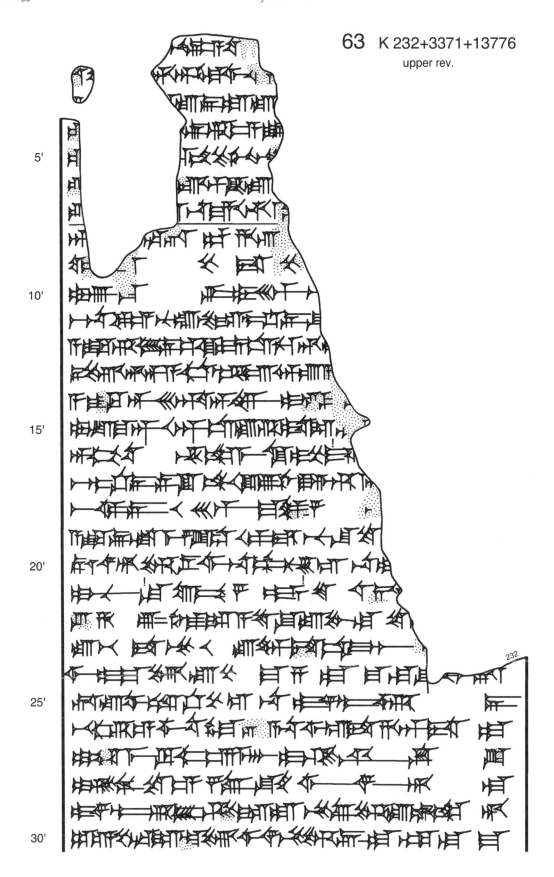

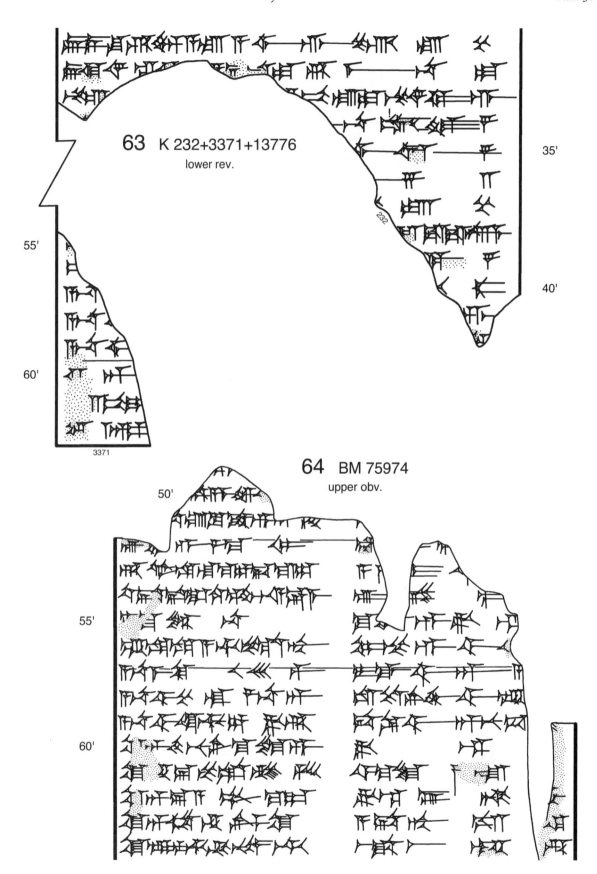

63   K 232+3371+13776
lower rev.

35'

40'

55'

60'

3371

64   BM 75974
upper obv.

50'

55'

60'

Plate 37   *Hymns to Gula*   67

64   BM 75974
lower obv.

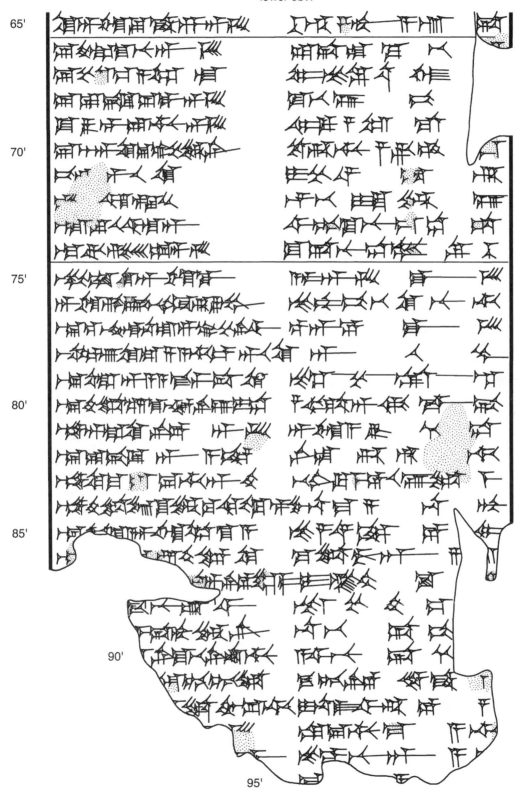

64 BM 75974
upper rev.

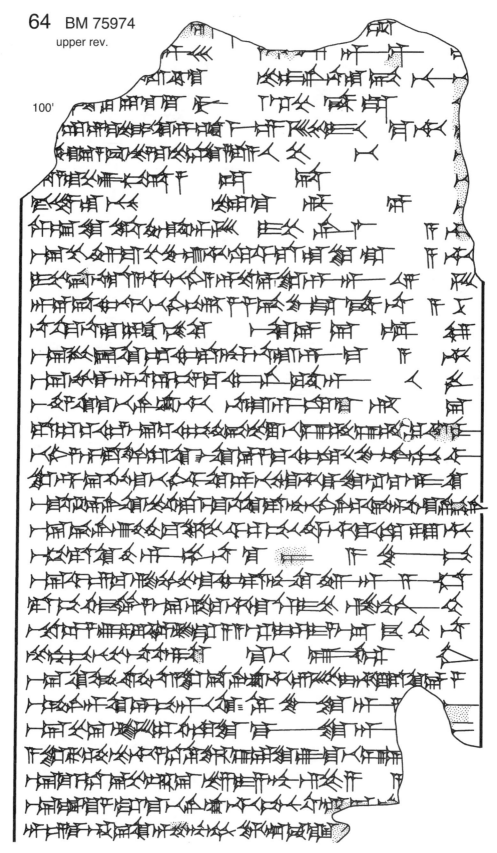

Plate 39　　　　　　　　　　　　　　*Hymns to Gula*　　　　　　　　　　　　　　69

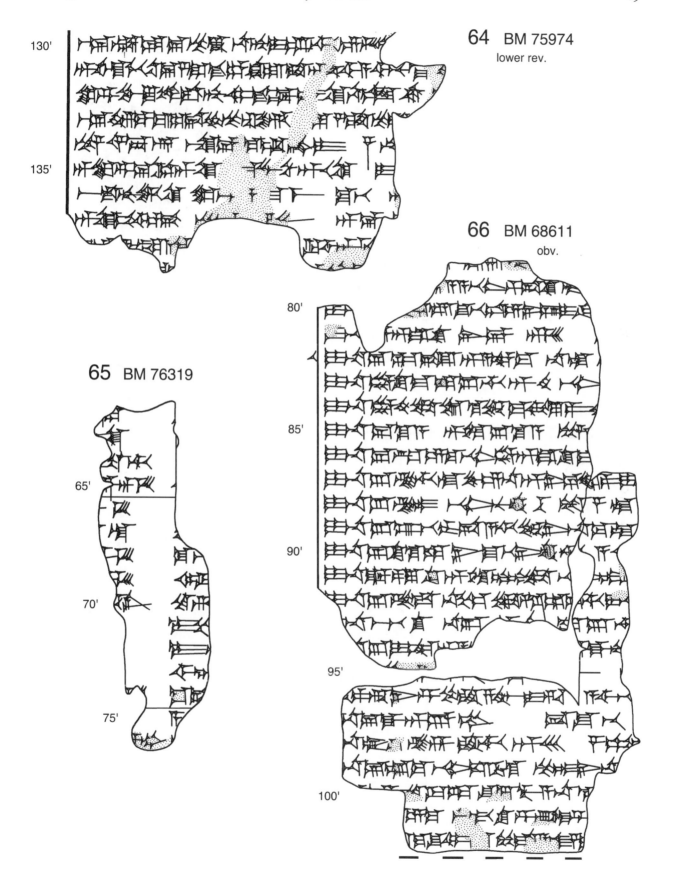

64　BM 75974
lower rev.

66　BM 68611
obv.

65　BM 76319

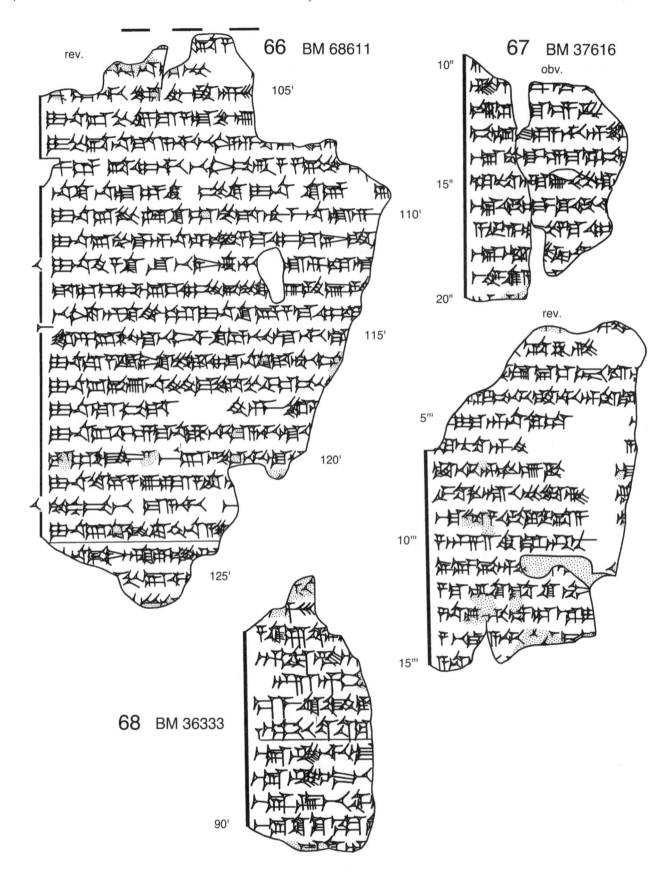

rev. **66** BM 68611

105'

110'

115'

120'

125'

67 BM 37616

10"

obv.

15"

20"

rev.

5'''

10'''

15'''

68 BM 36333

90'

Plate 41 *Akkadian Praise Poetry* 71

69 80-7-19, 115

obv.

rev.

71 K 15067

72 Sm 1810

70 K 9221+11328

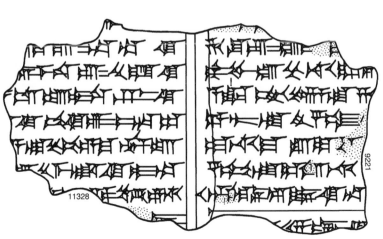

73 K 13975

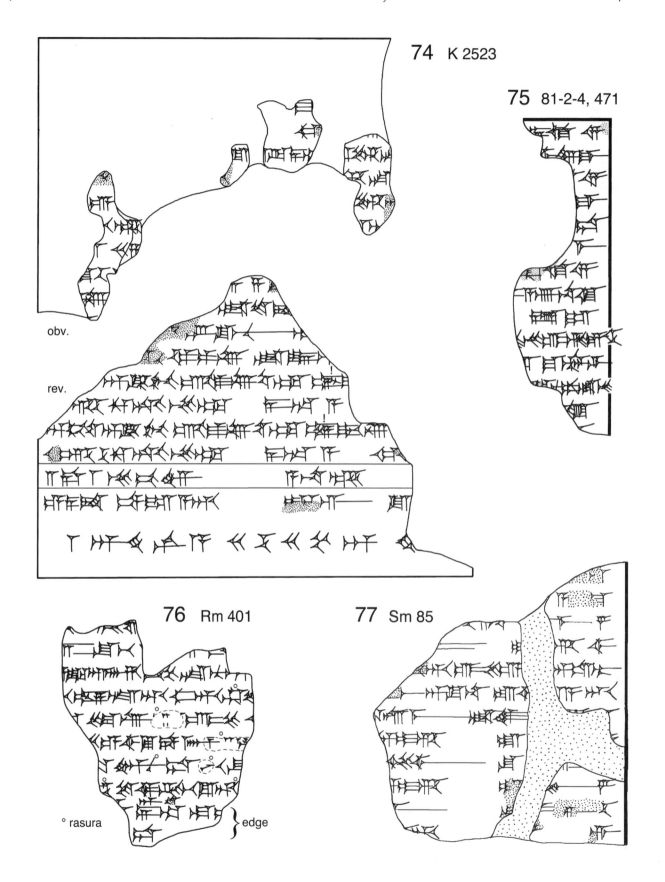

74 K 2523

75 81-2-4, 471

obv.

rev.

76 Rm 401

° rasura

} edge

77 Sm 85

Plate 43 *Akkadian Praise Poetry* 73

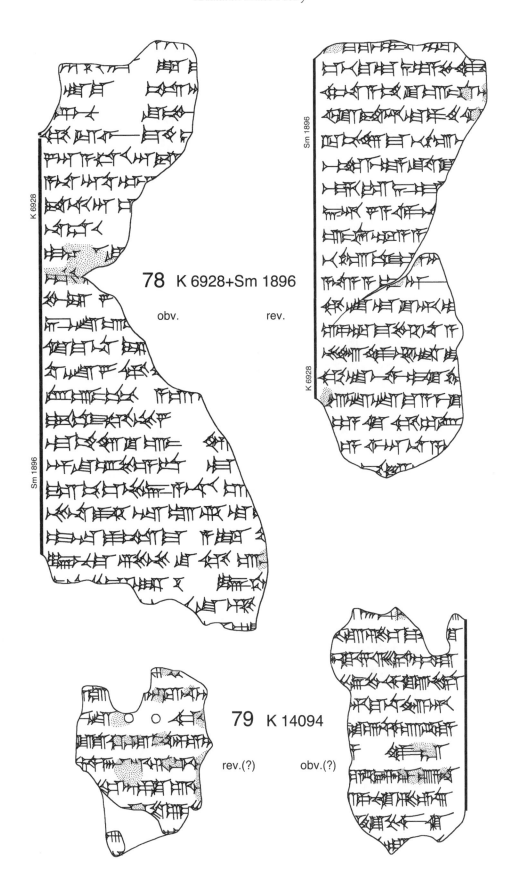

78 K 6928+Sm 1896

obv.   rev.

79 K 14094

rev.(?)   obv.(?)

80 CBS 1702

obv.

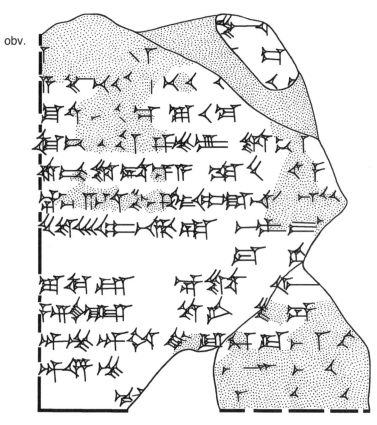

rev.

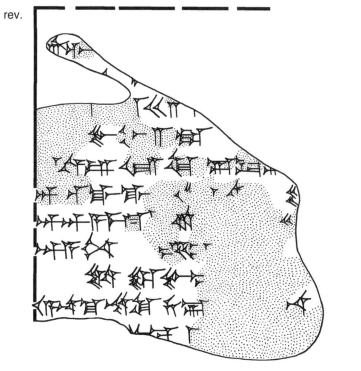

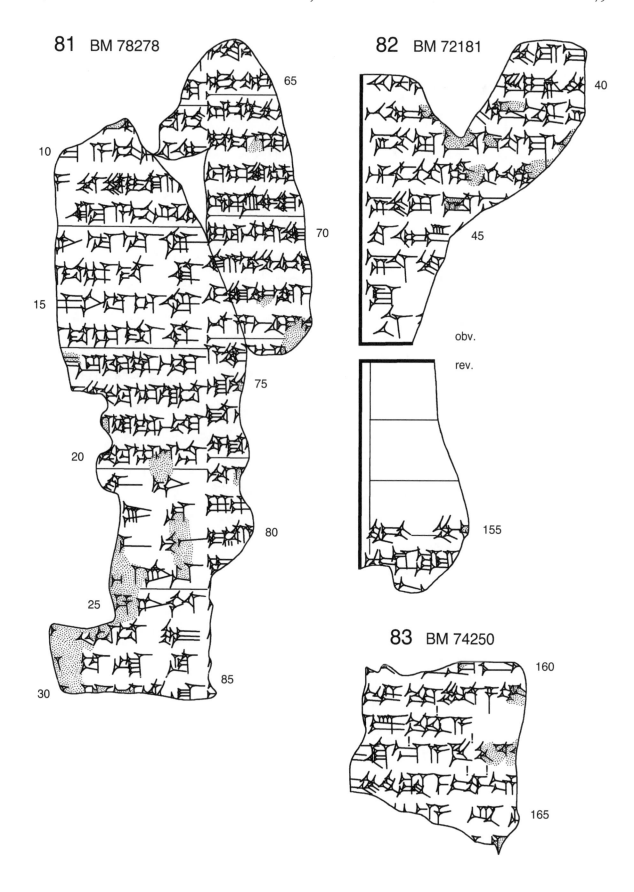

81 BM 78278

82 BM 72181

obv.

rev.

83 BM 74250

84 BM 76492

obv.

Plate 47   *Marduk Prayer No. 1*   77

84 BM 76492

rev.

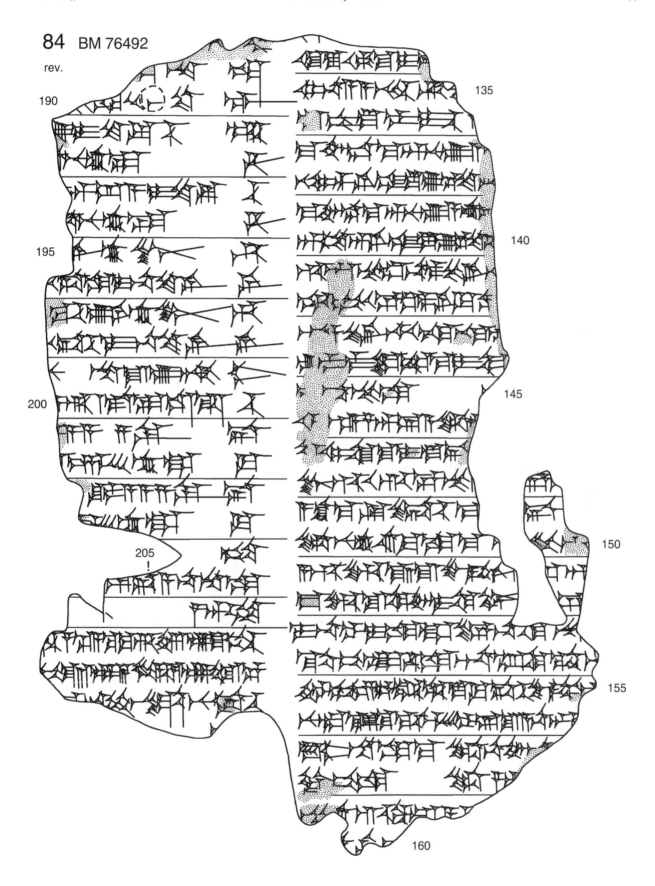

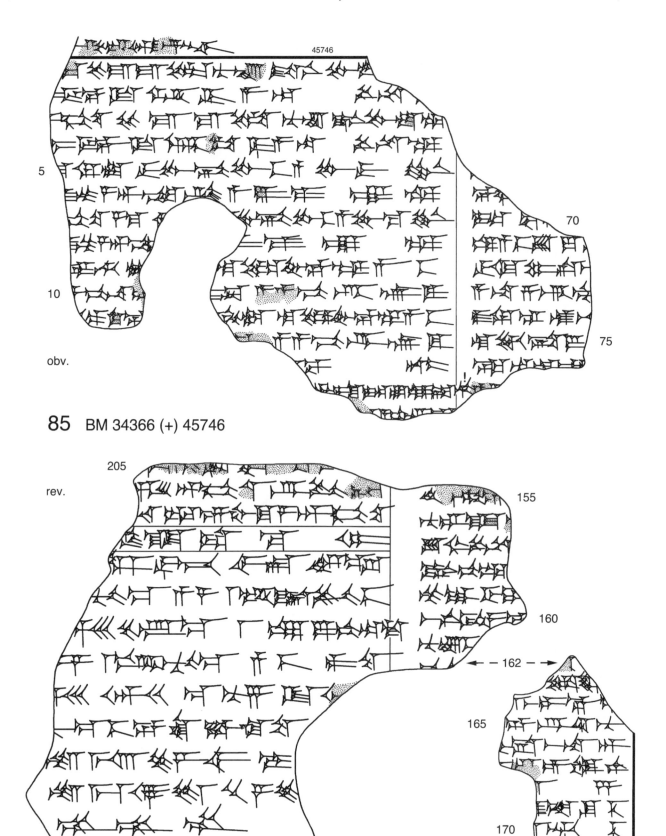

85 BM 34366 (+) 45746

Plate 49   *Marduk Prayer No. 1*   79

86 BM 45618   obv.

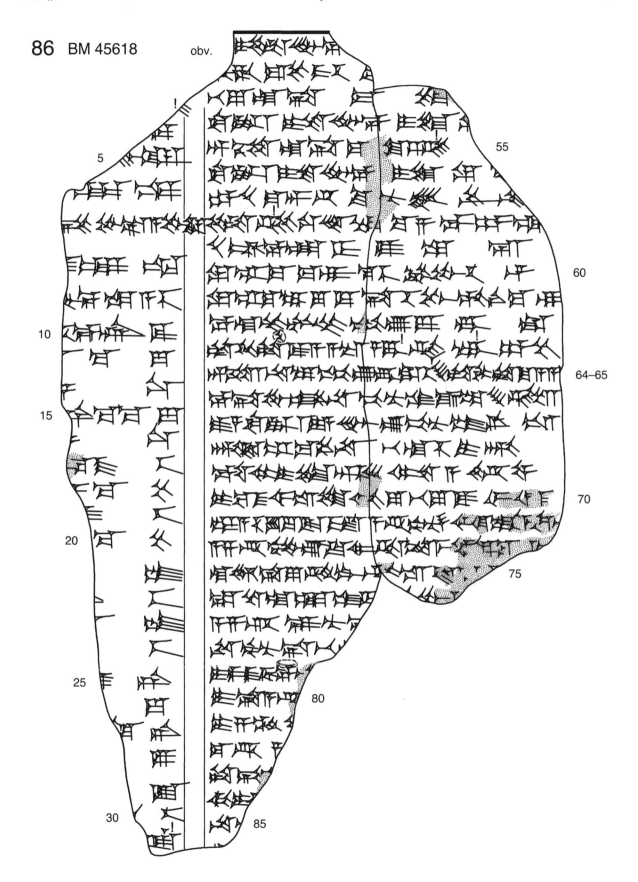

86 BM 45618

rev.

87 BM 66652

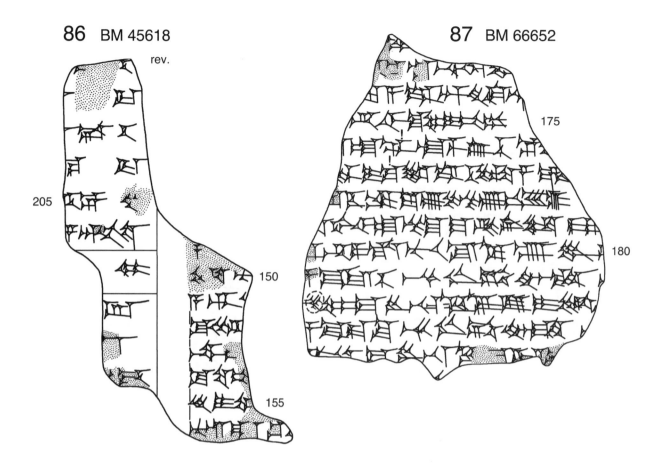

88 BM 34218+34334

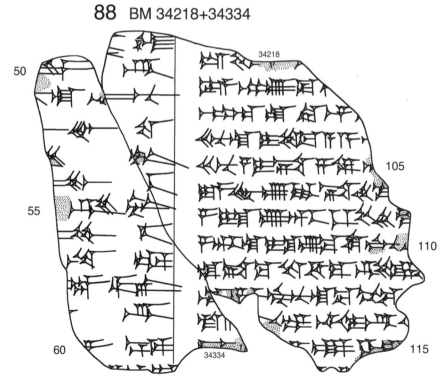

Plate 51 *Marduk Prayer No. 1* 81

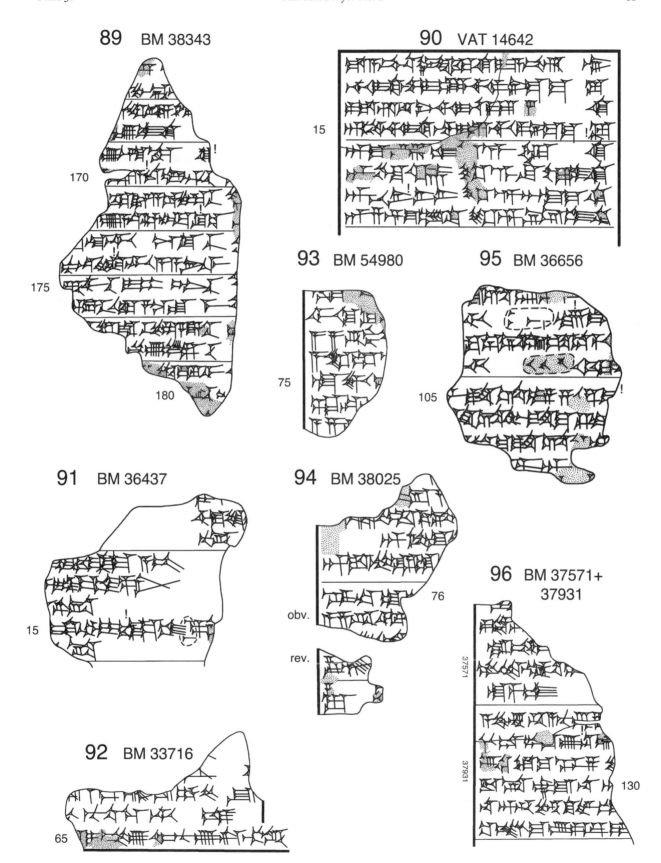

89 BM 38343

170

175

180

90 VAT 14642

15

93 BM 54980

75

95 BM 36656

105

91 BM 36437

15

94 BM 38025

obv.

rev.

76

96 BM 37571+ 37931

37571

37931

130

92 BM 33716

65

97 BM 61649+61672+62689+62816+
82987+82988+F 9

col. i

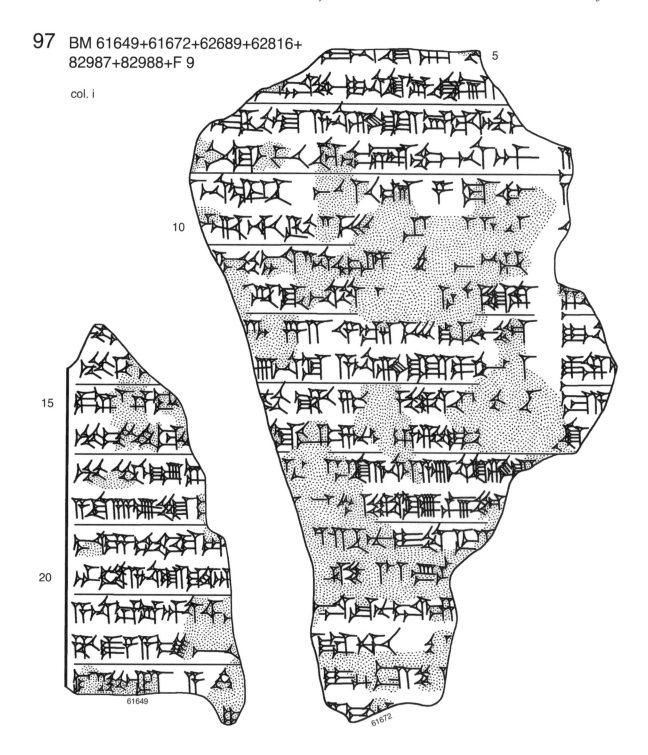

97   BM 61649+61672+62689+62816+
82987+82988+F 9

col. ii

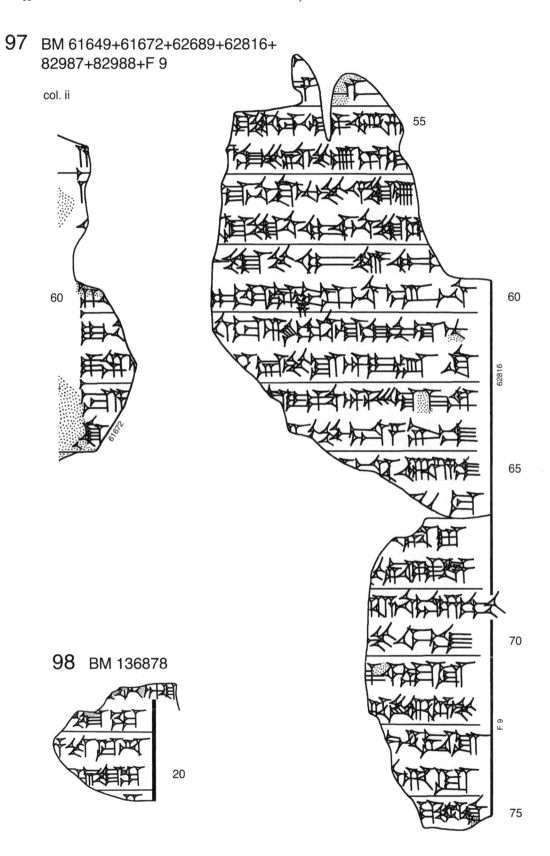

98   BM 136878

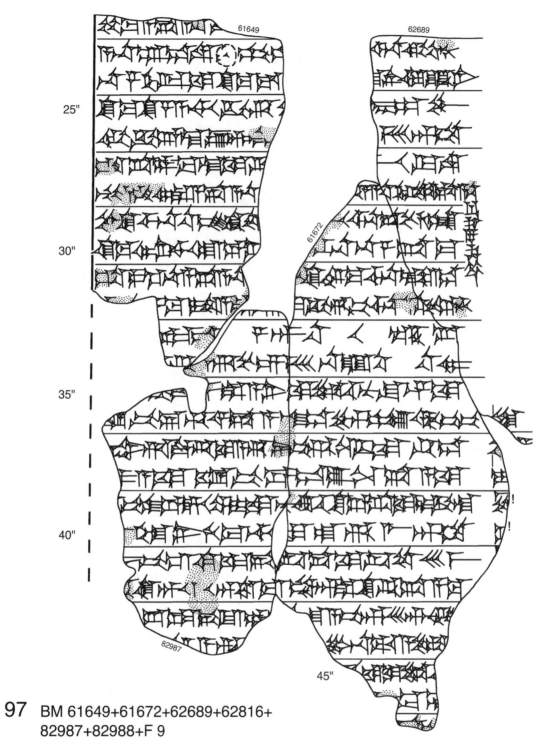

97 BM 61649+61672+62689+62816+
82987+82988+F 9

col. iv

Plate 55   *Marduk Prayer No. 2*   85

97 BM 61649+61672+62689+
        62816+82987+82988+F 9

col. iii

° insert

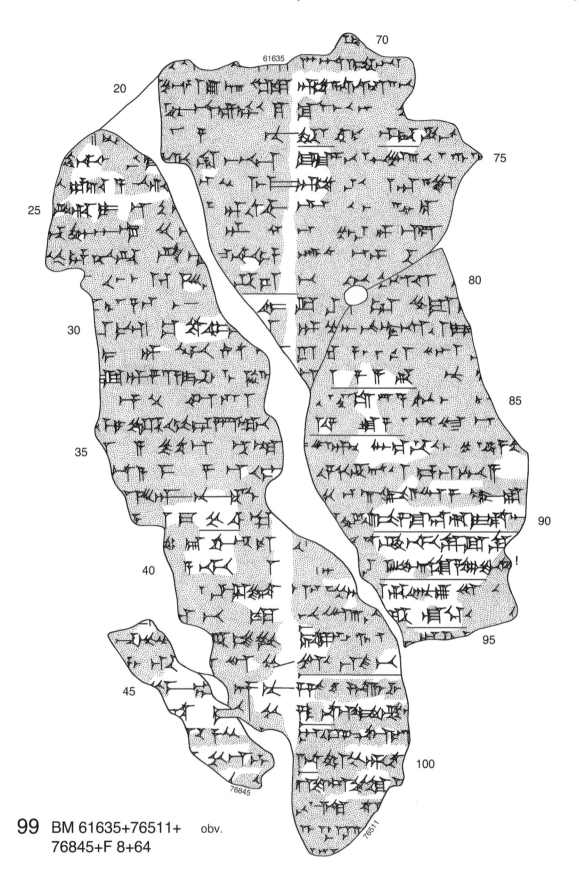

99 BM 61635+76511+   obv.
       76845+F 8+64

99 BM 61635+76511+
76845+F 8+64

rev.

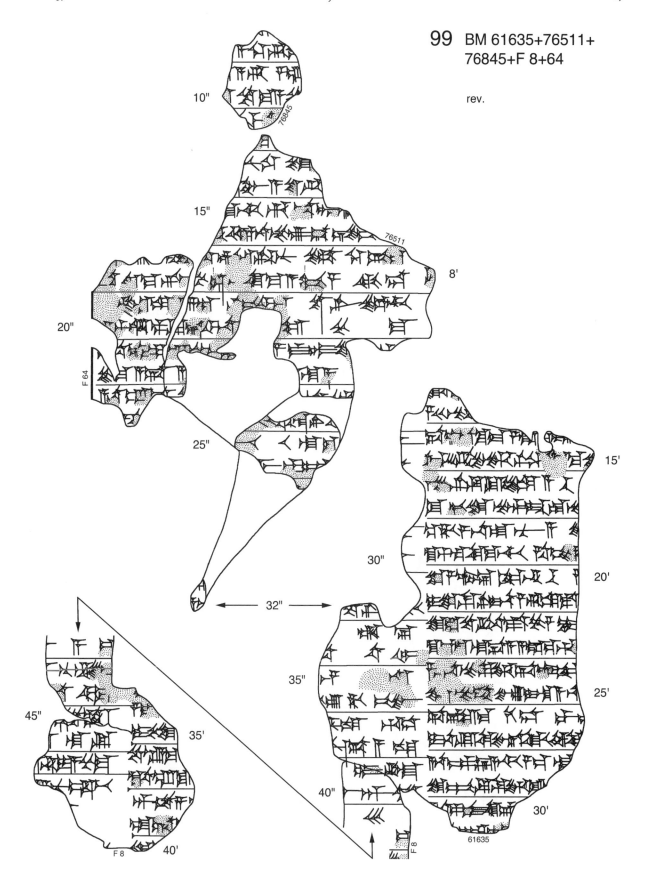

100   Si 857

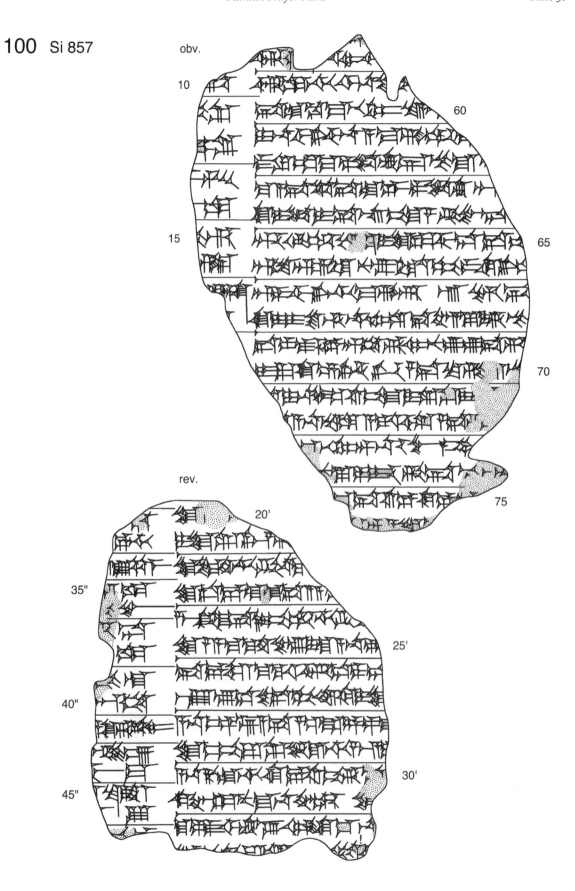

Plate 59   *Marduk Prayer No. 2*   89

101 VAT 11152+11170

102 BM 66558

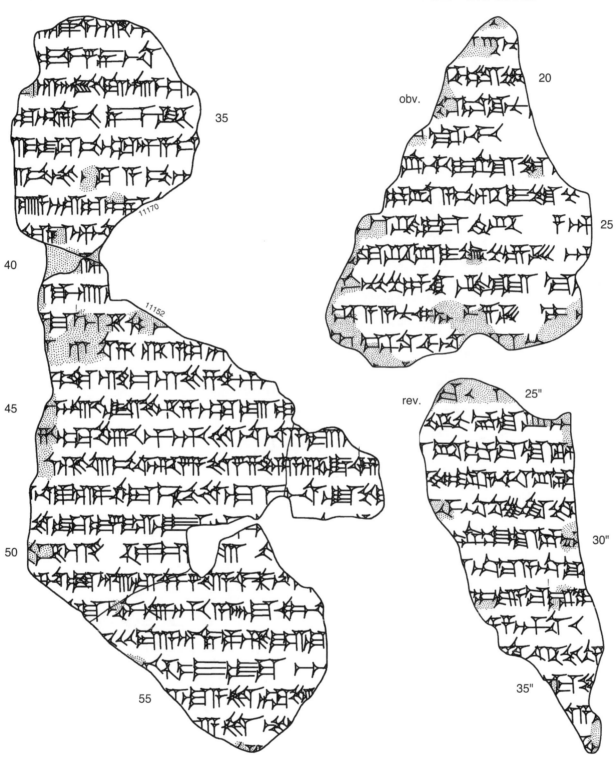

103 BM 41295

obv.

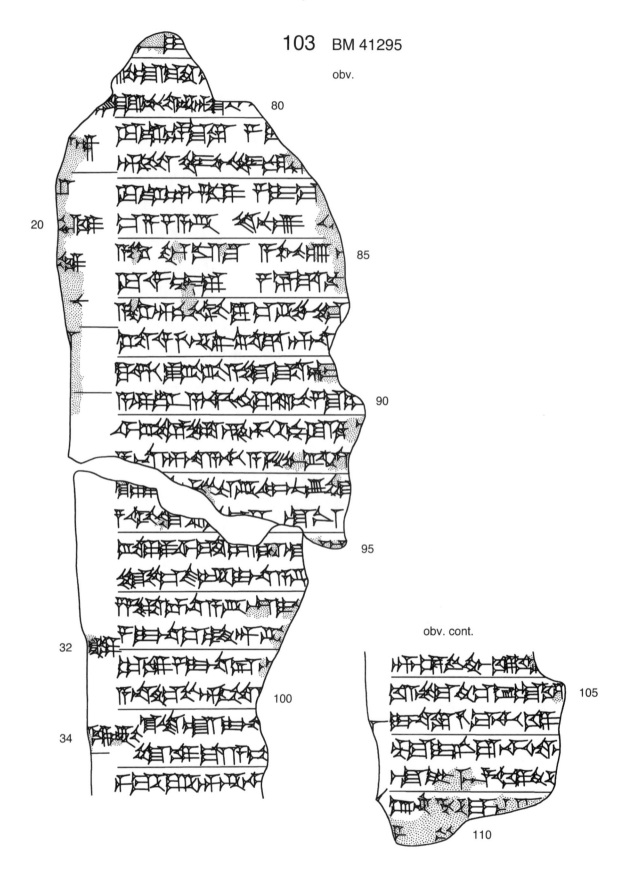

obv. cont.

103   BM 41295

rev.

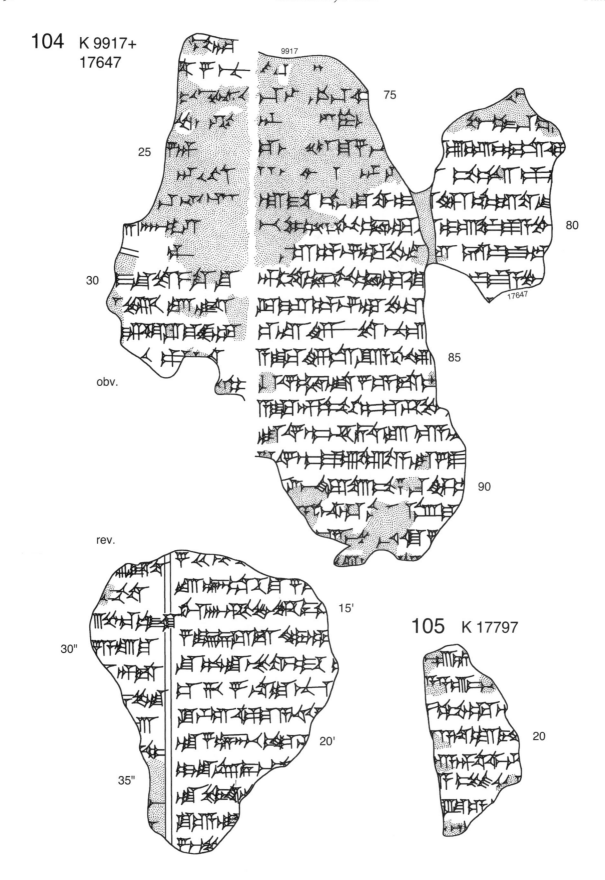

104 K 9917+
17647

25

30

obv.

75

80

85

90

rev.

15'

20'

30"

35"

105 K 17797

20

Plate 63　　　　　　　*Marduk Prayer No. 2*　　　　　　　93

106　HSM 6836

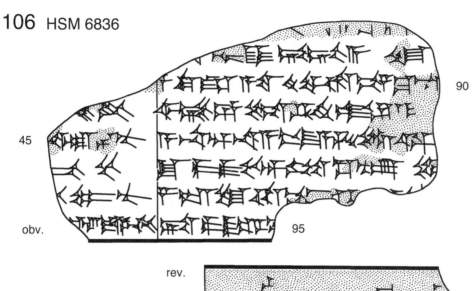

45

90

obv.

95

rev.

100

104–5

107　F 4

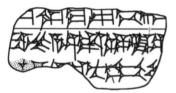

12

108　F 5

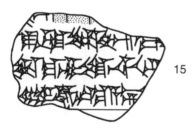

15

110　BM 37659

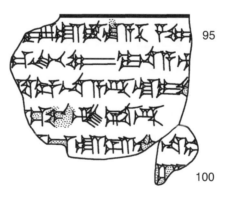

95

100

109　BM 35285

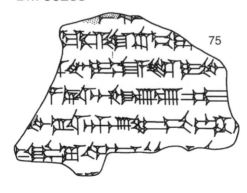

75

111　BM 37354

95

115 BM 54644+
66895

obv.

112 (K 3183+)+
Sm 1732

113 K 18397

114 Sm 1751

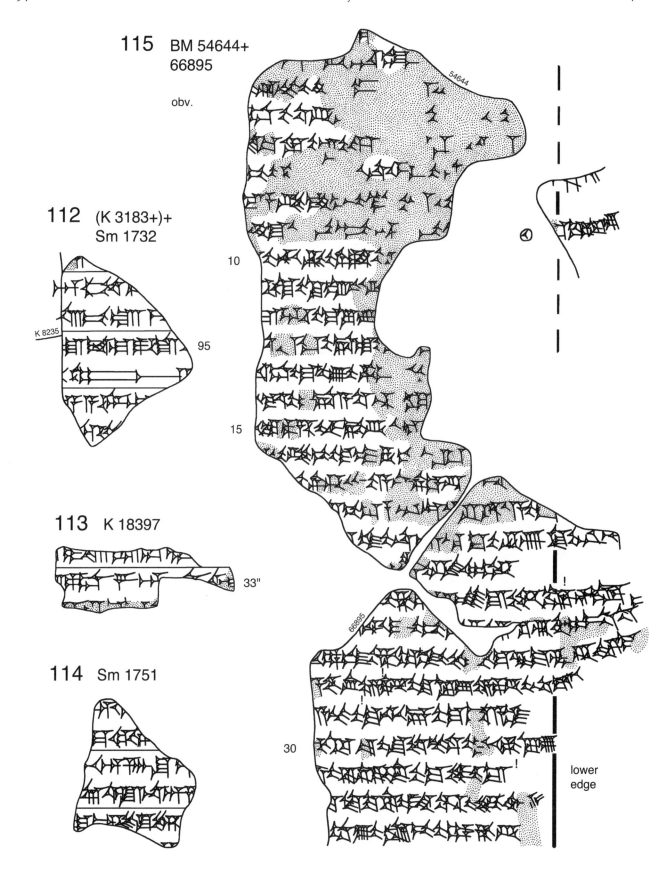

Plate 65   *Marduk Prayer No. 2*   95

115 BM 54644+66895

rev.

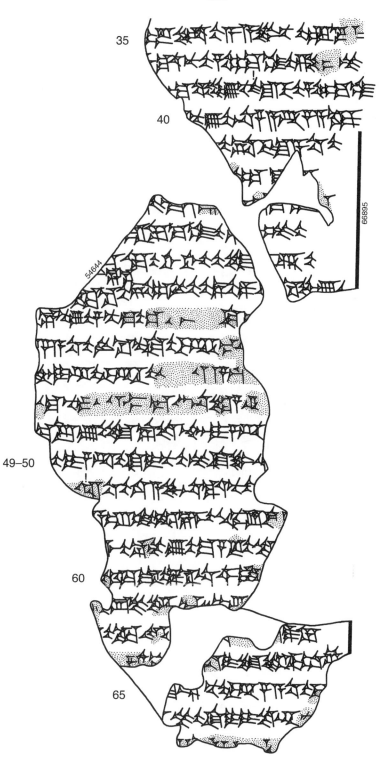

35

40

66895

54644

49–50

60

65

116   BM 54203

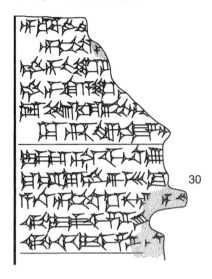

30

119   BM 36726

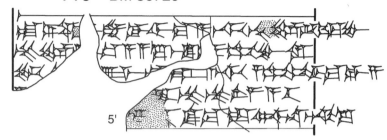

5'

120   BM 87226

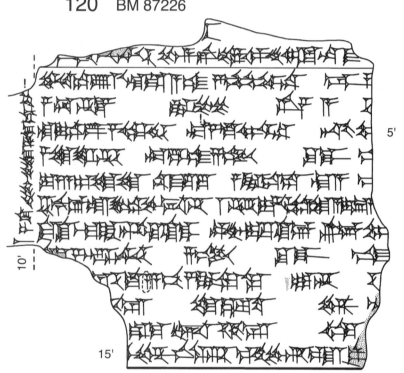

5'

10'

15'

117   BM 66609

55

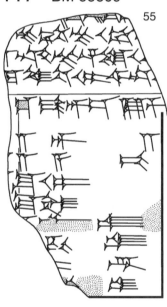

118   BM 55300

obv.

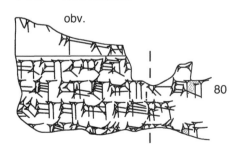

80

rev.

121   BM 37392

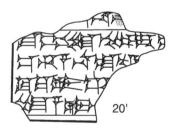

20'

Plate 67 *Marduk Prayer No. 2* 97

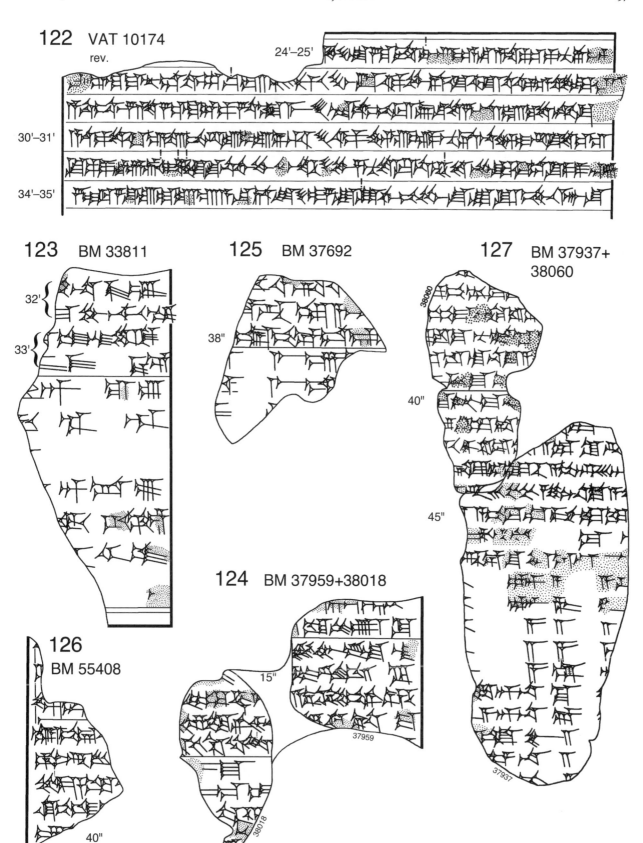

122 VAT 10174
rev.

24'–25'

30'–31'

34'–35'

123 BM 33811

32'

33'

125 BM 37692

38"

127 BM 37937+
38060

40"

45"

124 BM 37959+38018

15"

37959

126
BM 55408

40"

38018

37937

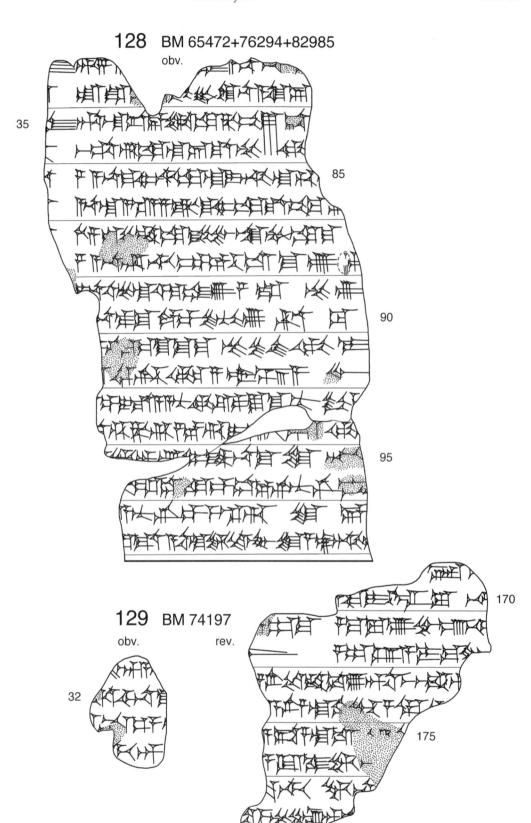

128 BM 65472+76294+82985

obv.

35

85

90

95

129 BM 74197

obv.   rev.

170

32

175

Plate 69 Šamaš Hymn 99

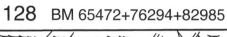

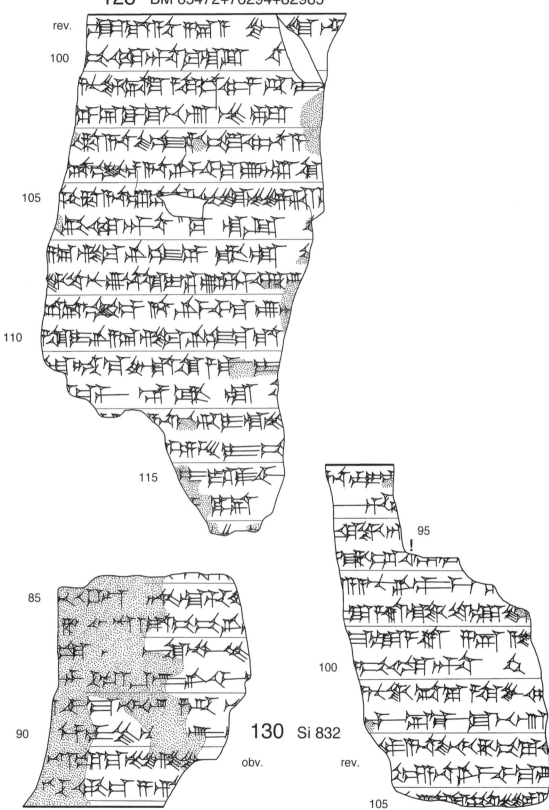

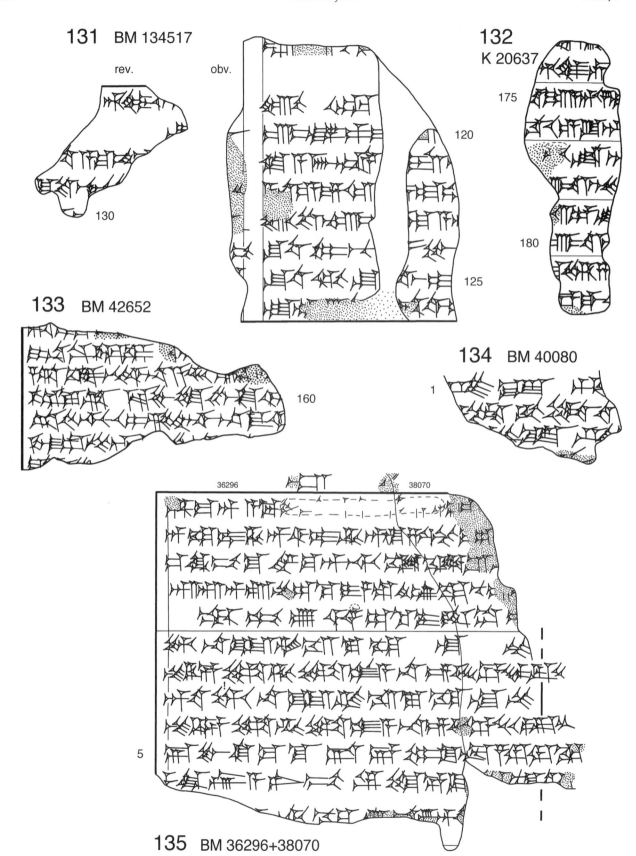

131   BM 134517

rev.   obv.

130

120

125

132
K 20637

175

180

133   BM 42652

160

134   BM 40080

1

36296   38070

5

135   BM 36296+38070

Plate 71   Šamaš Hymn   101

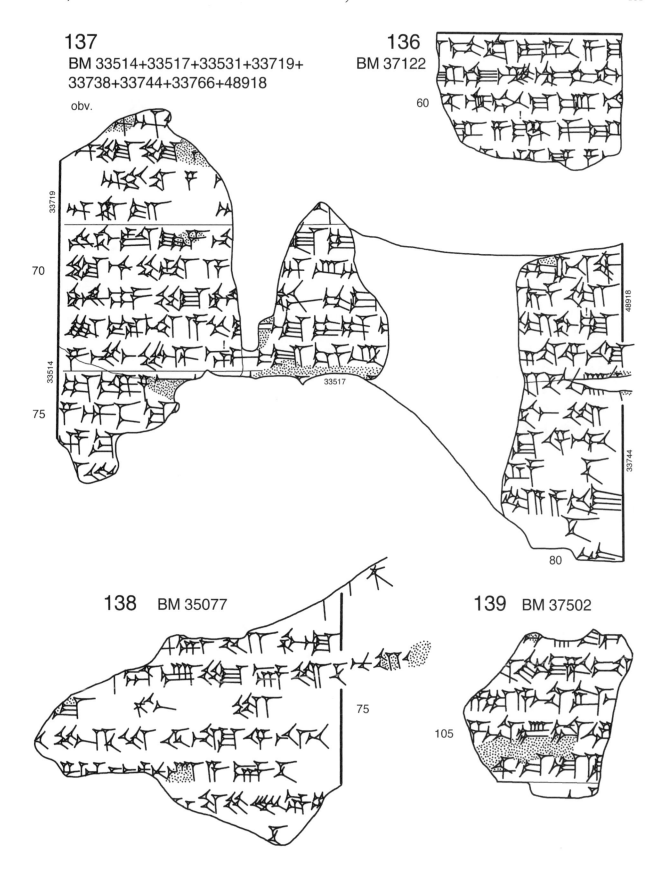

137
BM 33514+33517+33531+33719+
33738+33744+33766+48918

136
BM 37122

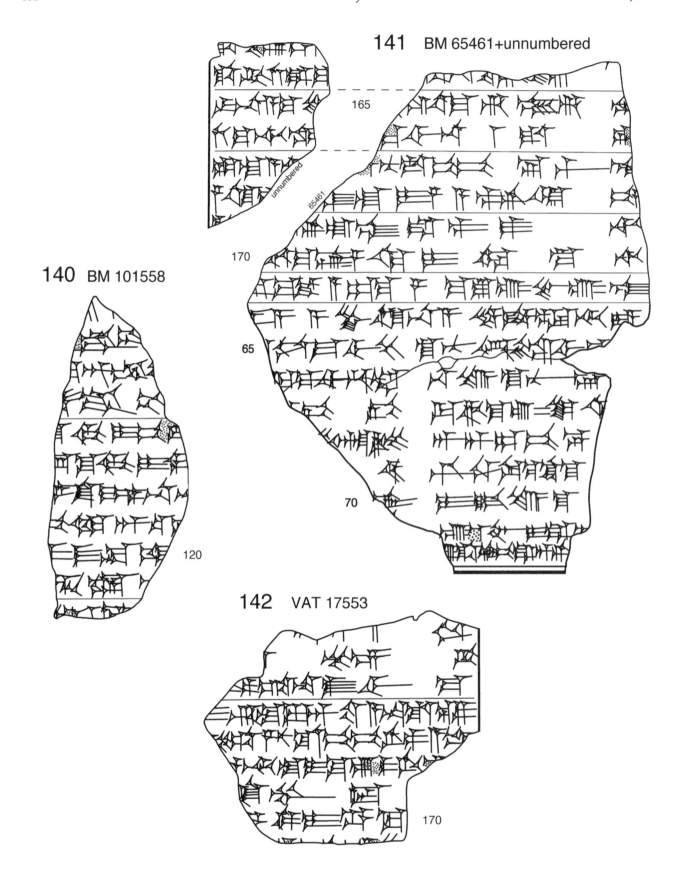

140 BM 101558

141 BM 65461+unnumbered

142 VAT 17553

Plate 73   *Ludlul bēl nēmeqi*   103

143   79-7-8, 225

obv.

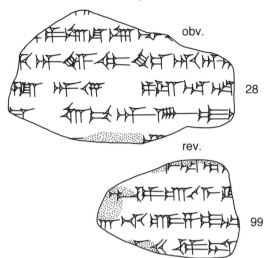

28

rev.

99

144   K 1757+18963

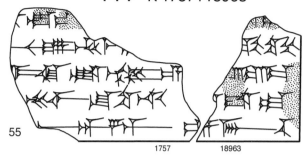

55

1757   18963

146   BM 73592

obv.   rev.

145   BM 66345

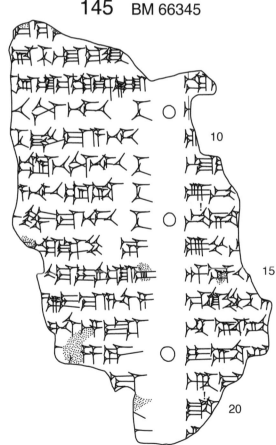

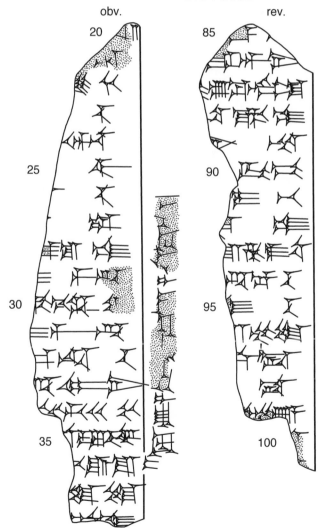

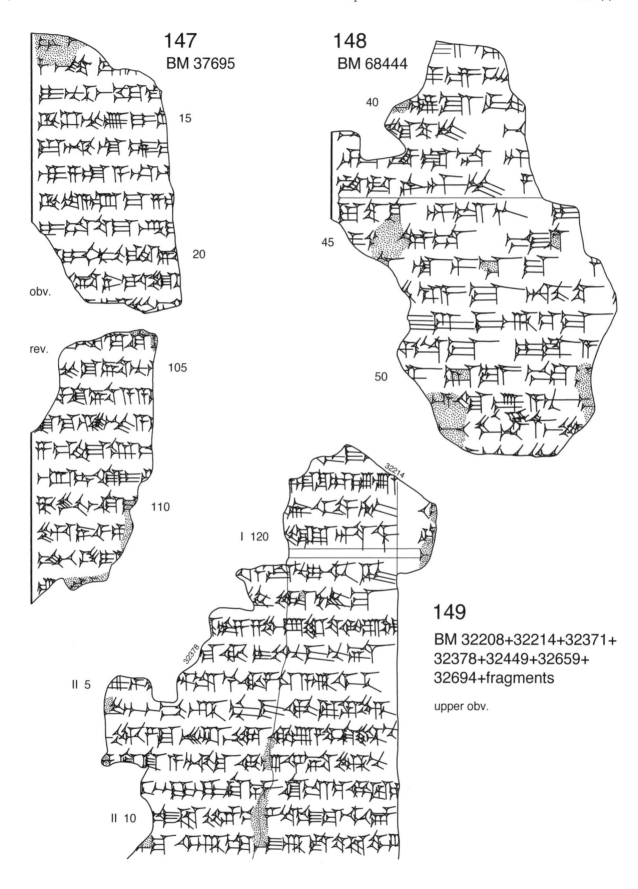

147
BM 37695

15

20

obv.

rev.

105

110

148
BM 68444

40

45

50

I 120

II 5

II 10

149

BM 32208+32214+32371+
32378+32449+32659+
32694+fragments

upper obv.

149

BM 32208+32214+32371+
32378+32449+32659+
32694+fragments

lower obv.

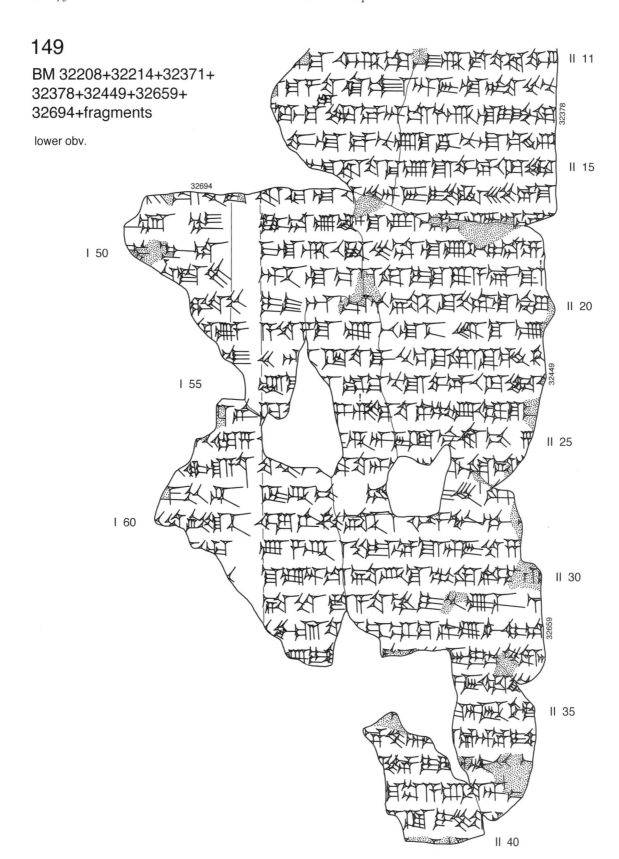

149

BM 32208+32214+32371+
32378+32449+32659+
32694+fragments

rev.

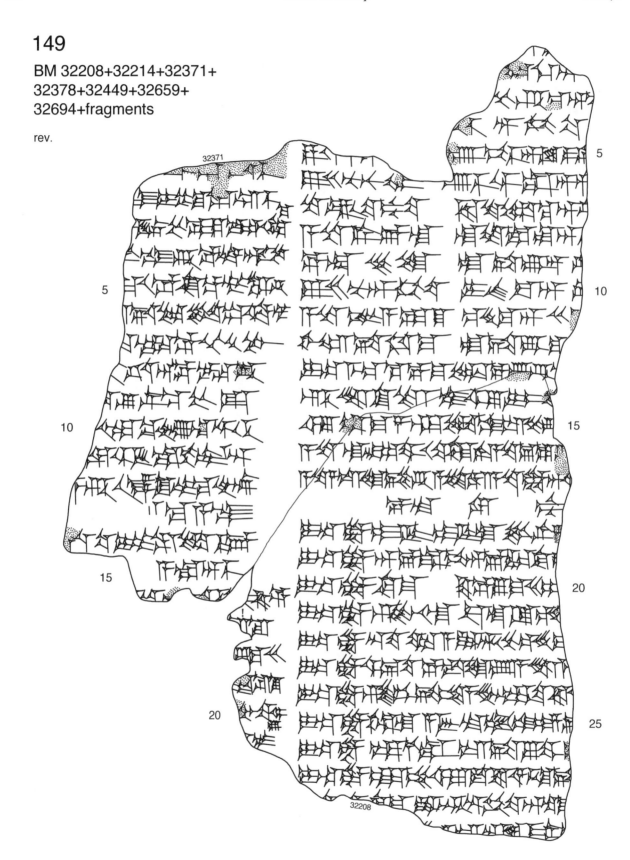

Plate 77   *Ludlul bēl nēmeqi*   107

150

BM 65956+67872+93047

obv.

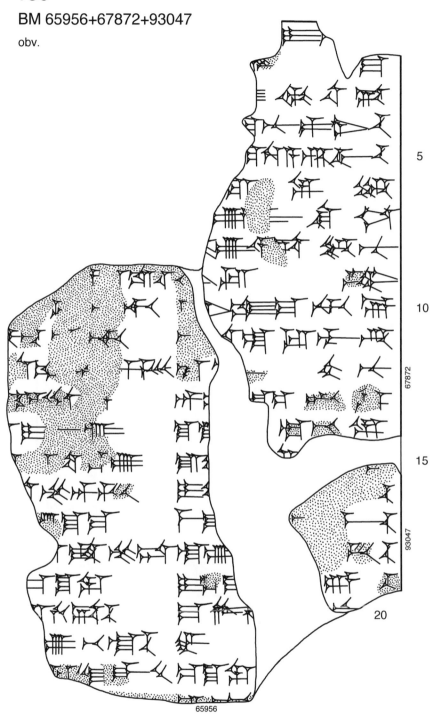

150
BM 65956+67872+93047
rev.

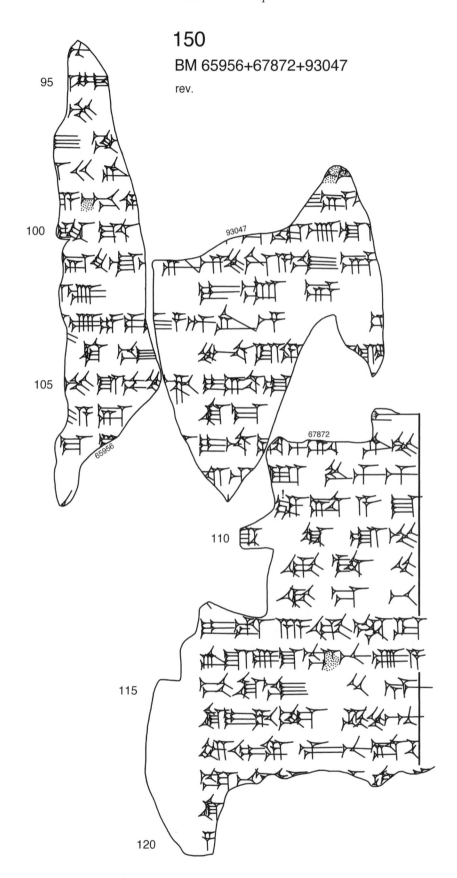

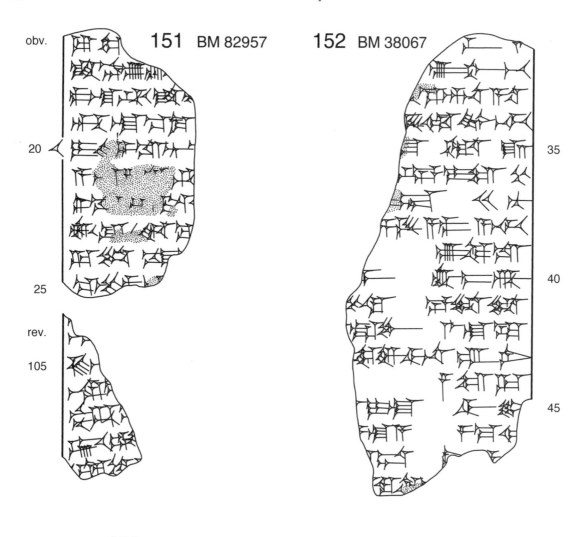

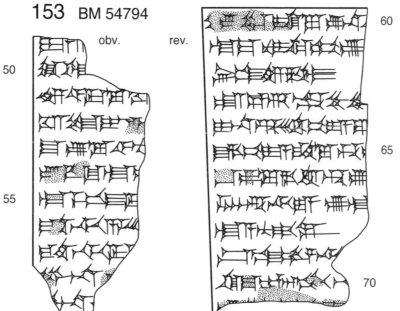

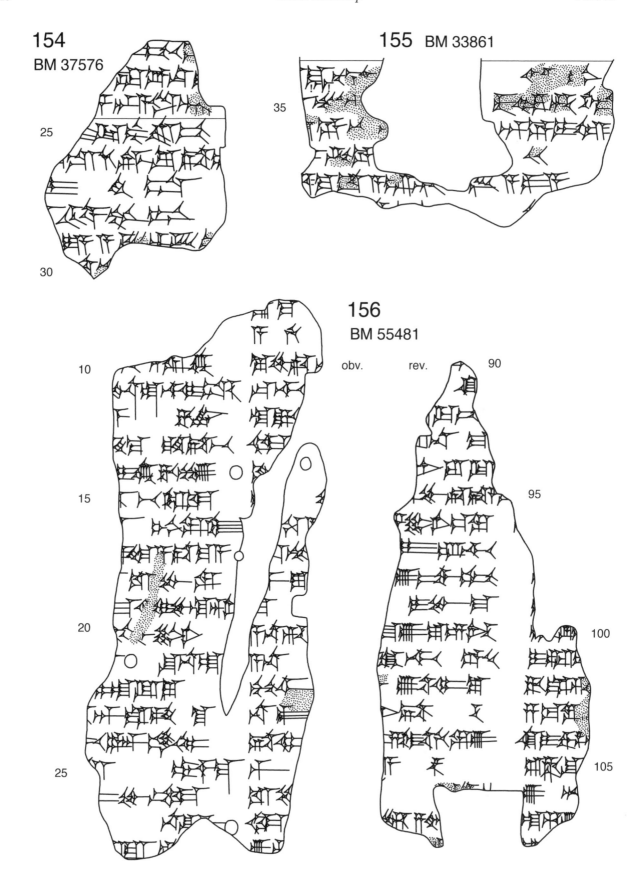

157
BM 77093

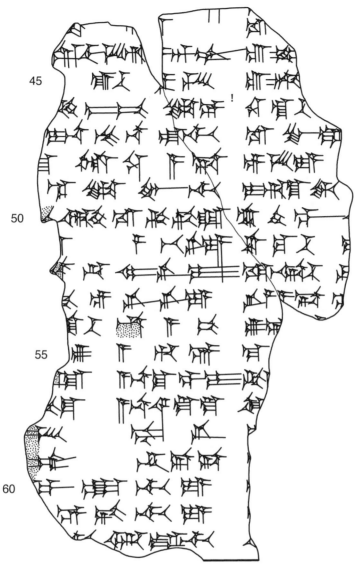

45

50

55

60

158   BM 68435

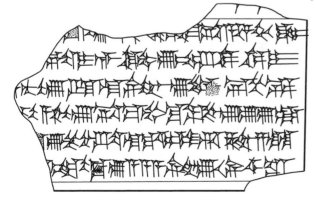

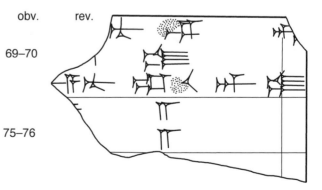

obv.   rev.

69–70

75–76

159 Si 728

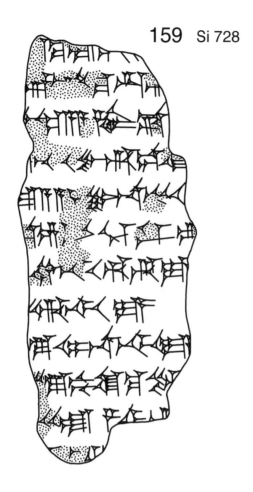

160 BM 123392

obv.(?)

rev.(?)

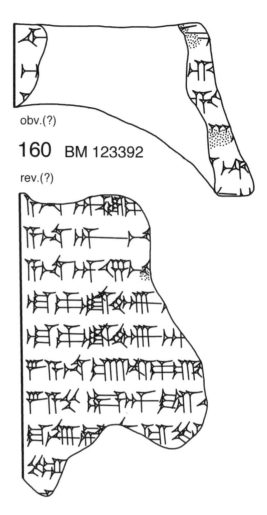

161 BM 38002

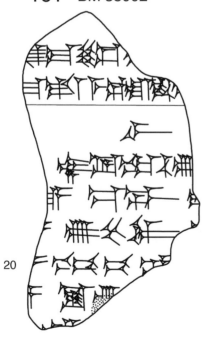

20

162 BM 74201

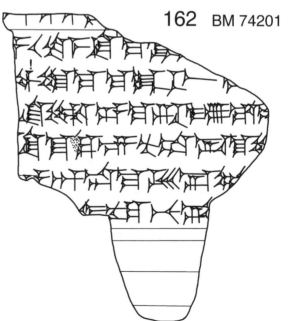

Plate 83 *Ludlul bēl nēmeqi* 113

163
BM 34650
obv.

164 BM 77253

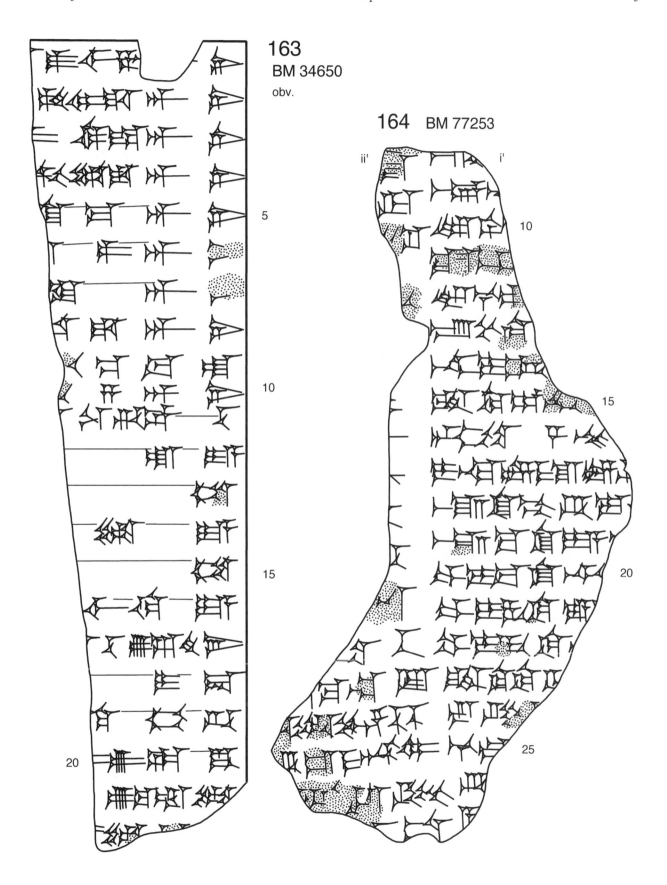

163
BM 34650
rev.

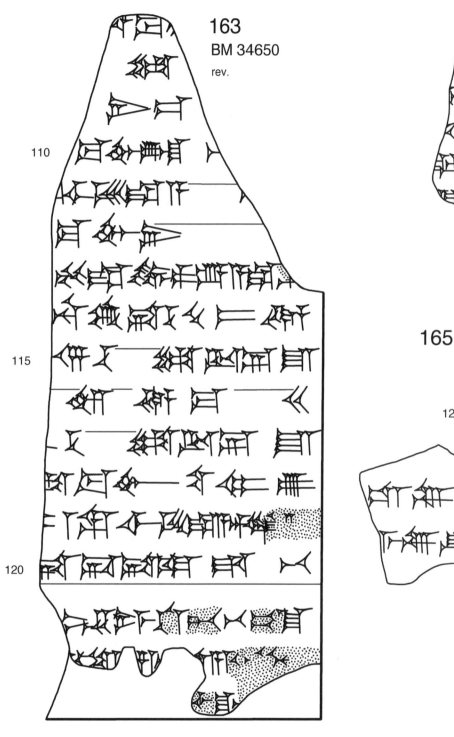

110

115

120

165 K 8576

obv.

rev.

120

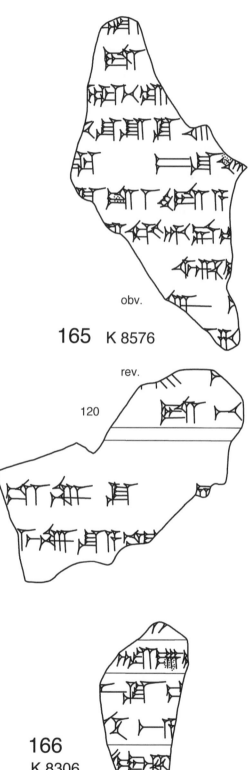

166
K 8306

Plate 85   Marduk's Address to the Demons   115

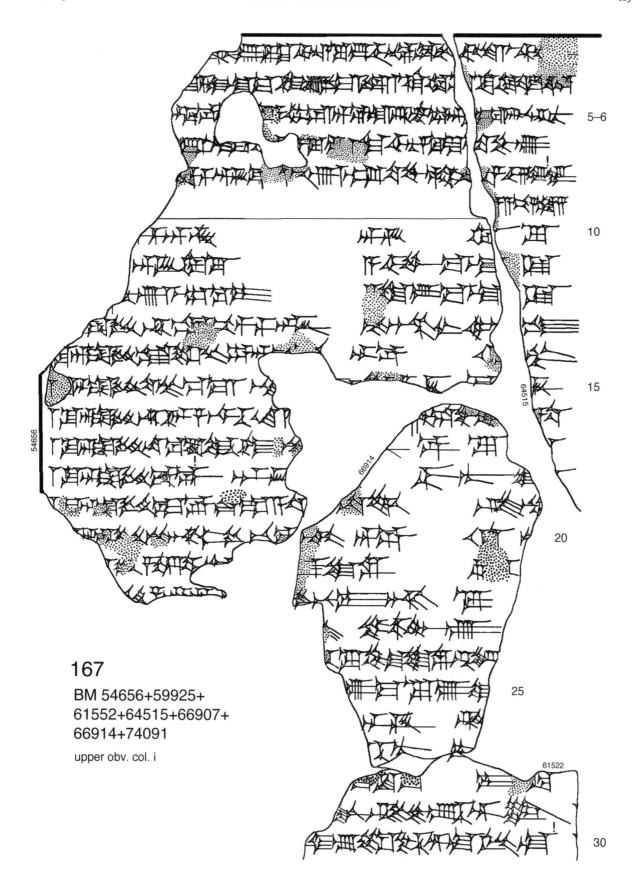

167

BM 54656+59925+
61552+64515+66907+
66914+74091

upper obv. col. i

167

BM 54656+59925+
61552+64515+66907+
66914+74091 (+) 59211

lower obv. cols. i and ii

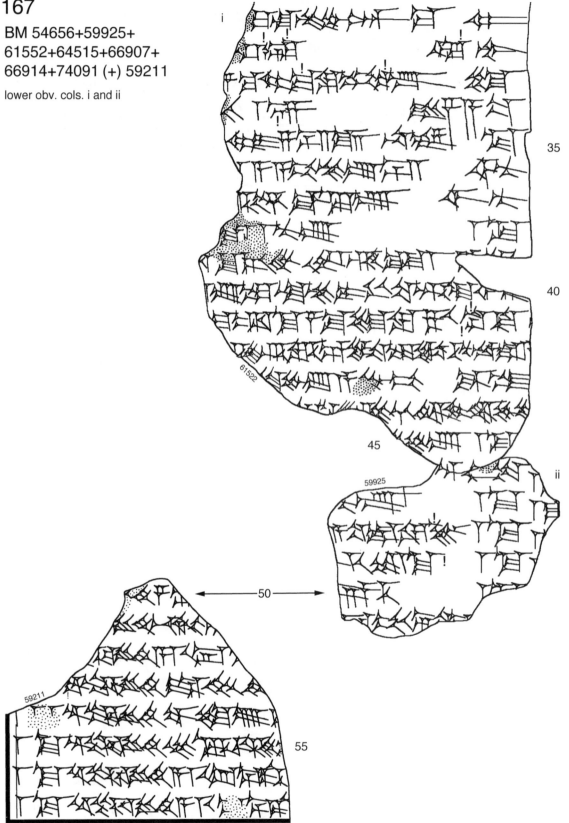

Plate 87   *Marduk's Address to the Demons*   117

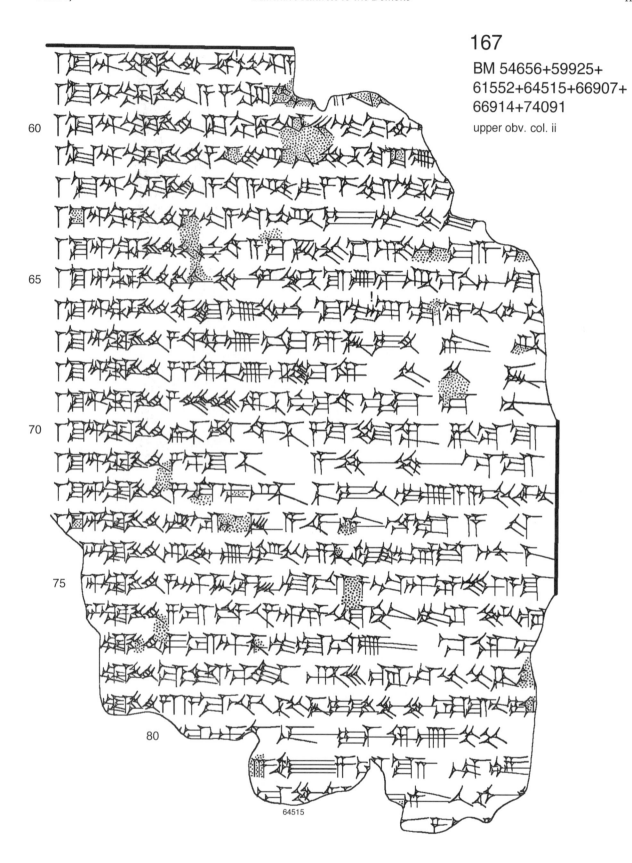

167

BM 54656+59925+
61552+64515+66907+
66914+74091

upper obv. col. ii

60

65

70

75

80

64515

167

BM 54656+59925+
61552+64515+66907+
66914+74091

rev. col. iii

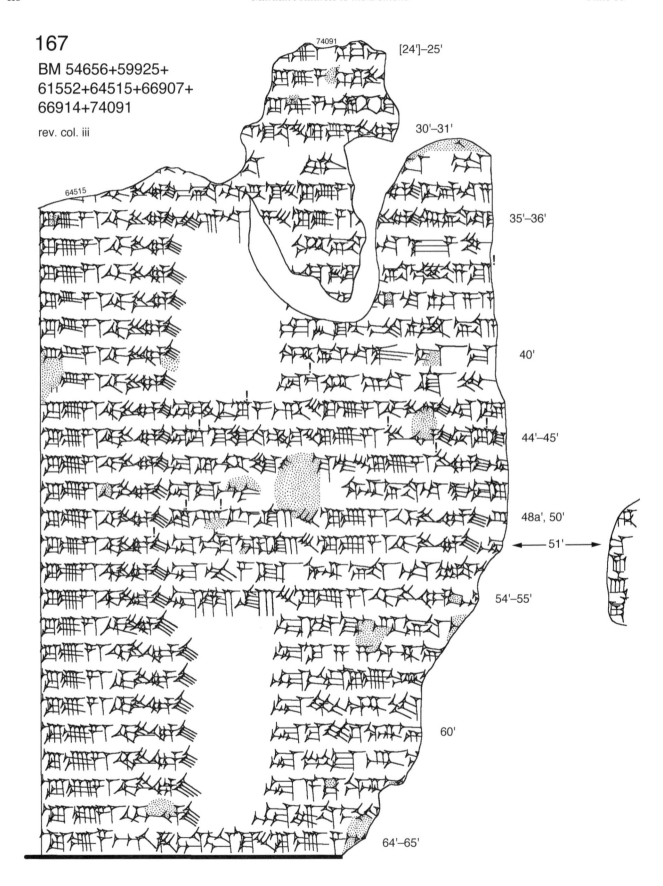

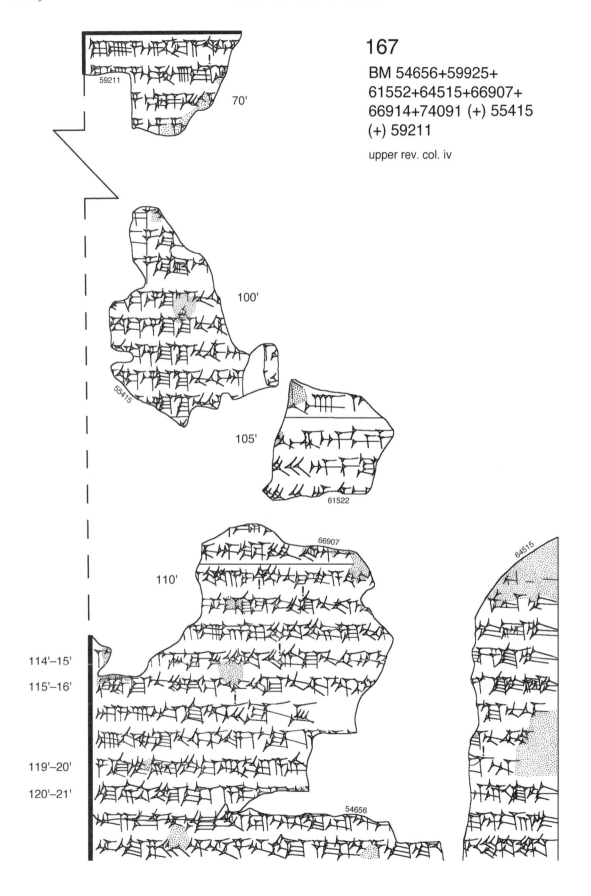

167
BM 54656+59925+
61552+64515+66907+
66914+74091 (+) 55415
(+) 59211

upper rev. col. iv

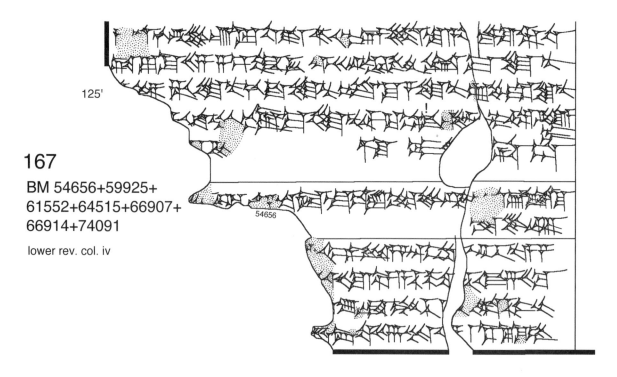

167

BM 54656+59925+
61552+64515+66907+
66914+74091

lower rev. col. iv

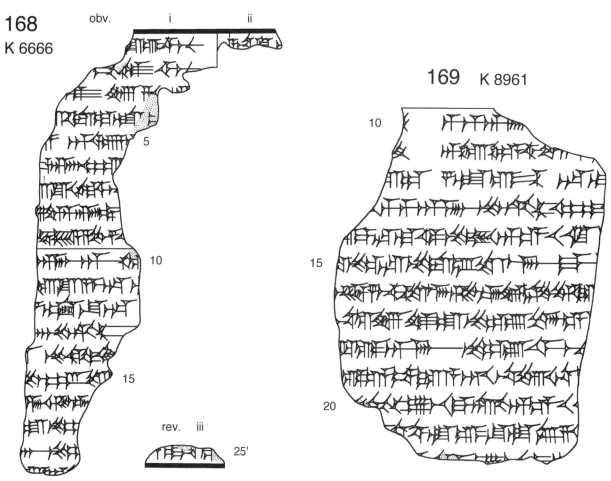

170   BM 72748

upper obv.

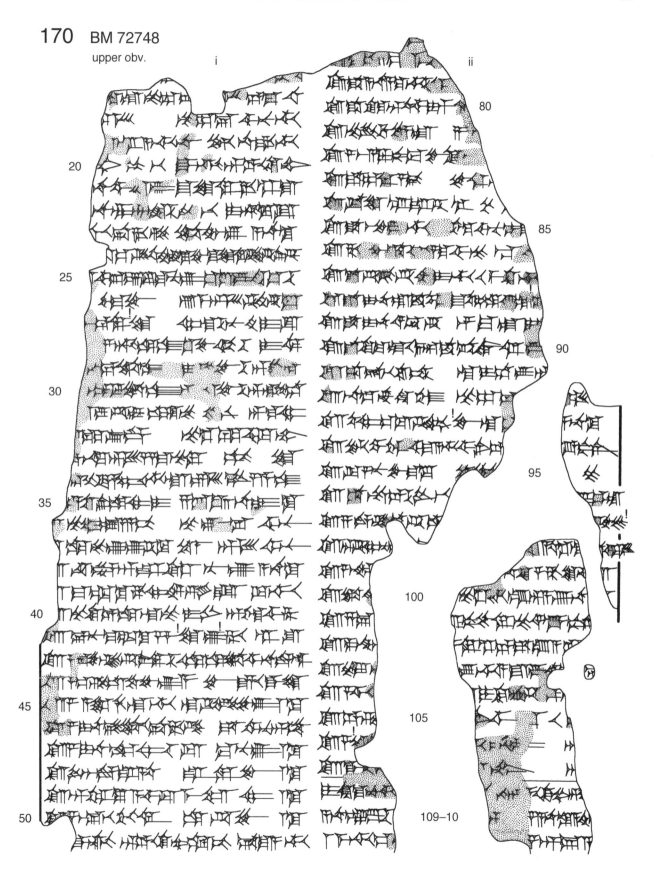

170   BM 72748

lower obv.

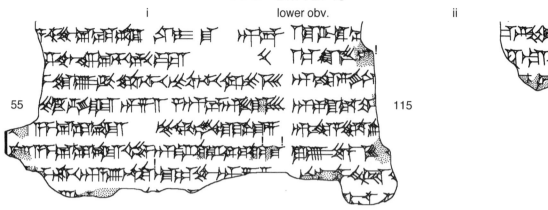

i   ii

55   115

171
K 13768+
Sm 164

45

50

55

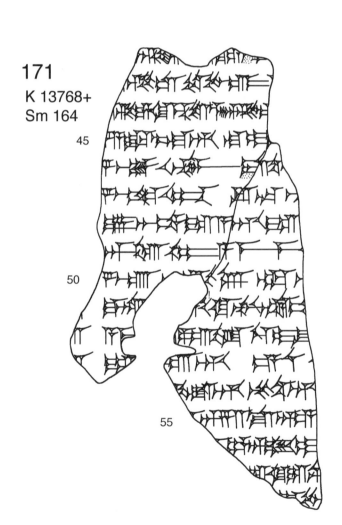

172
BM 66922
+68471

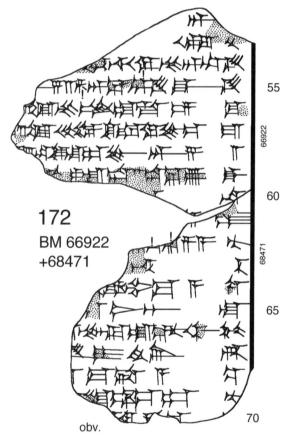

55

66922

60

68471

65

obv.   70

rev.

10'

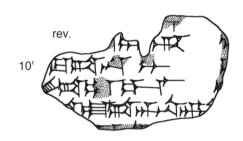

170 BM 72748

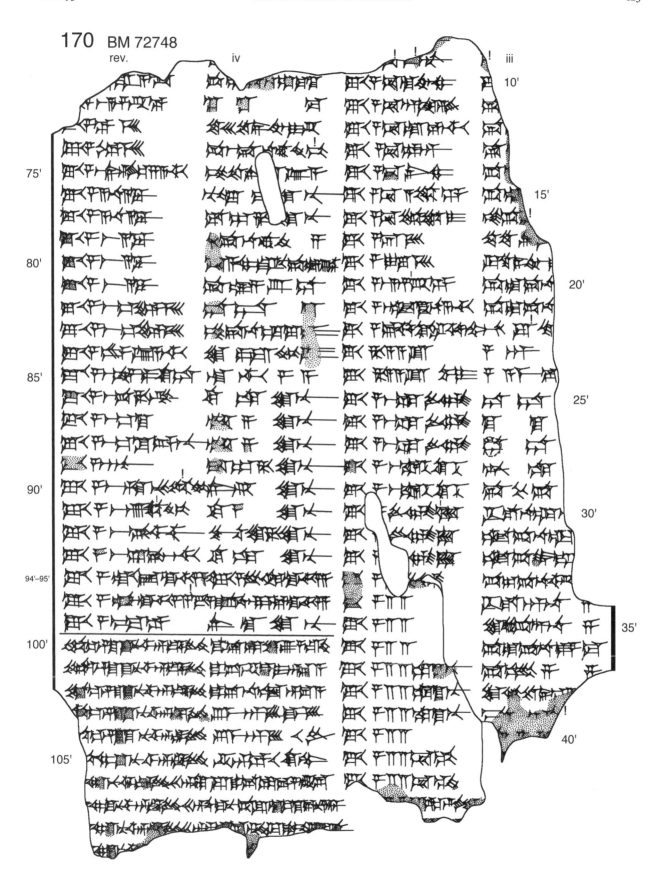

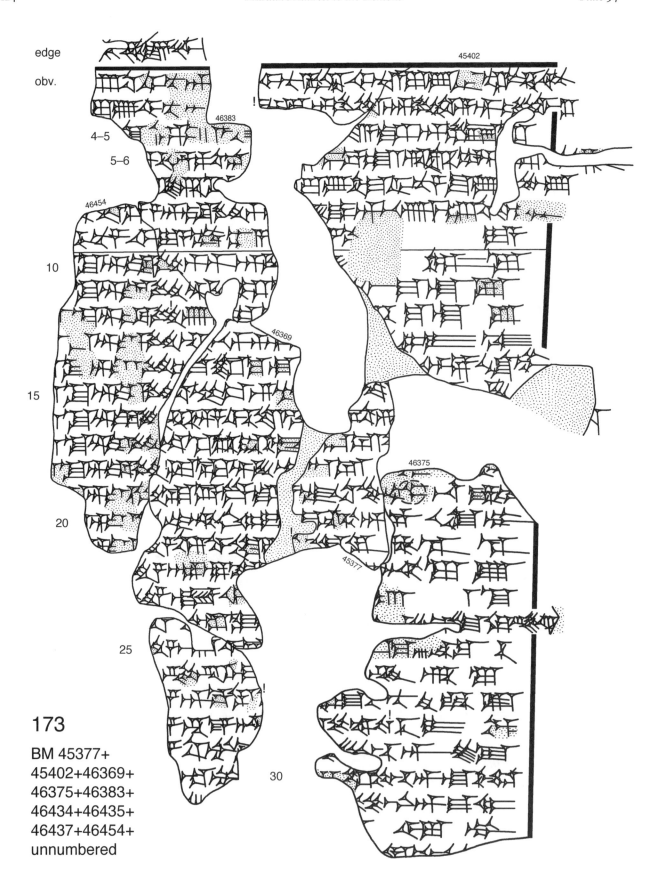

edge

obv.

45402

46383

4–5

5–6

46454

10

46369

15

46375

20

45377

25

30

173

BM 45377+
45402+46369+
46375+46383+
46434+46435+
46437+46454+
unnumbered

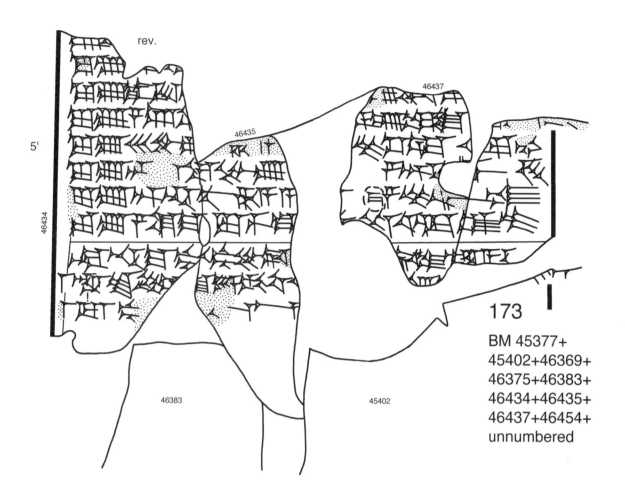

173

BM 45377+
45402+46369+
46375+46383+
46434+46435+
46437+46454+
unnumbered

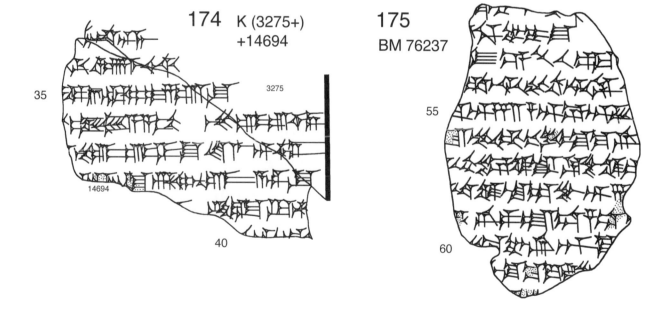

174 K (3275+)
+14694

175
BM 76237

176
BM 45403+
unnumbered

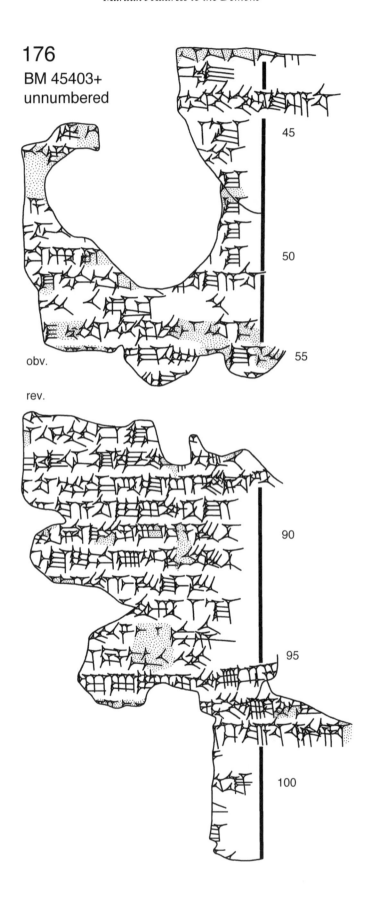

obv.

rev.

45

50

55

90

95

100

177   BM 45372+46401

178   BM 46499

179   BM 46442

180   BM 46501

181
81-7-28,
unnumbered

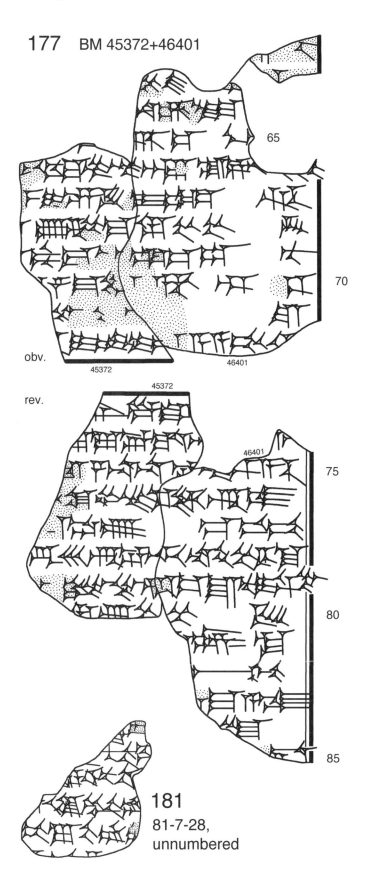
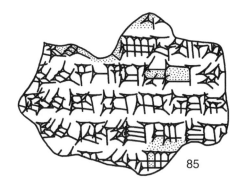
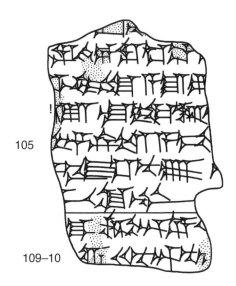
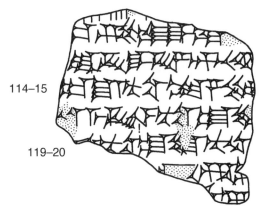

182
K (3349+)
17113+18488

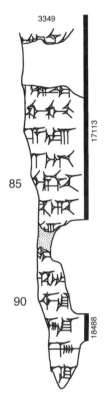

183   K 10857

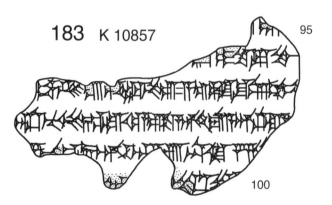

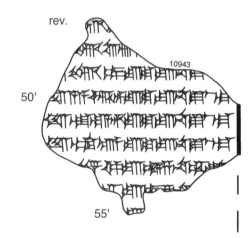

obv.   110

184   K 9595+10943+11586

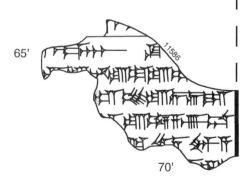

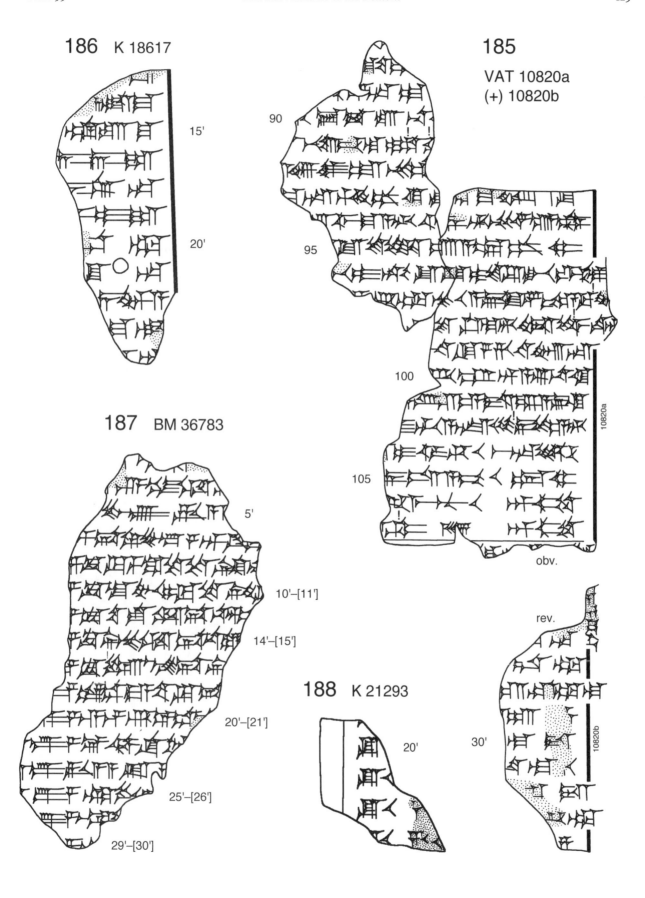

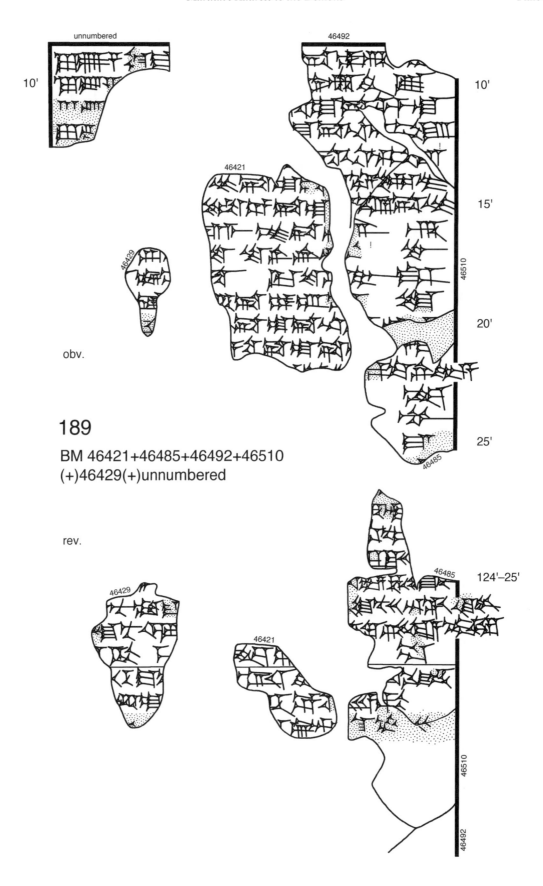

189

BM 46421+46485+46492+46510
(+)46429(+)unnumbered

Plate 101   *Marduk's Address to the Demons*   131

190

BM 54638+
54639+54957

obv.

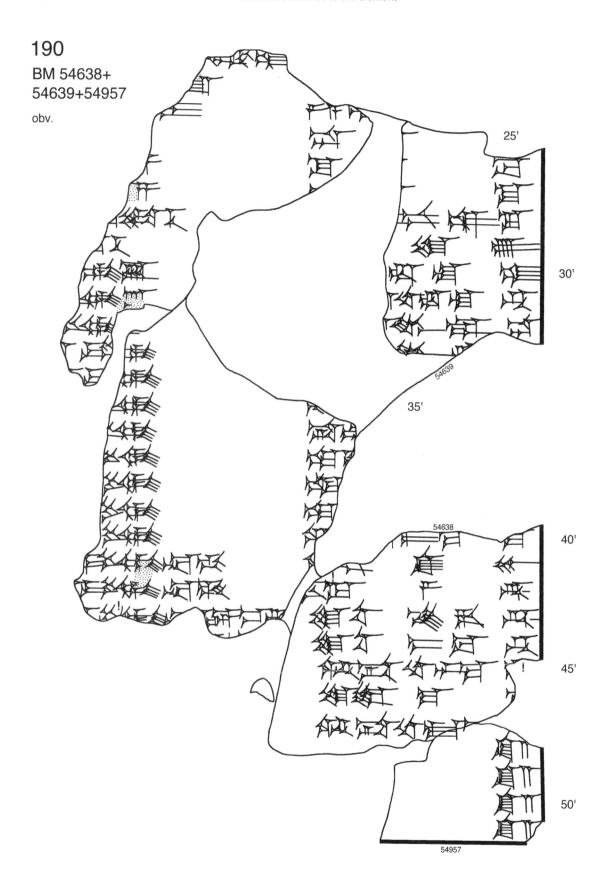

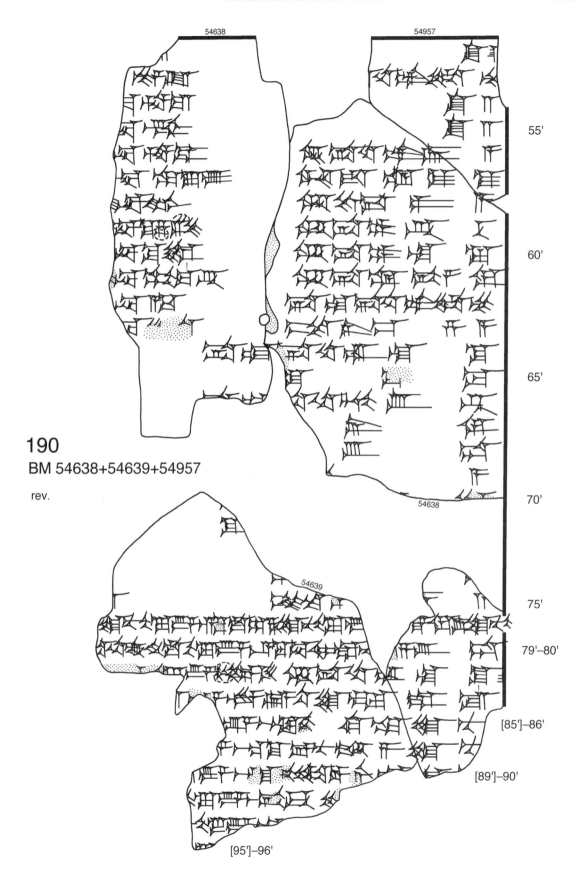

190
BM 54638+54639+54957

rev.

Plate 103   *Marduk's Address to the Demons*   133

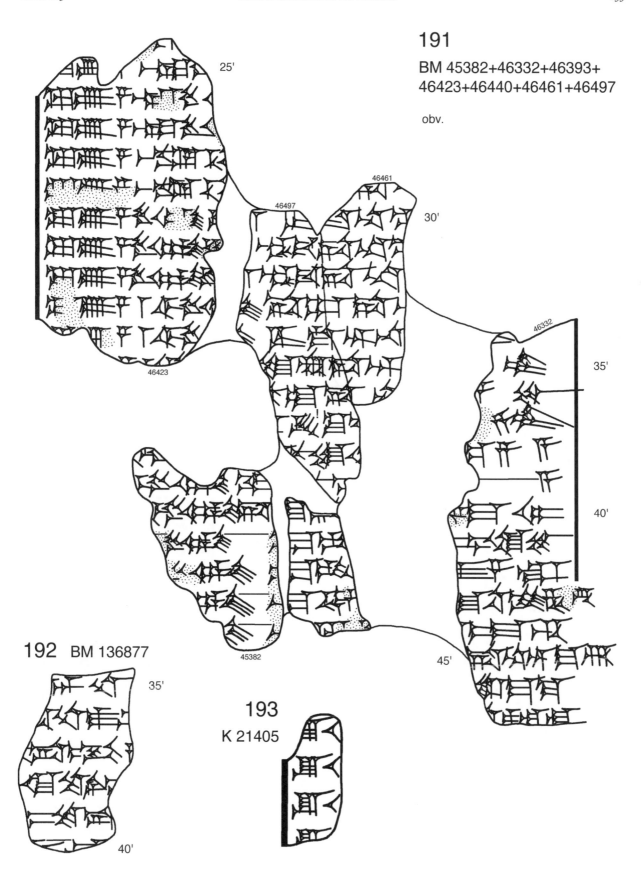

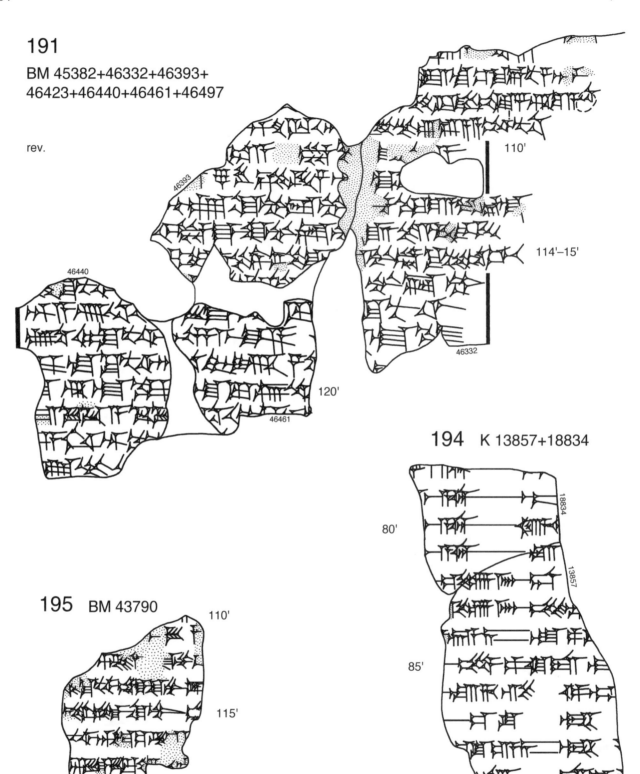

191

BM 45382+46332+46393+
46423+46440+46461+46497

rev.

195   BM 43790

194   K 13857+18834

Plate 105   *Marduk's Address to the Demons*   135

196

BM 45373+46318+
46323+46368+
46484+unnumbered

obv.

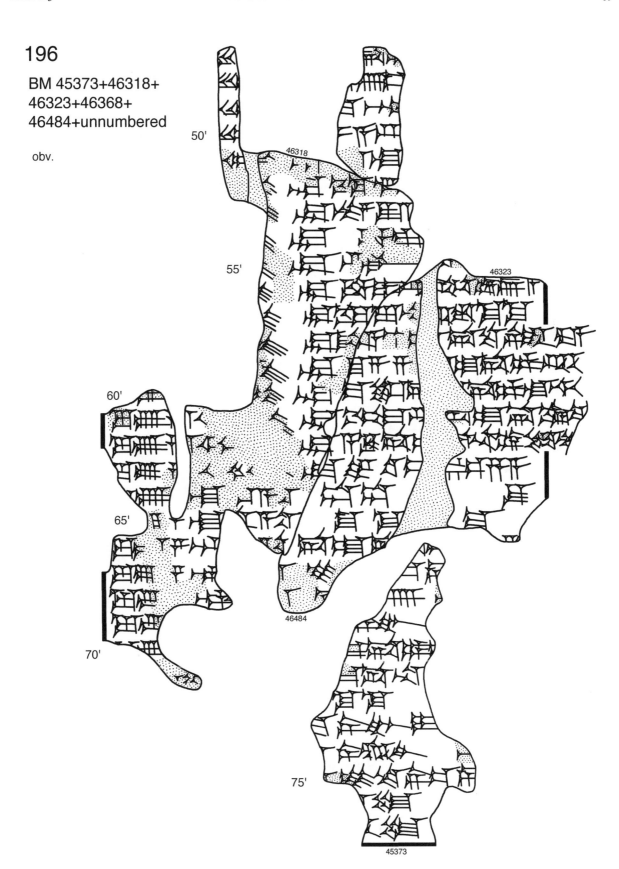

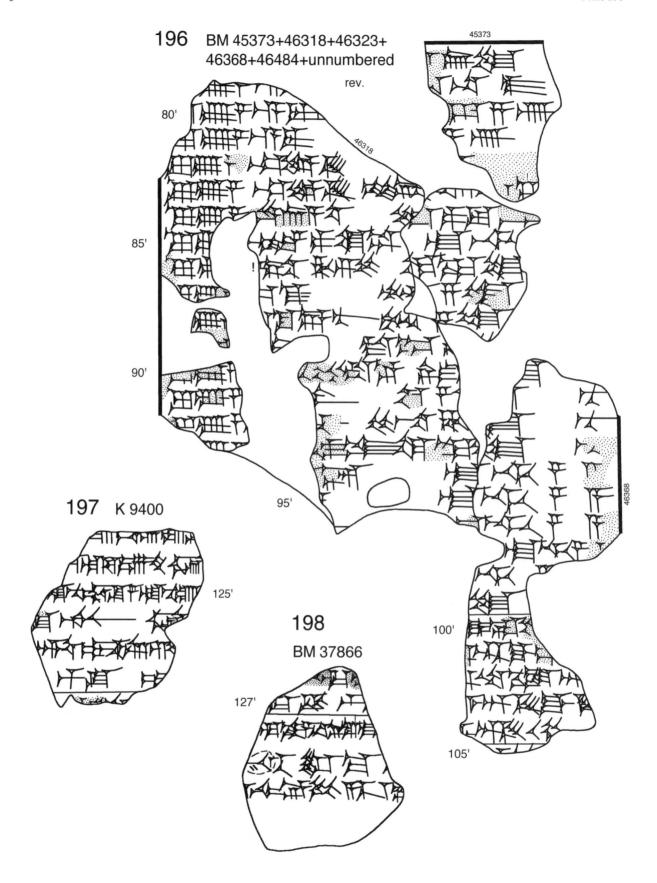

196 BM 45373+46318+46323+
46368+46484+unnumbered

rev.

197 K 9400

198

BM 37866

Plate 107   *Marduk's Address to the Demons*   137

199   K (3307+)+6726

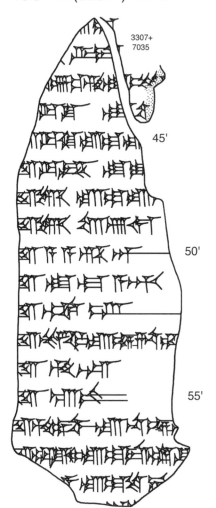

200

K 11362+
12229

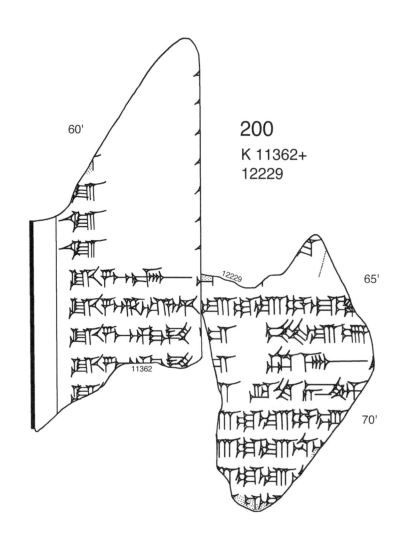

201   BM 46558

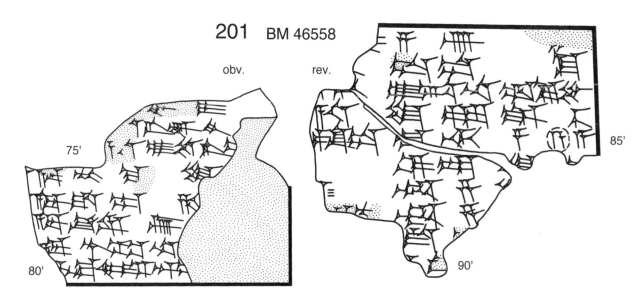

Plate 109   *Marduk's Address to the Demons*   139

205 BM 55305

25
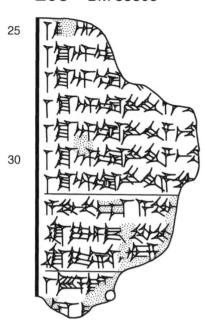
30

206 BM 71975

50
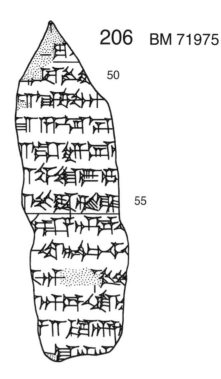
55

207 BM 71949   obv.   75   rev.

80
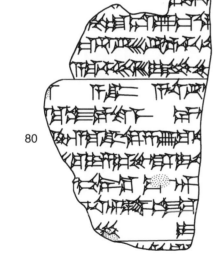
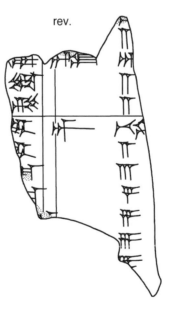

208 BM 36646

   70'

209 BM 68038+
68385

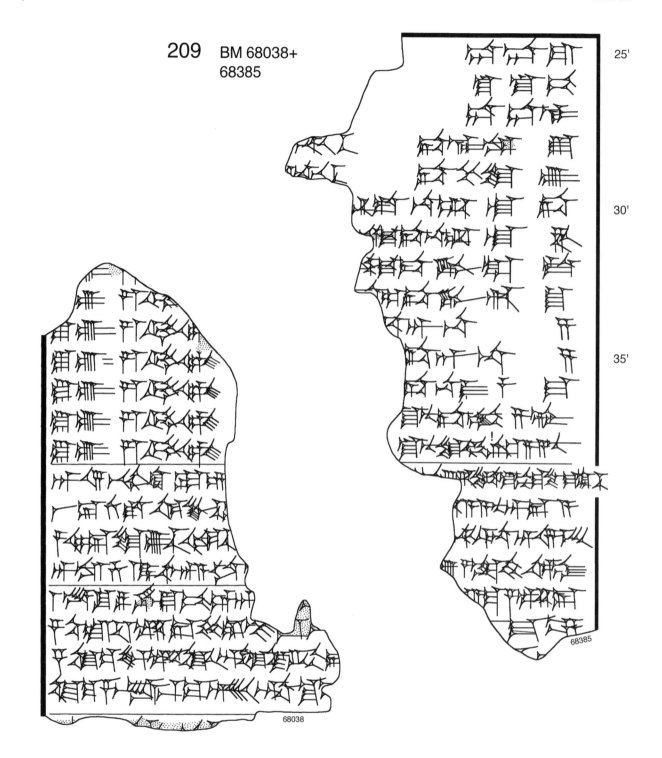

25'

30'

35'

68385

68038

Plate 111 *Marduk's Address to the Demons* 141

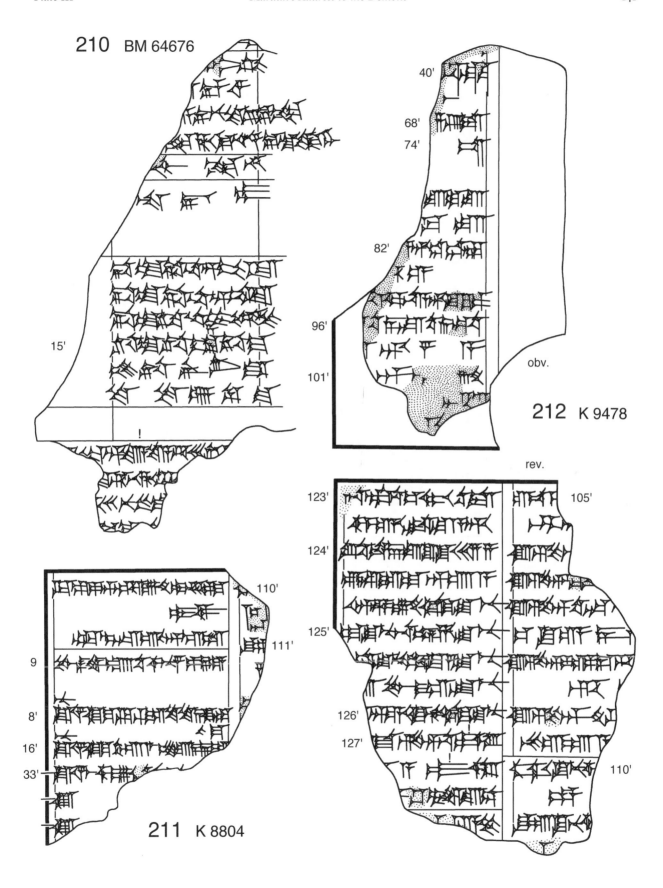

213   JRL 1053

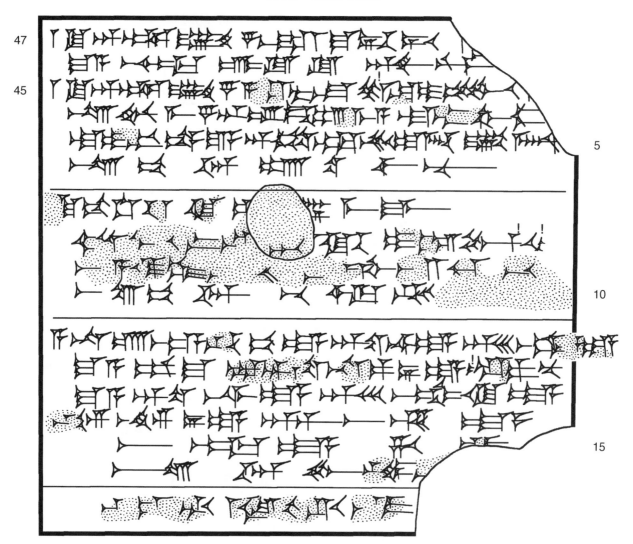

Plate 113   *Marduk's Address to the Demons*   143

214   BM 47529+47685

obv.

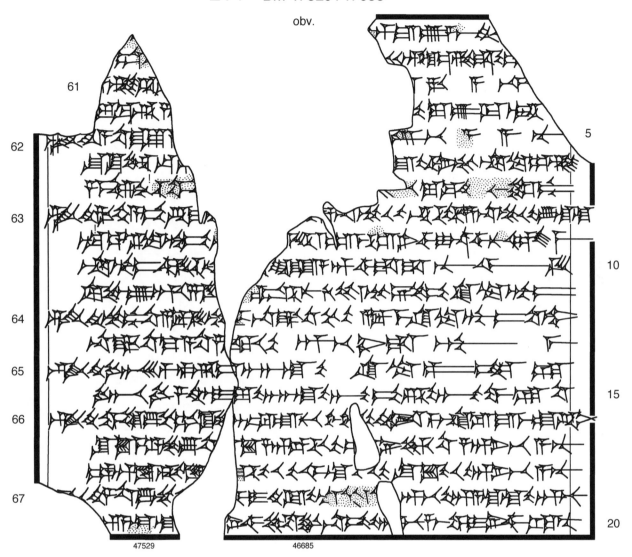

47529   46685

214   BM 47529+47685

rev.

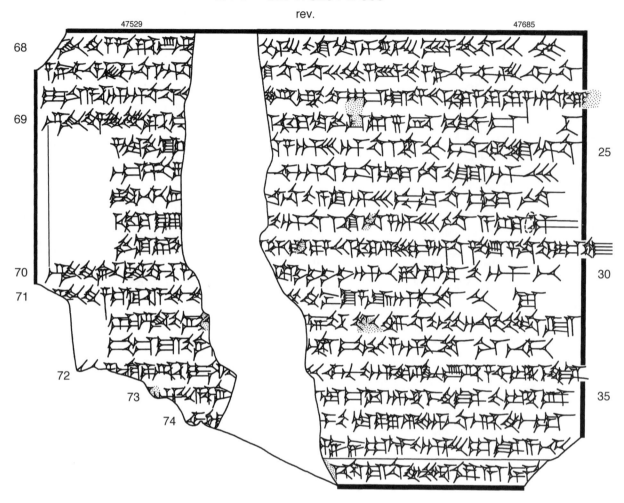

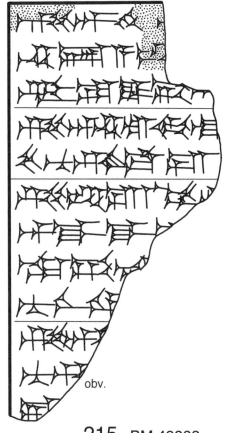

obv.

215   BM 48883

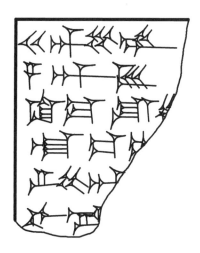

216   BM 37402

217   BM 46736

rev.

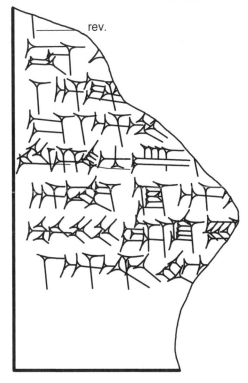

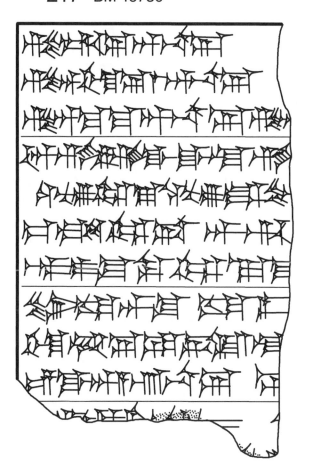

218
BM 38367

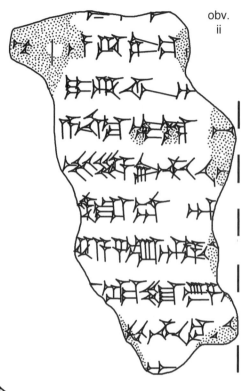

obv.
ii

upper rev.

iv   iii

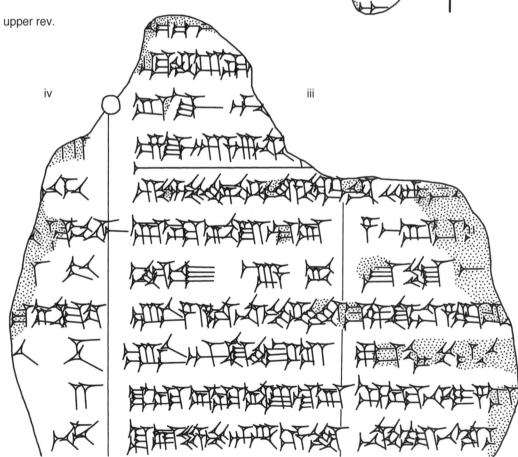

Plate 117   zi—pàd Incantations   147

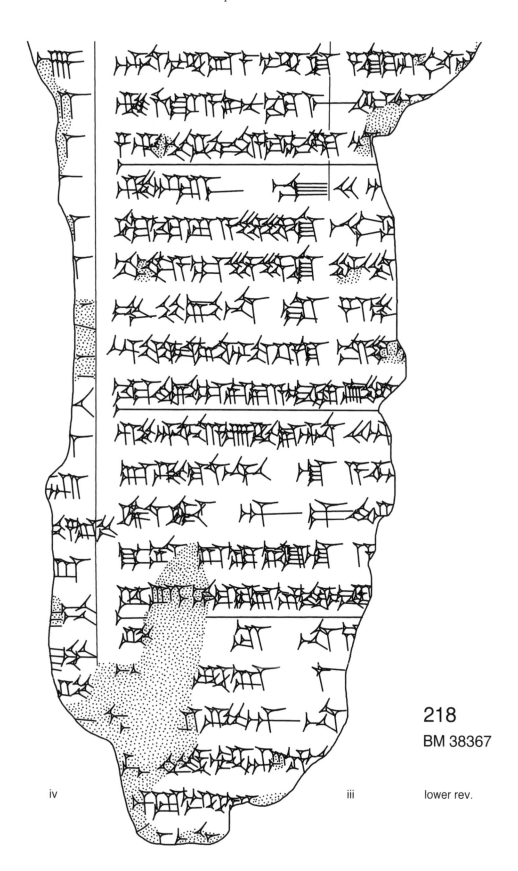

218
BM 38367

iv   iii   lower rev.

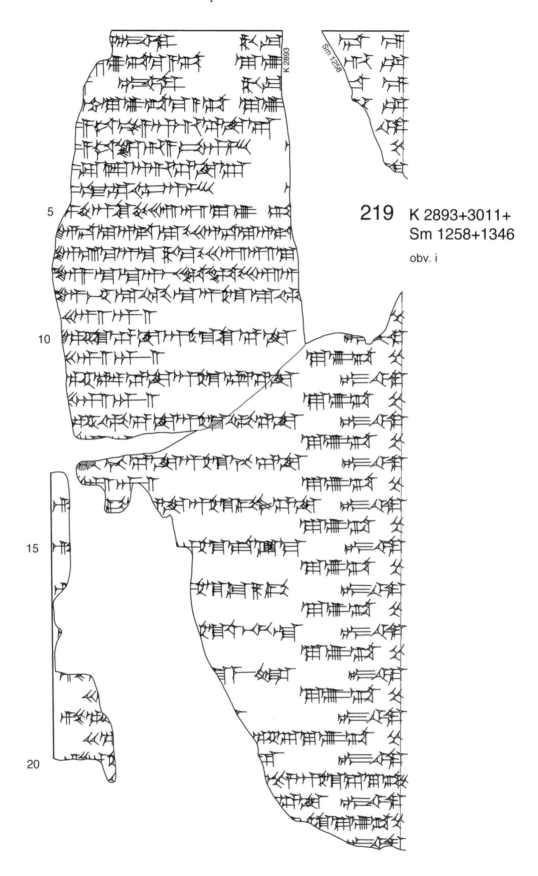

219 K 2893+3011+
Sm 1258+1346

obv. i

Plate 119   *zi—pàd Incantations*   149

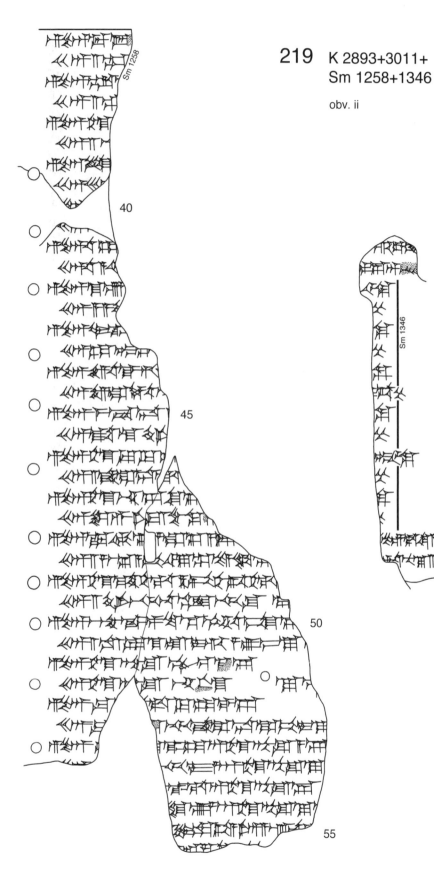

219 K 2893+3011+
Sm 1258+1346

obv. ii

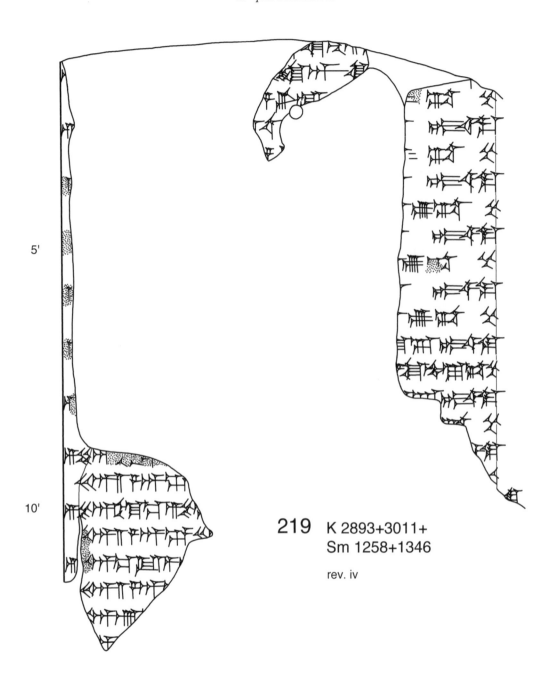

219 K 2893+3011+
Sm 1258+1346

rev. iv

upper edge, left fragment

Plate 121　　　　　*zi—pàd Incantations*　　　　　151

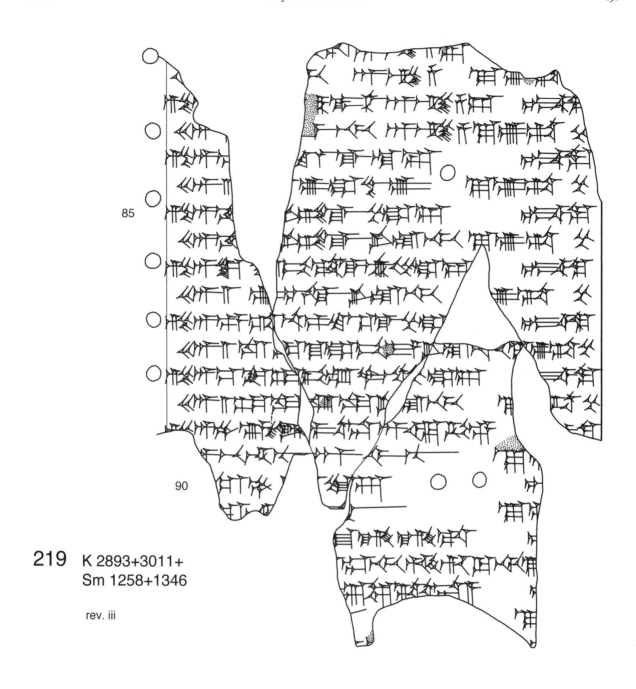

219 K 2893+3011+
Sm 1258+1346

rev. iii

upper edge, right fragment

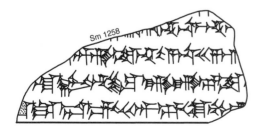

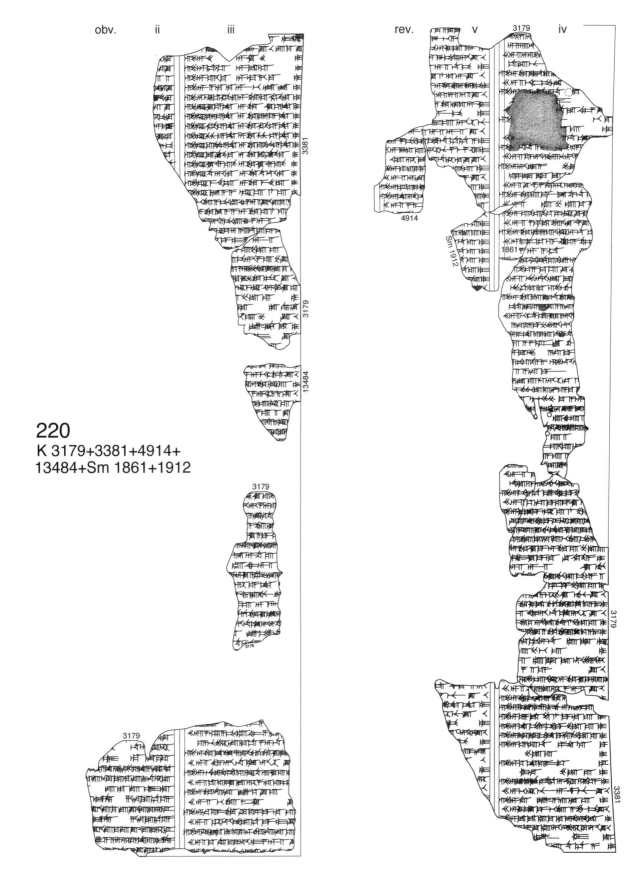

220
K 3179+3381+4914+
13484+Sm 1861+1912

Plate 123   *zi—pàd Incantations*   153

220 K 3179+3381+4914+13484+Sm 1861+1912

upper obv.   ii   iii

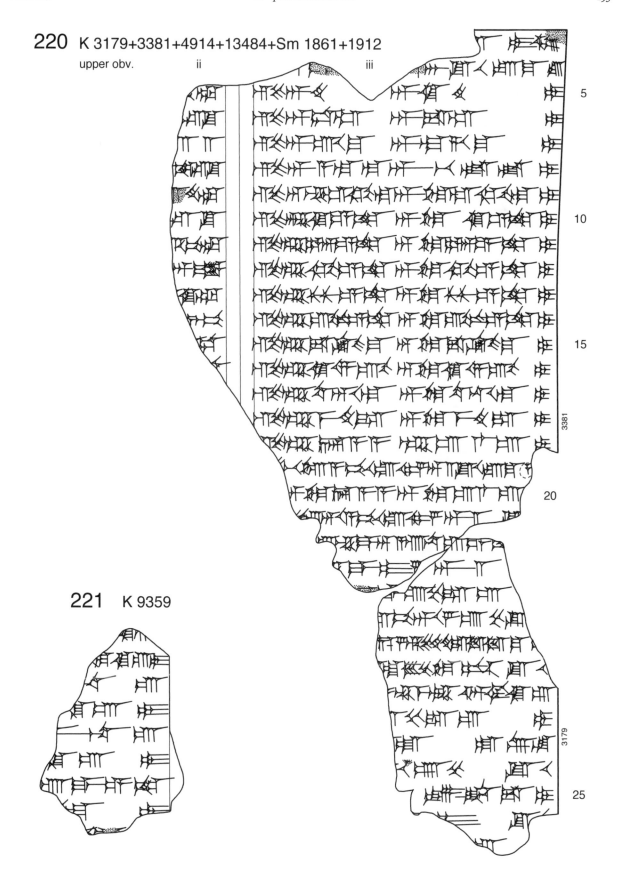

222   DT 91

obv.

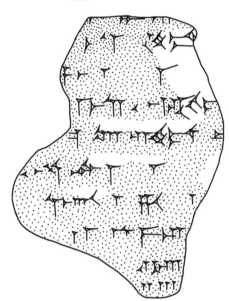

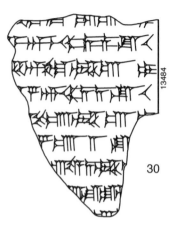

13484

30

220
K 3179+3381+4914+
13484+Sm 1861+1912

middle obverse

iii

rev.   60

64

37

40

43

3179

220   K 3179+3381+4914+13484+Sm 1861+1912

lower obv.

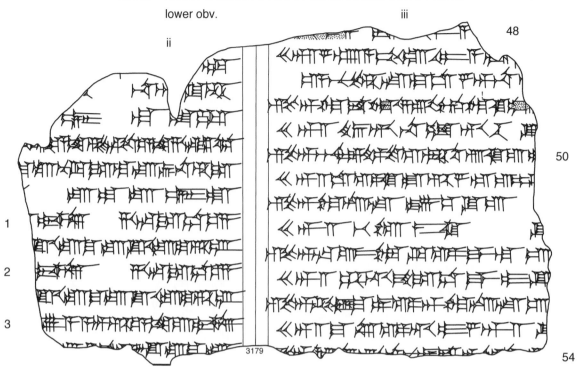

223   BM 44216

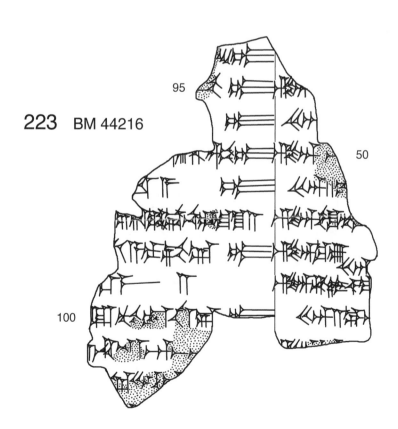

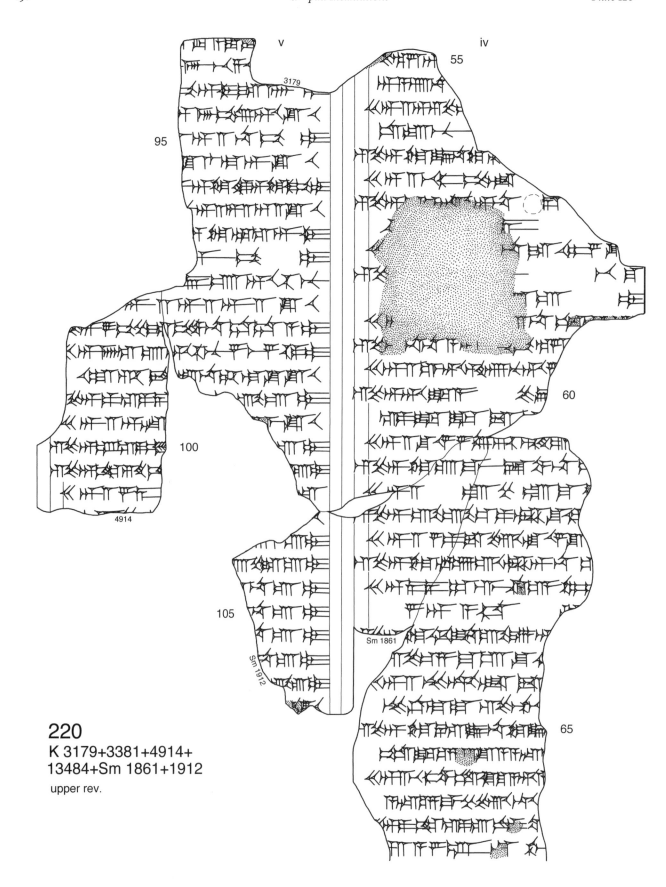

220
K 3179+3381+4914+
13484+Sm 1861+1912

upper rev.

Plate 127   *zi—pàd Incantations*   157

iv

220
K 3179+3381+4914+
13484+Sm 1861+1912

middle rev.

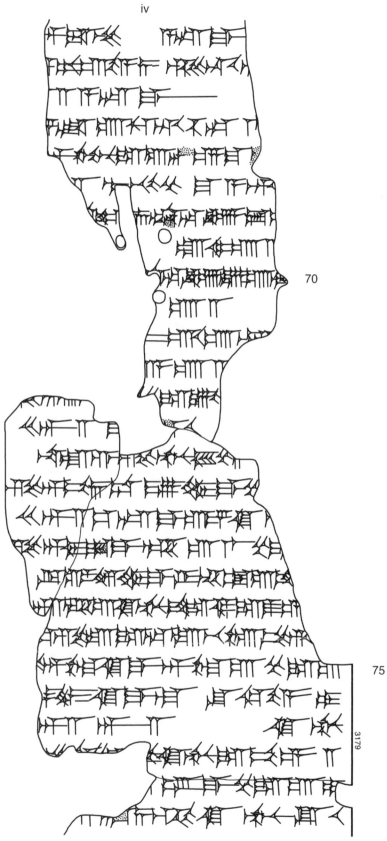

220
K 3179+3381+4914+
13484+Sm 1861+1912

lower rev.

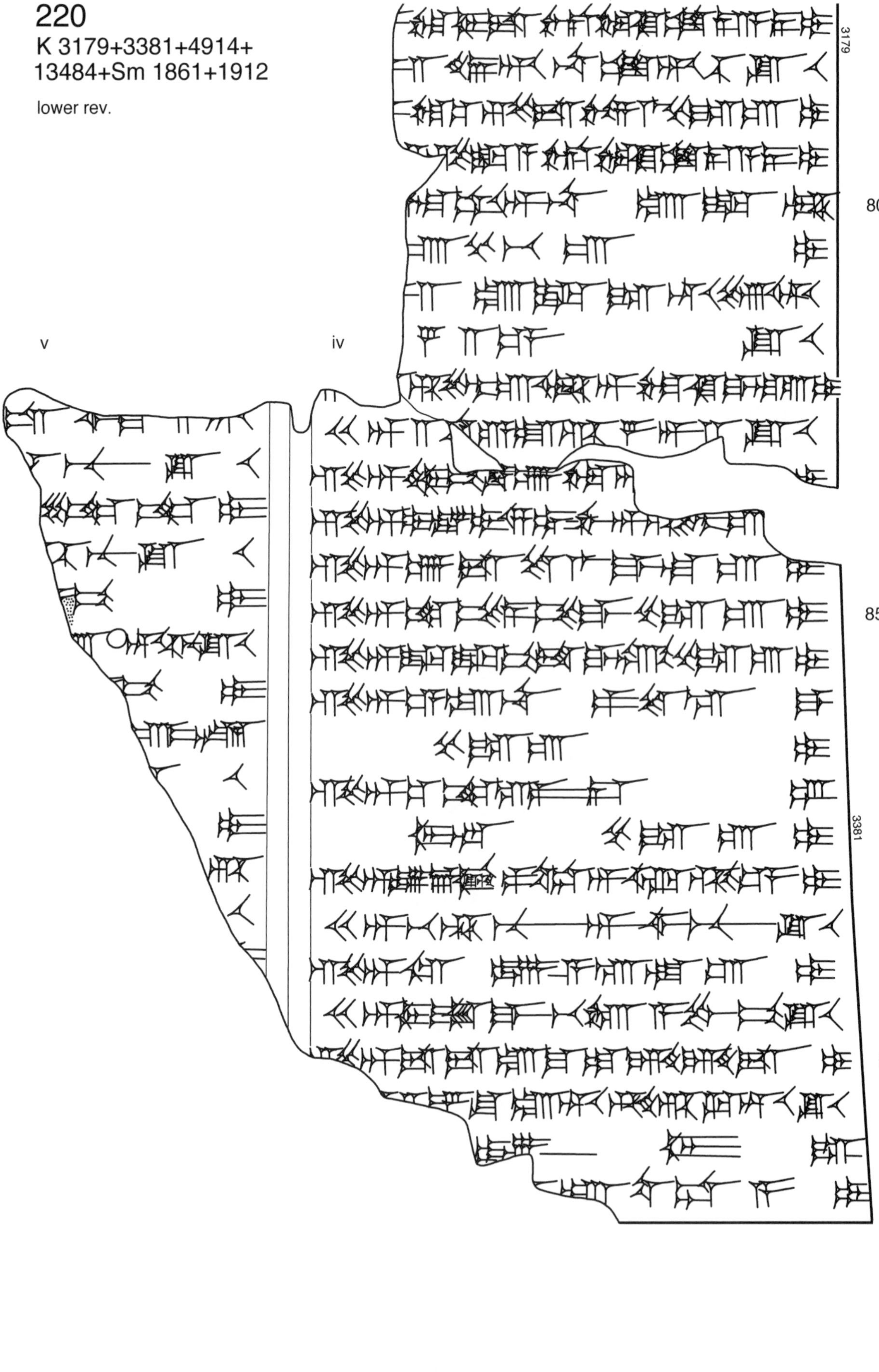

v

iv

3179

80

85

3381

90

Plate 129   *zi—pàd Incantations*   159

224   BM 40805

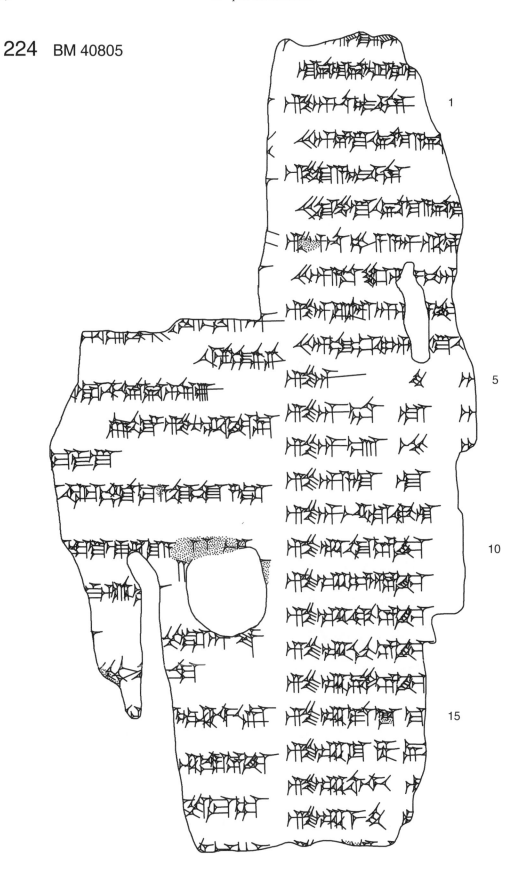

225 BM 48168

obv.   rev.

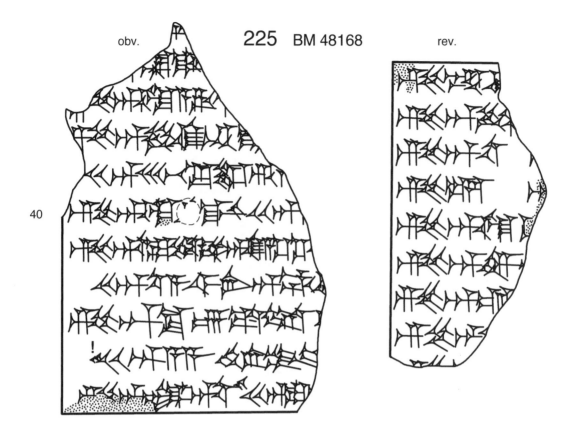

40

226 BM 72015

obv.?

80

rev.?

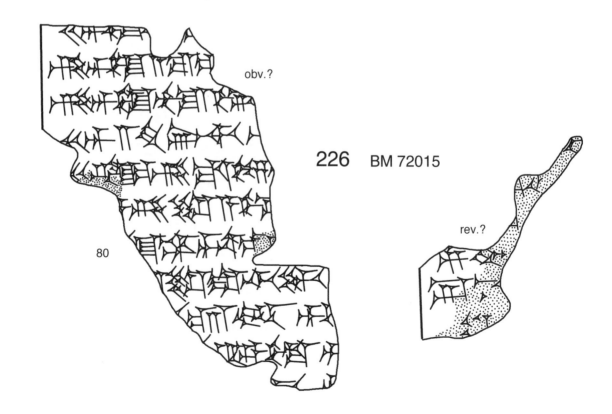

Plate 131

227 CBS 590 obv. i

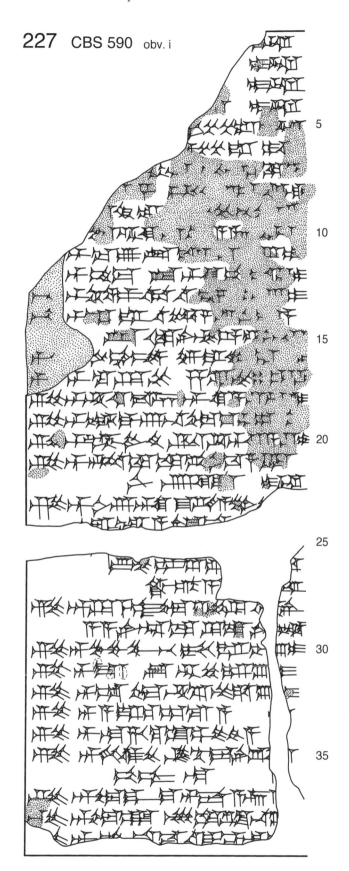

227 CBS 590

obv. ii

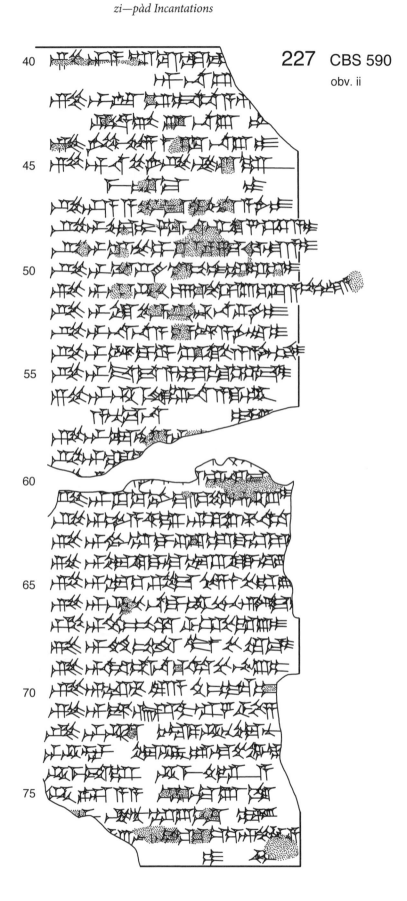

Plate 133   *zi—pàd Incantations*   163

227 CBS 590

rev. iii

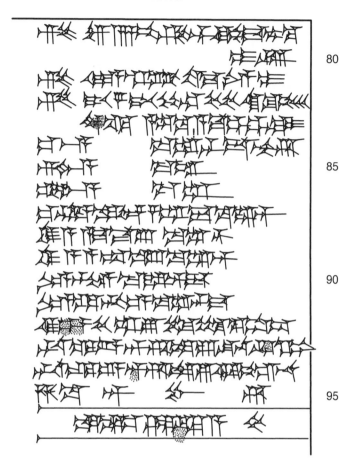

80

85

90

95

228 K 14763   ## 229 K 16753

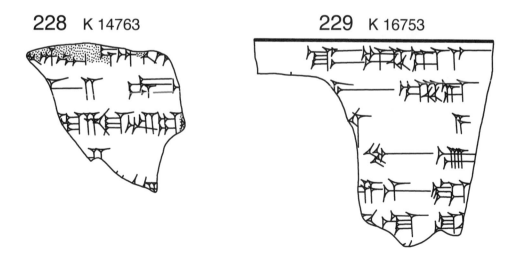

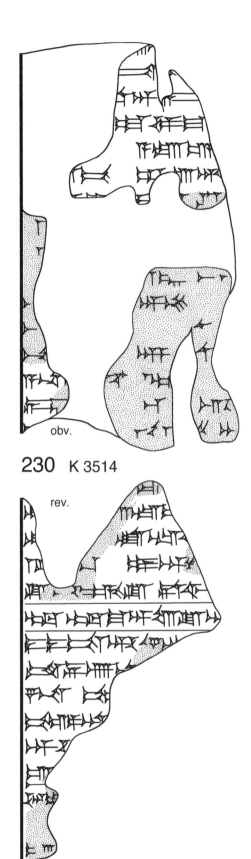

obv.

230 K 3514

rev.

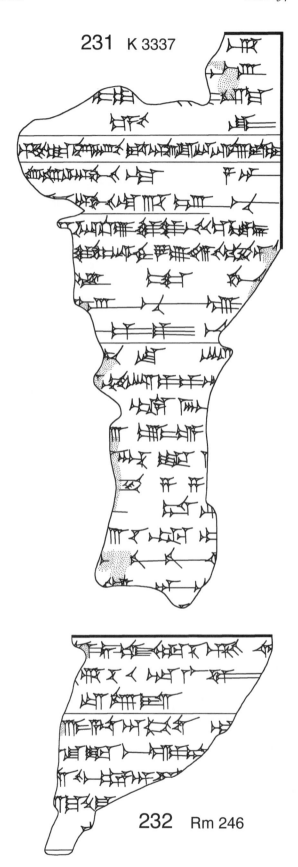

231 K 3337

232 Rm 246

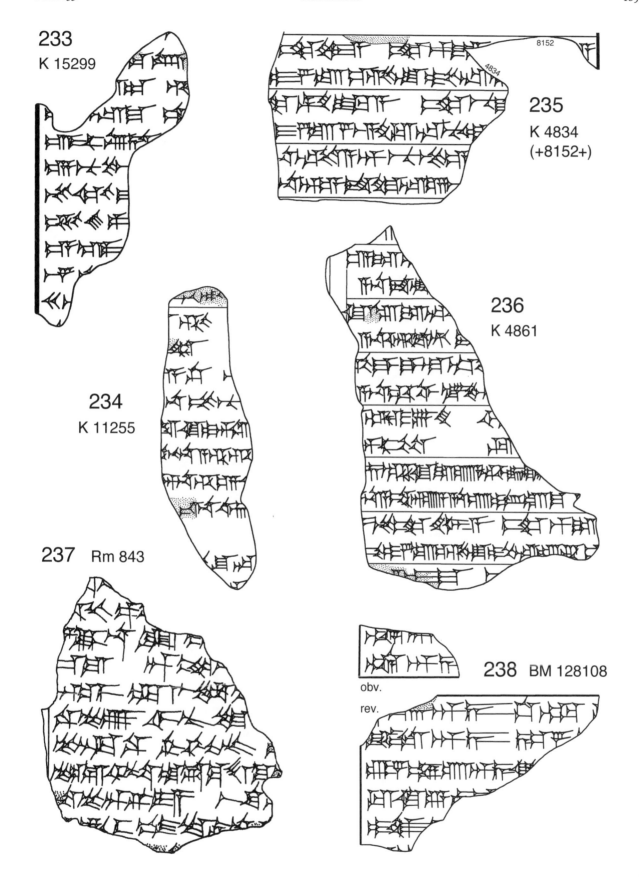

239

K 6335

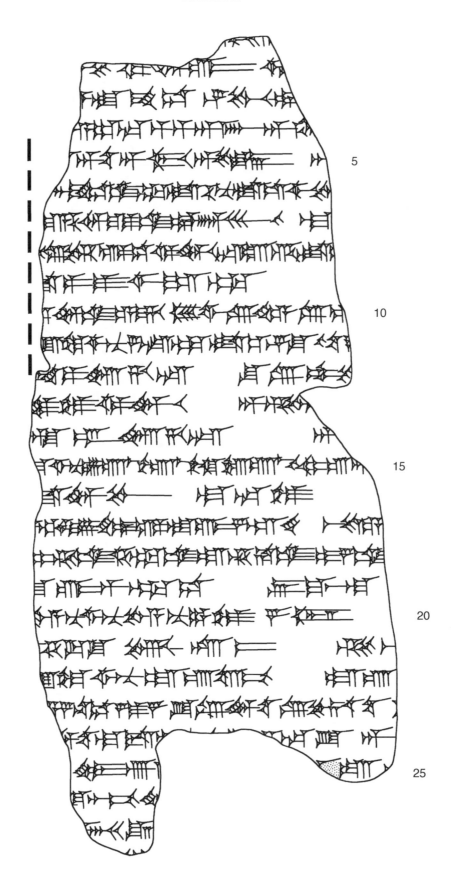

Plate 137

240   K 8104

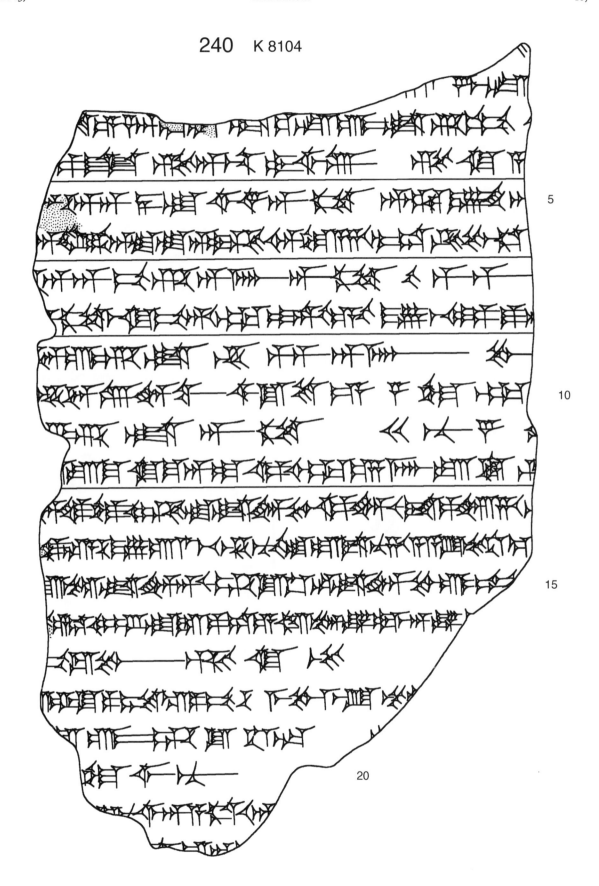

5

10

15

20

241   82-5-22, 535

obv.?   rev.?

Plate 139

242 Rm 595

243 K 10896

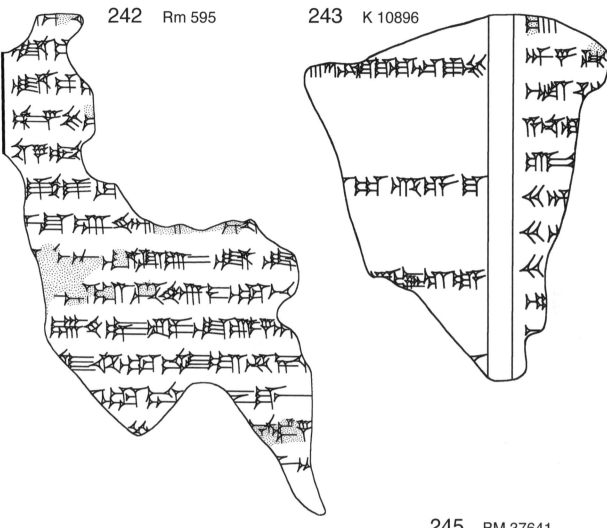

245 BM 37641

244 K 14713

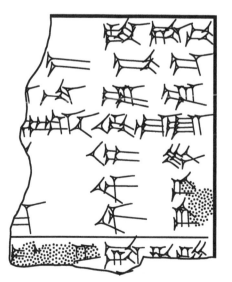

246

K 5416a+
BM 98584+
98589

obv.

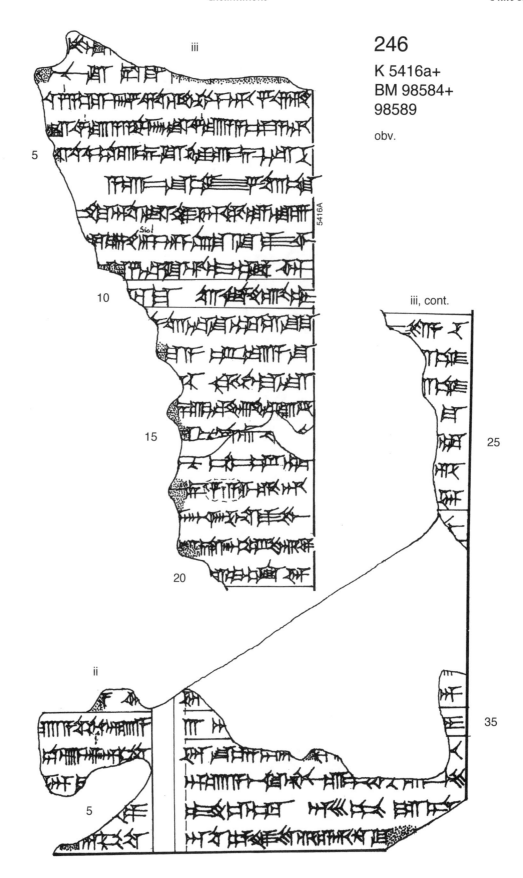

Plate 141   *Incantations*   171

iv

246

K 5416a+
BM 98584+
98589

rev.

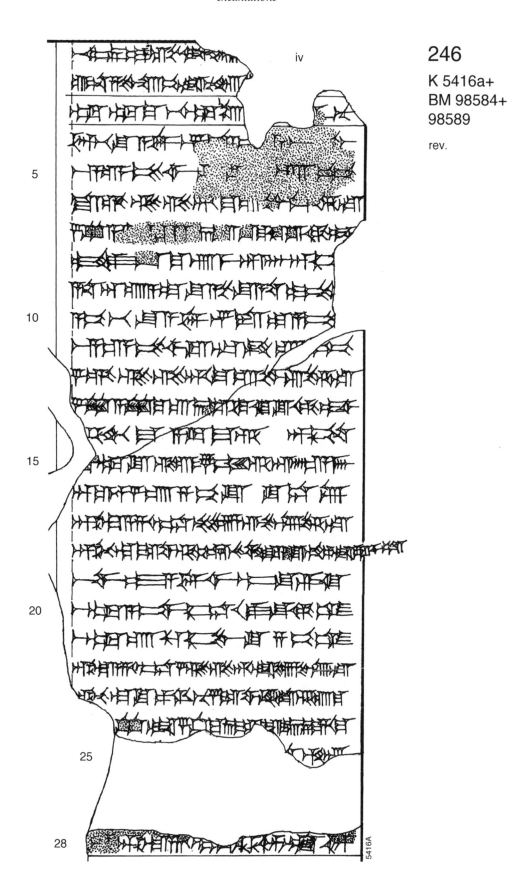

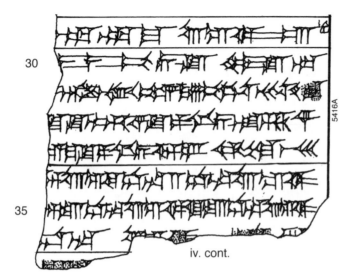

246

K 5416a+
BM 98584+
98589

rev., cont.

iv. cont.

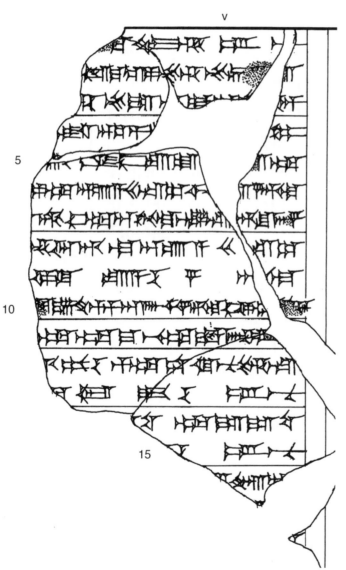

v

Plate 143   *Incantations*   173

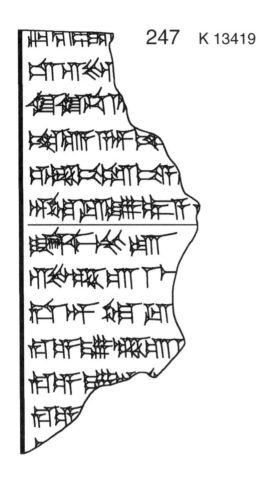

247   K 13419

248   K 10111

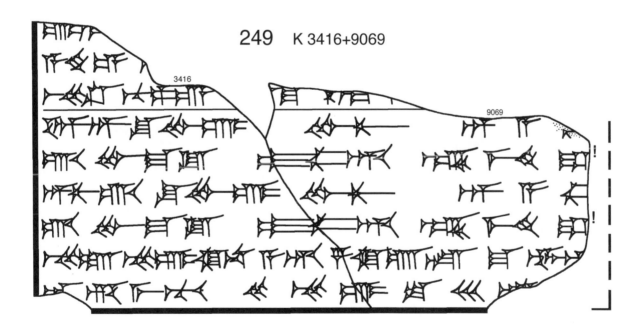

249   K 3416+9069

250 K 9355

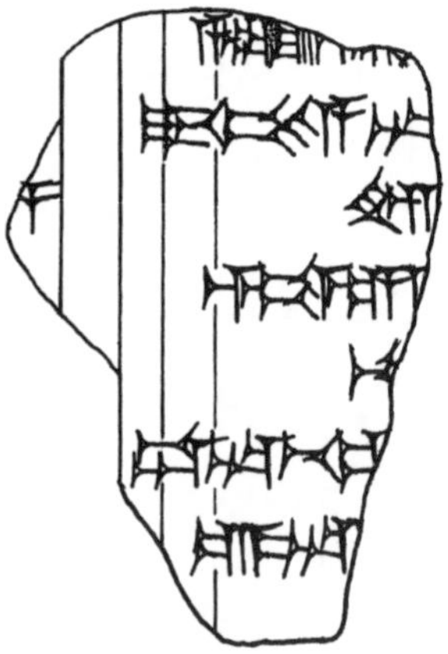

251 K 11984

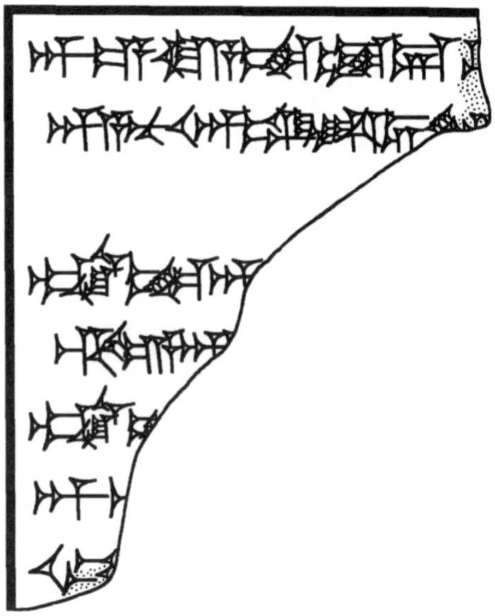

252

BM 68589

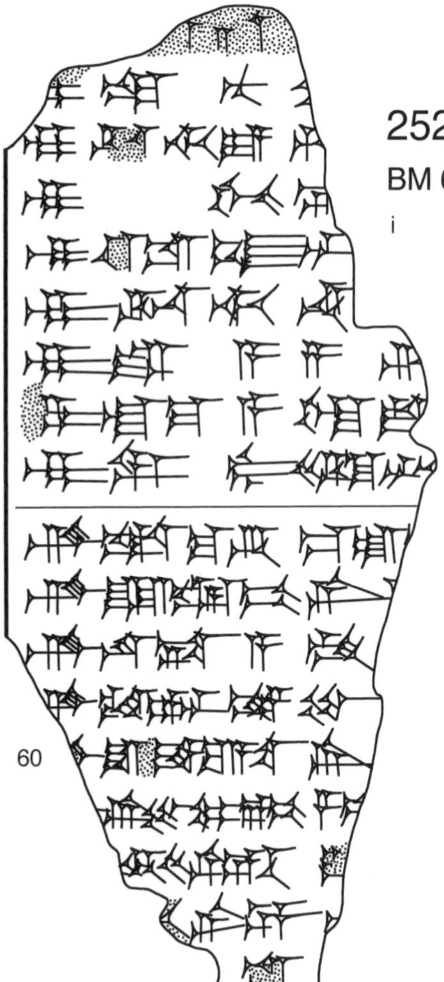

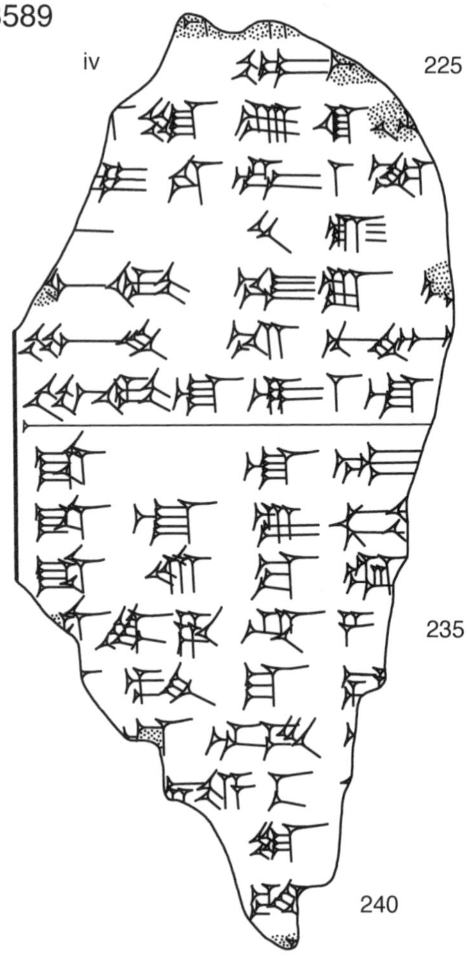

i   iv

50

55

60

65

225

230

235

240

Plate 145

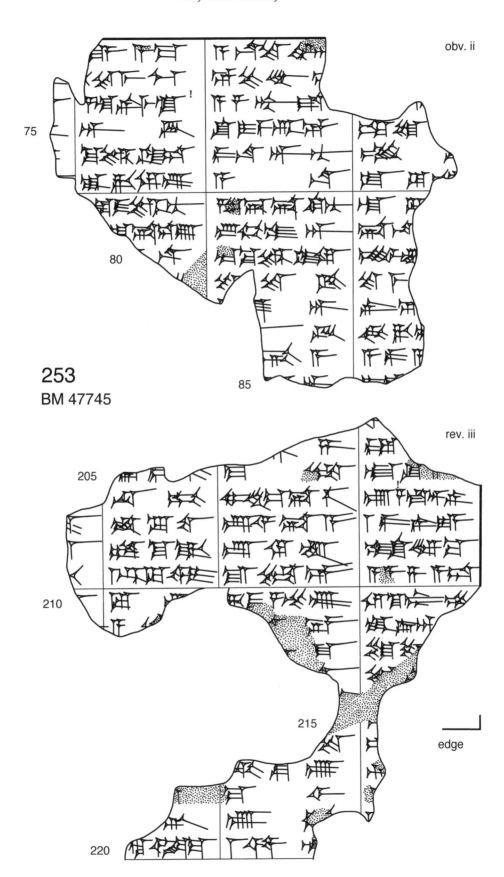

obv. ii

75

80

85

253

BM 47745

rev. iii

205

210

215

edge

220

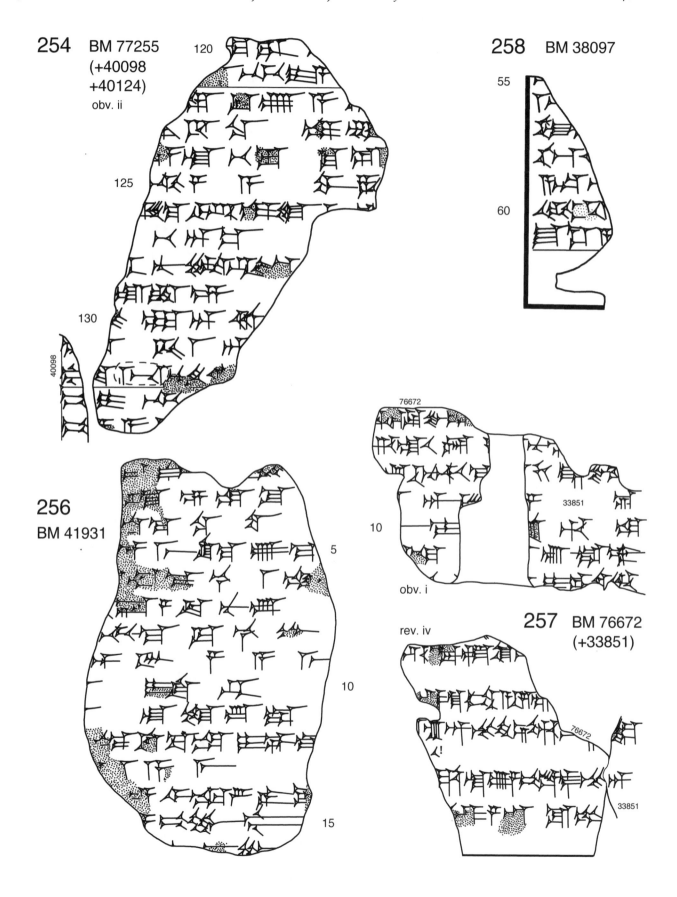

Plate 147   Babylonian Theodicy   177

255   BM 66882+76009+76506+76832+83044+83045+83046
upper obv.

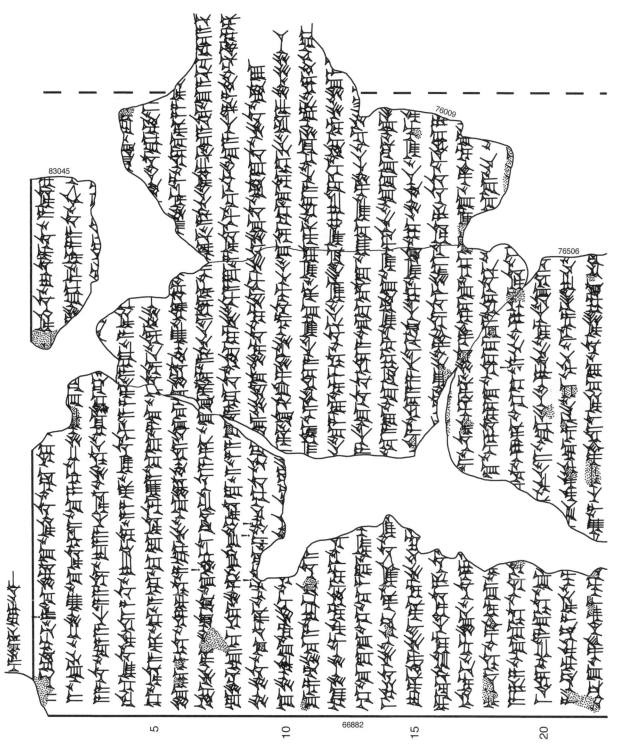

255   BM 66882+76009+76506+76832+83044+83045+83046
lower obv.

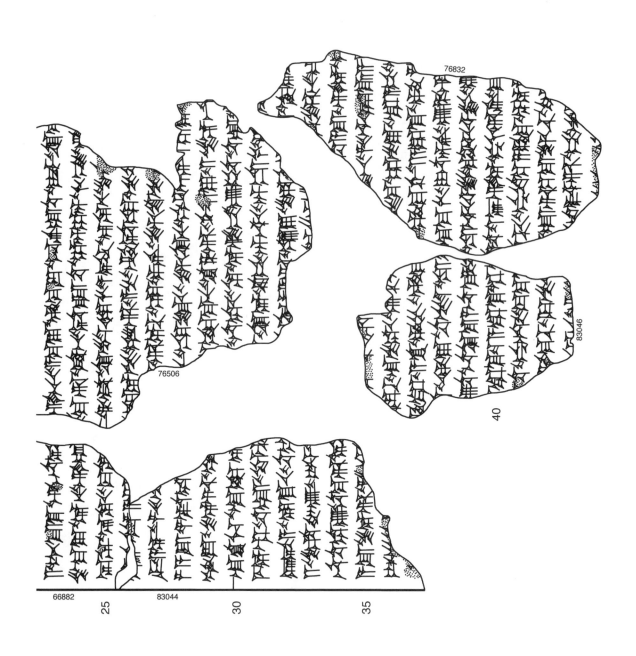

Plate 149 *Babylonian Theodicy* 179

255 BM 66882+76009+76506+76832+83044+83045+83046

upper rev.

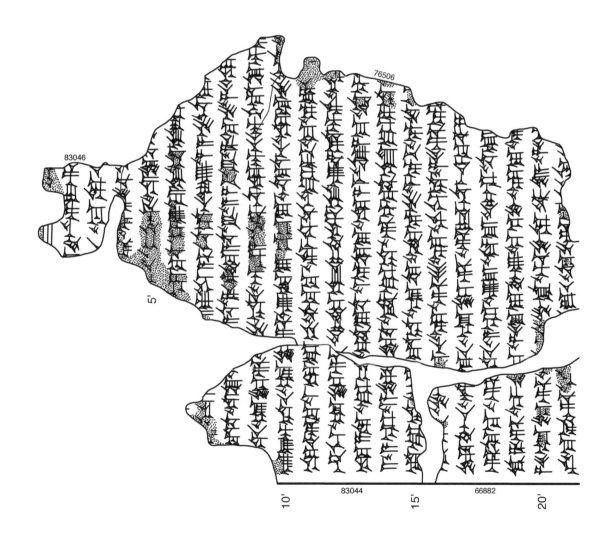

255 BM 66882+76009+76506+76832+83044+83045+83046
lower rev.

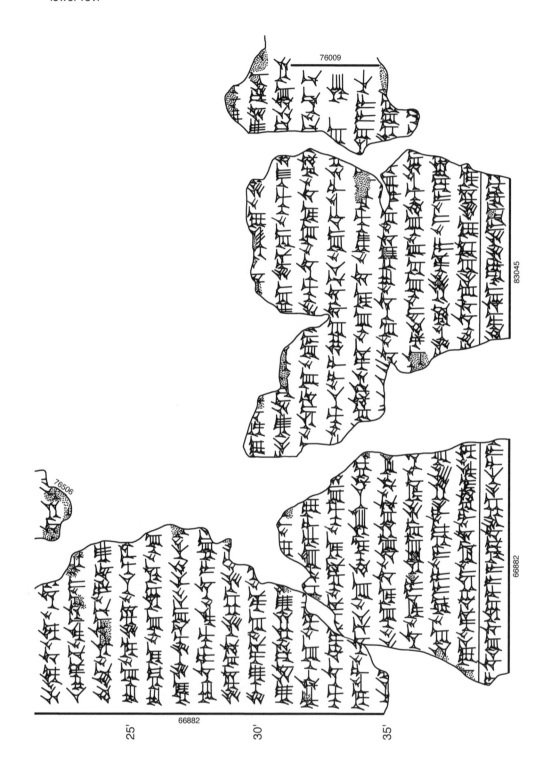

Plate 151   *Counsels of Wisdom*   181

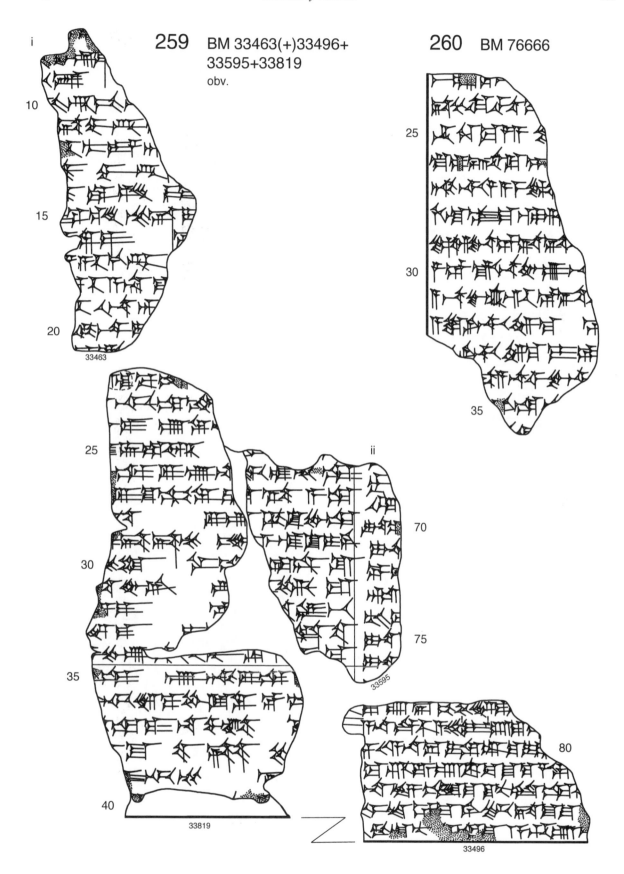

259   BM 33463(+)33496+
33595+33819
obv.

260   BM 76666

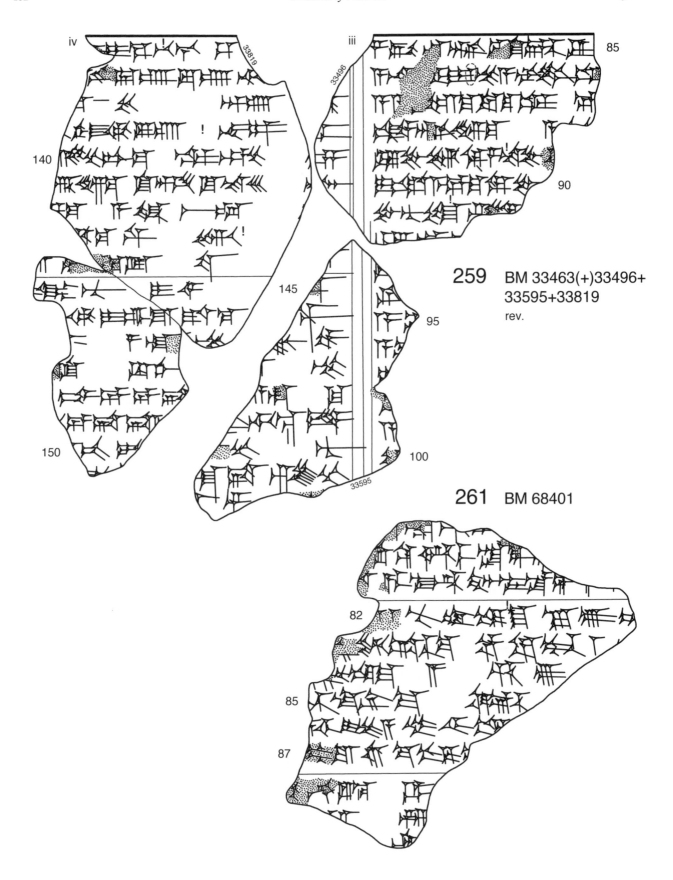

259 BM 33463(+)33496+
33595+33819
rev.

261 BM 68401

Plate 153 *Counsels of Wisdom* 183

262 BM 38484+38488   263 82-5-22, 555

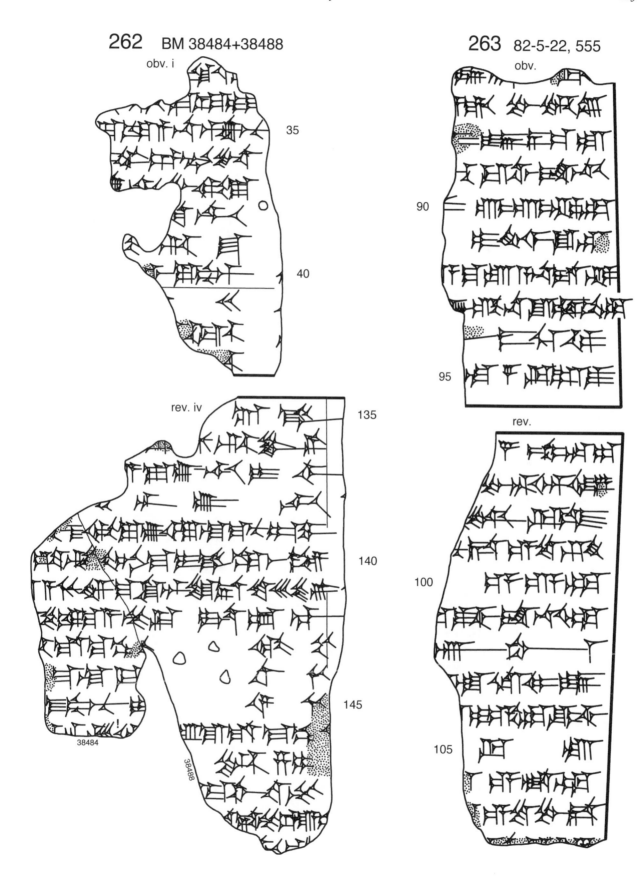

264
BM 51070
obv.

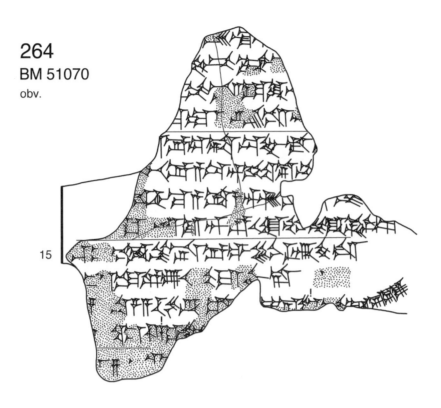

15

265
BM 80065

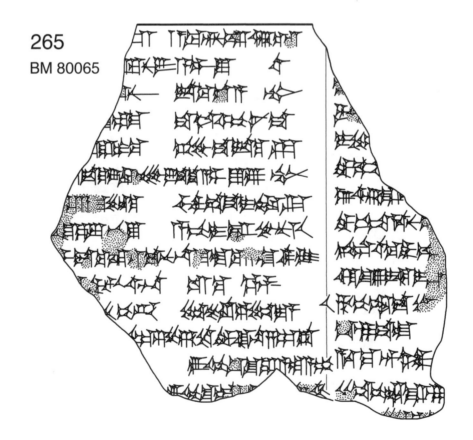

Plate 155   *Instructions of Šuruppak*   185

266 BM 50522+52767+52946+77468

obv.

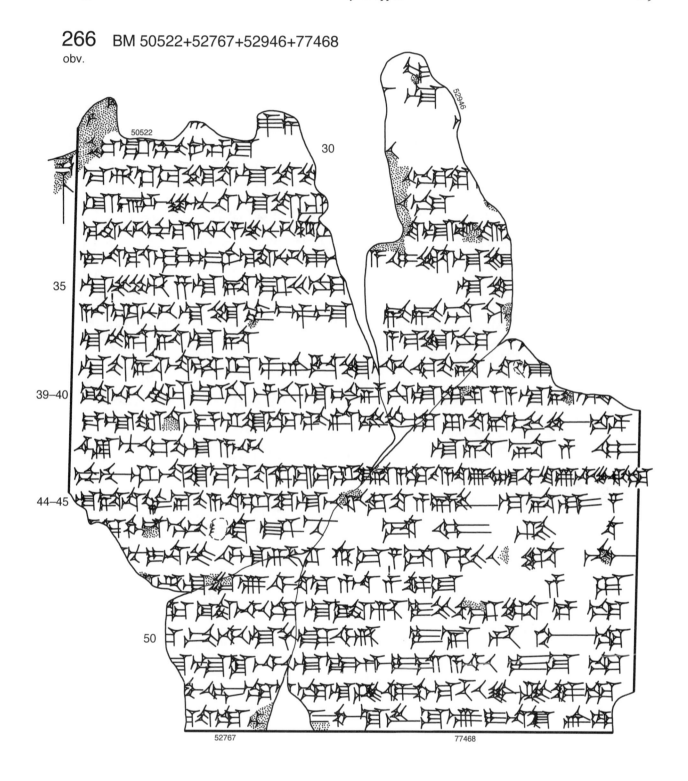

266   BM 50522+52767+52946+77468
rev.

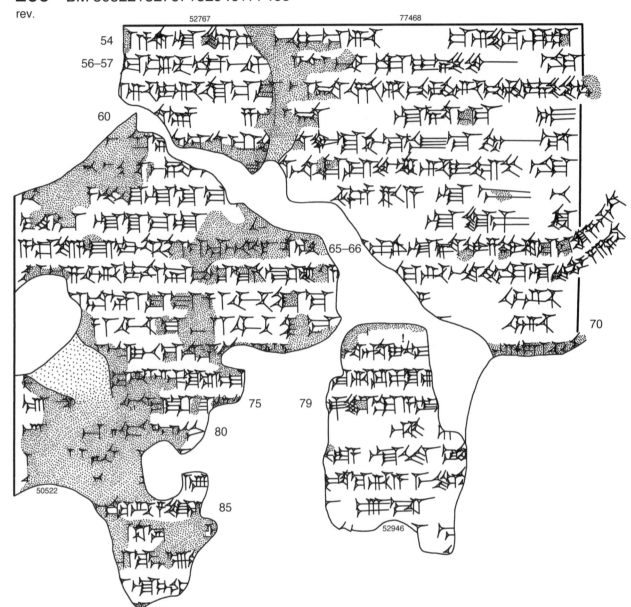

Plate 157   Admonitions   187

267 K 9471
obv.

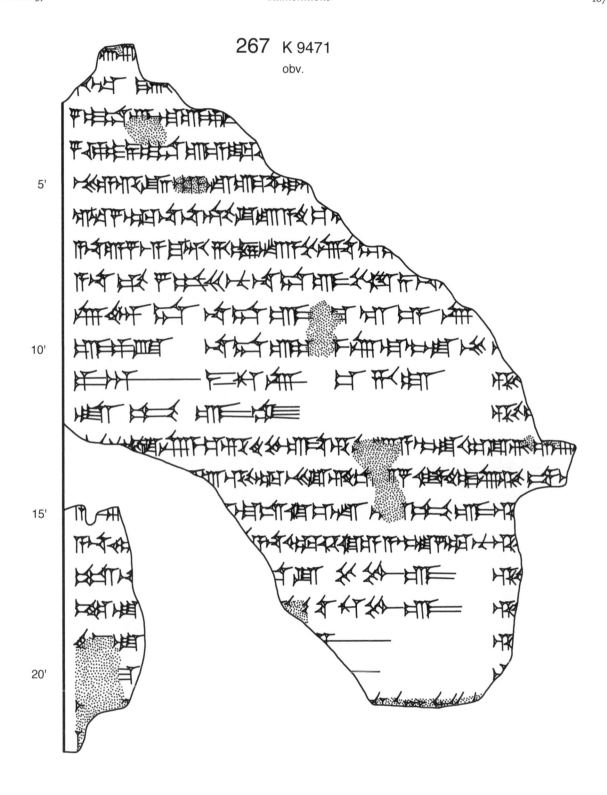

267 K 9471

rev.

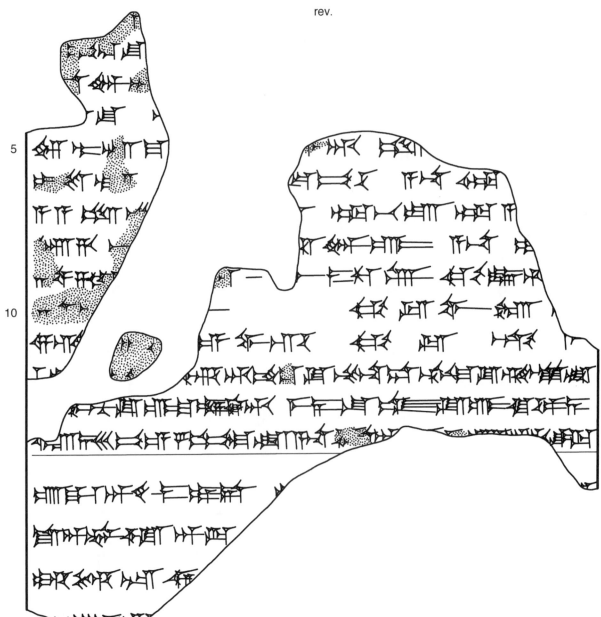

Plate 159

obv.   **268** K 8954   rev.

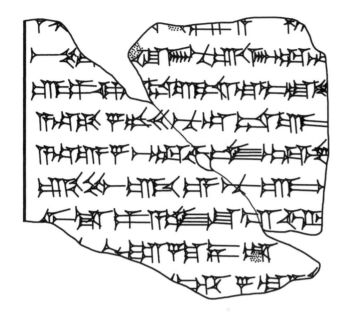

obv.   **269** F 224   rev.

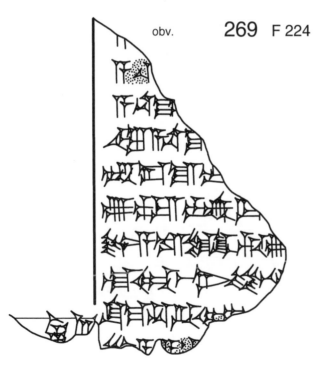

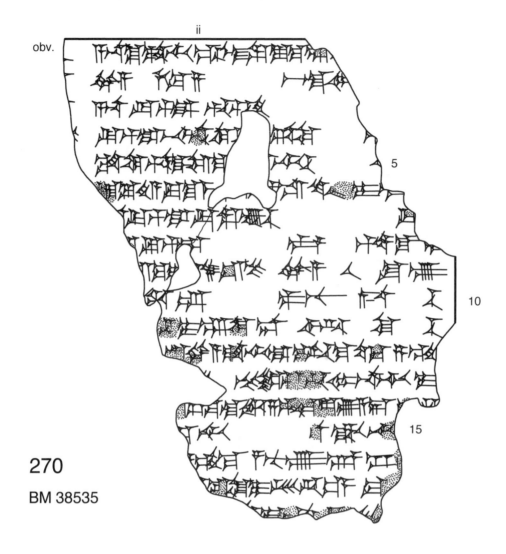

270

BM 38535

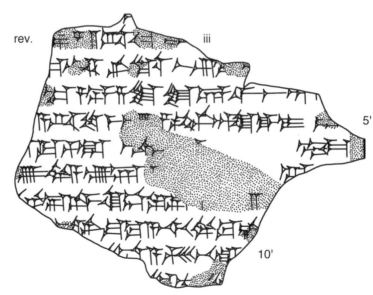

272

Ash. Mus. 1924-2050

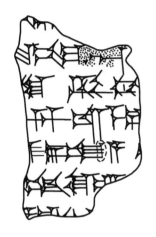

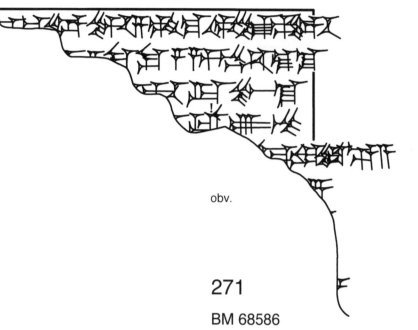

obv.

271

BM 68586

273

K 13841

rev.

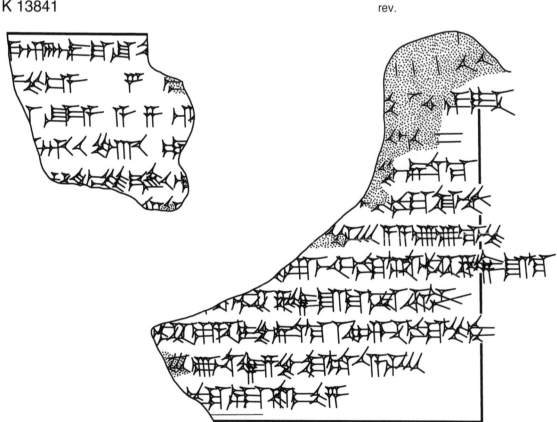

274   CBS 2266+2301+8803+8803a+11300+N 921

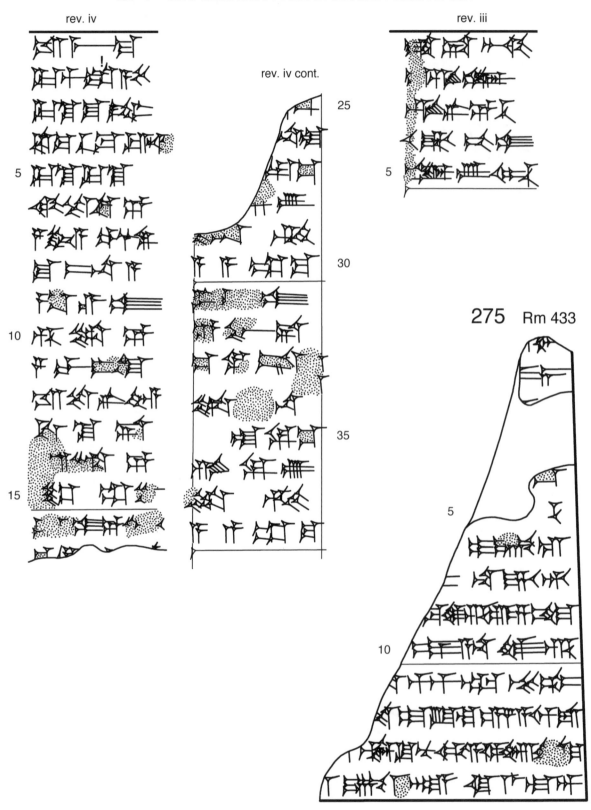

275   Rm 433

Plate 163

274   CBS 2266+2301+8803+8803a+11300+N 921

rev. v   rev. v cont.   rev. vi

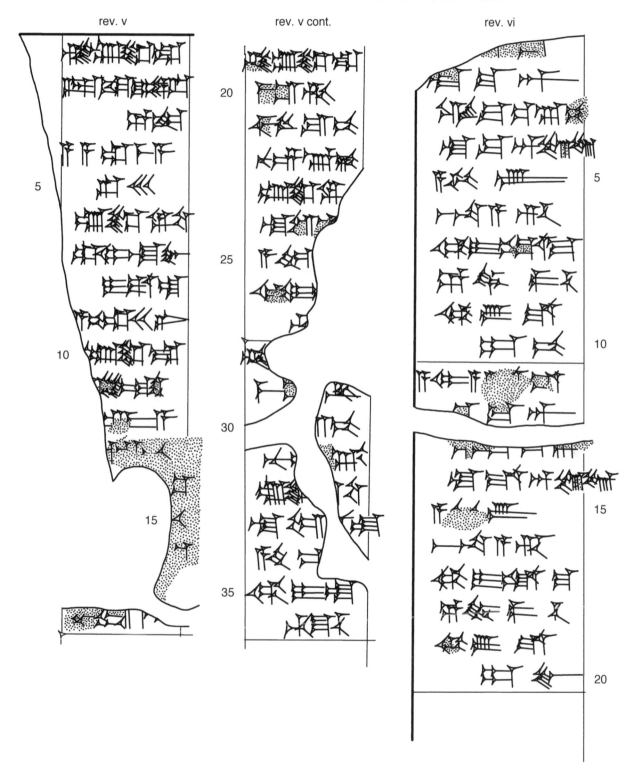

276 BM 34654 obv.

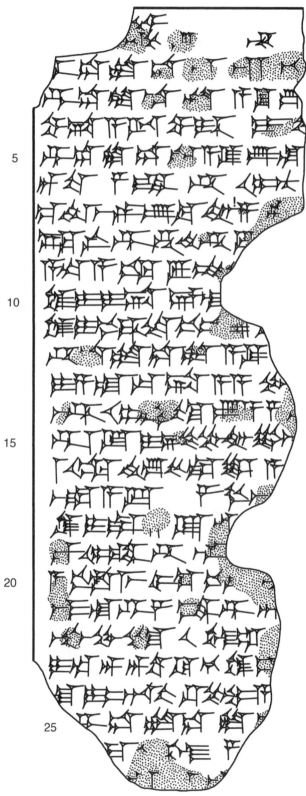

276   BM 34654   rev.

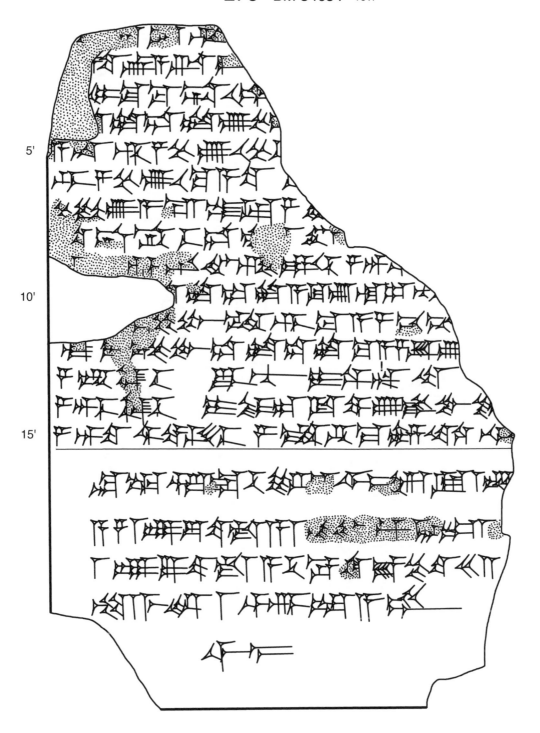

277 BM 35622

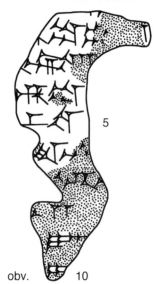

obv.   5   10

rev.

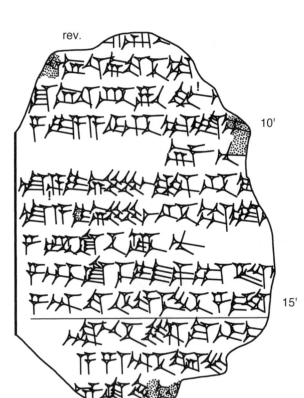

10'

15'

278 BM 46735

rev.(?)

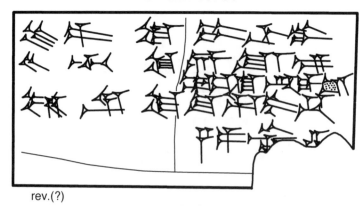

obv.(?)

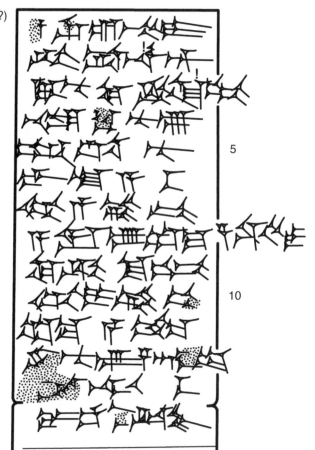

5

10

Plate 167   Proverbs and Precepts   197

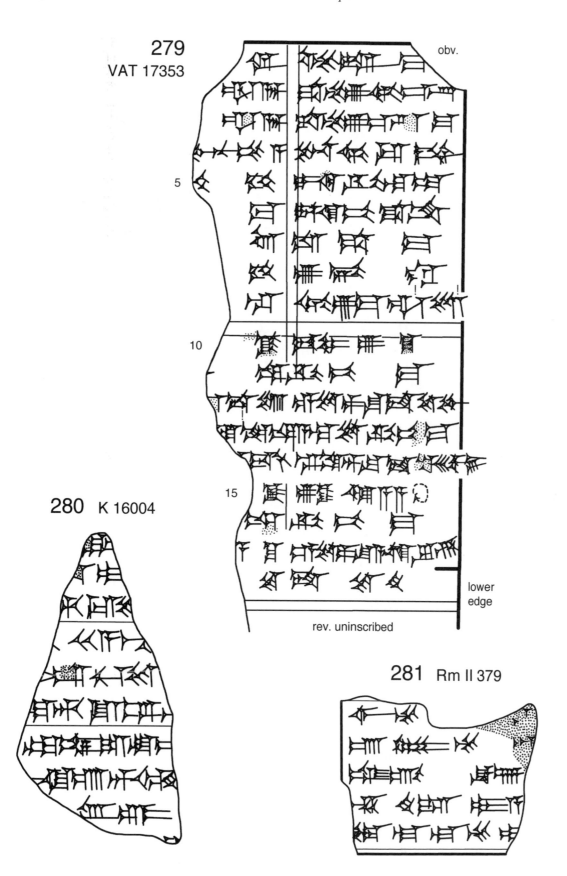

282

Rm II 311+
80-7-19, 282
(+289)

obv. ii

rev. iv

80-7-19, 289

Rm II 311

80-7-19, 282

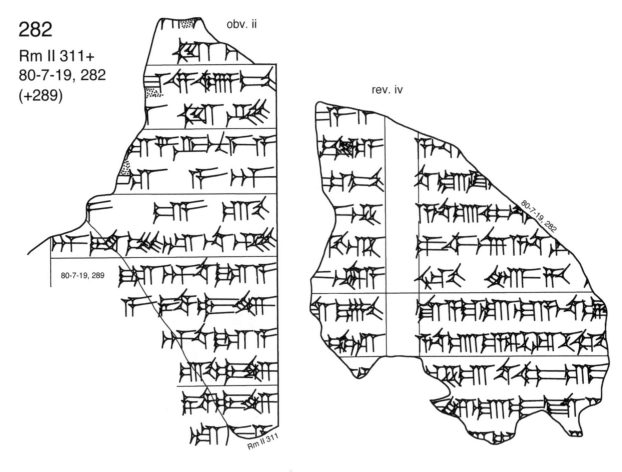

283

K (8206)+
14056

14056

8206

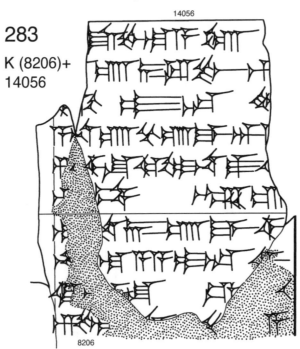

285   K 14143

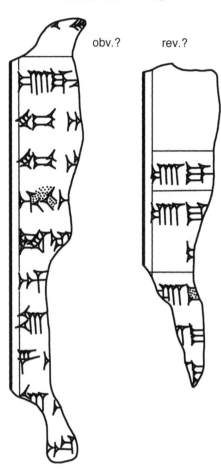

obv.?   rev.?

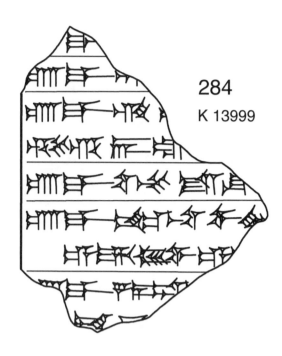

284

K 13999

287   Sm 1784

286   81-2-4, 376

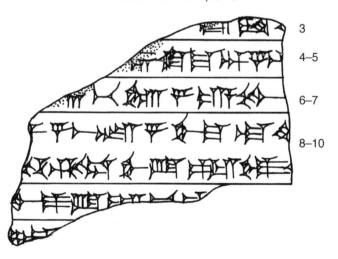

3

4–5

6–7

8–10

288 K 6080

289
K (7654+)
17246

290 K 11224

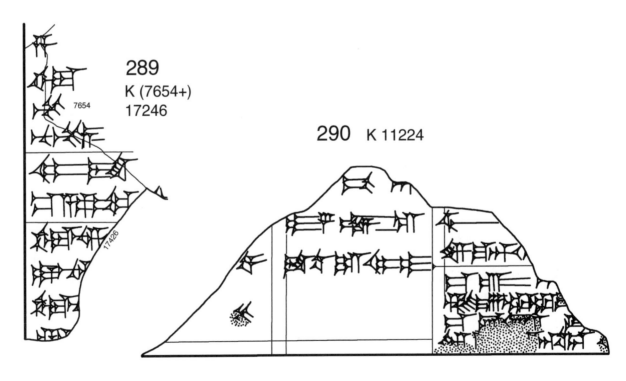

Plate 171 Proverbs and Precepts 201

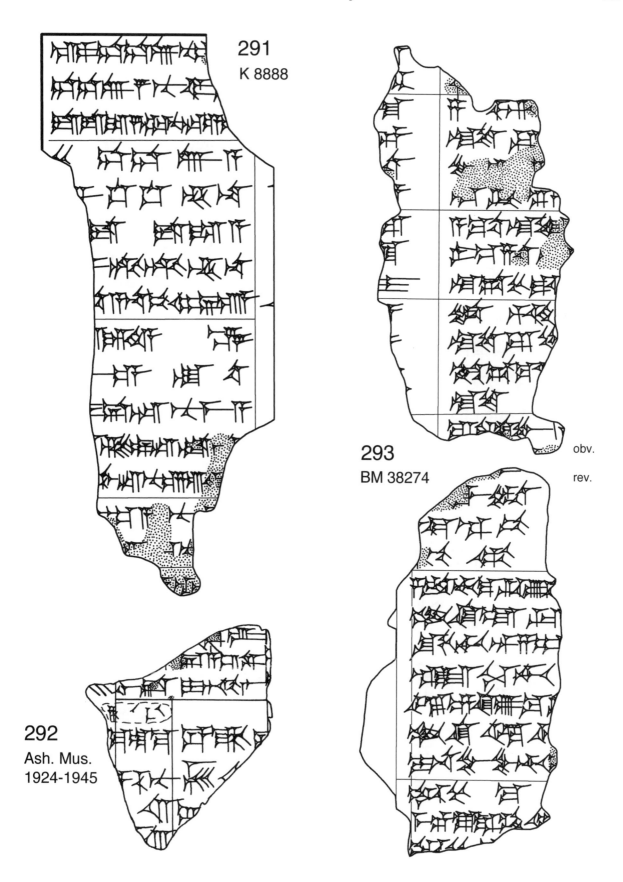

291
K 8888

293
BM 38274

obv.

rev.

292
Ash. Mus.
1924-1945

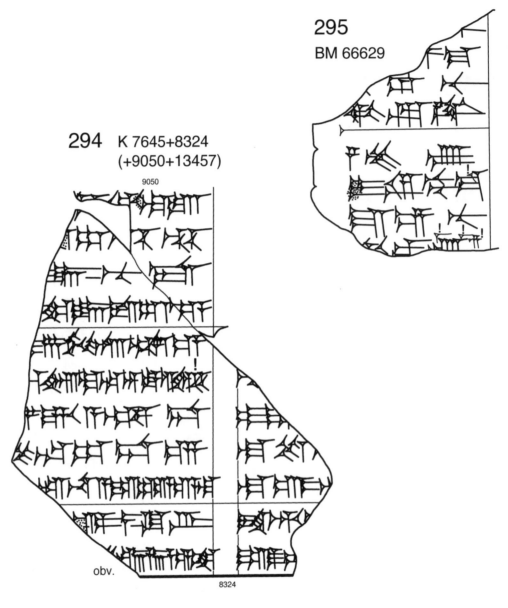

294   K 7645+8324 (+9050+13457)

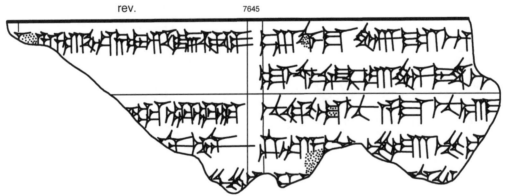

295   BM 66629

Plate 173   Proverbs and Precepts   203

296 BM 38554b

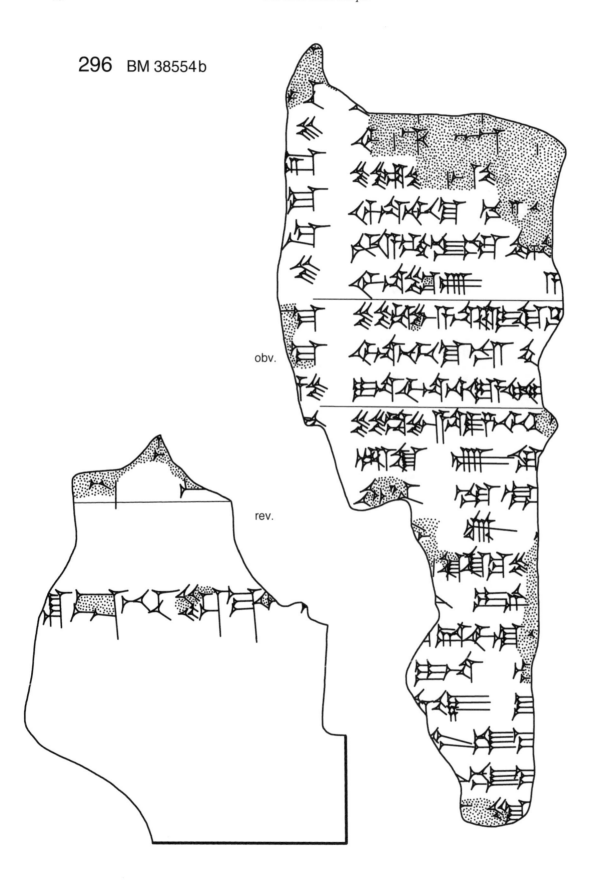

obv.

rev.

297 BM 121076

298 BM 66647 rev.

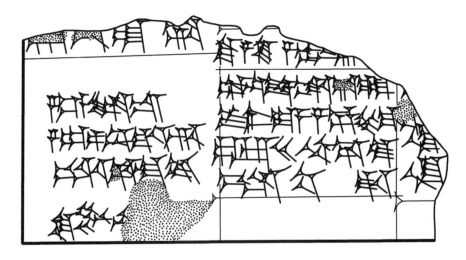

299

BM (56607+) 68060+68590+
76257+82989

obv.

299

BM (56607+) 68060+68590+
76257+82989

rev.

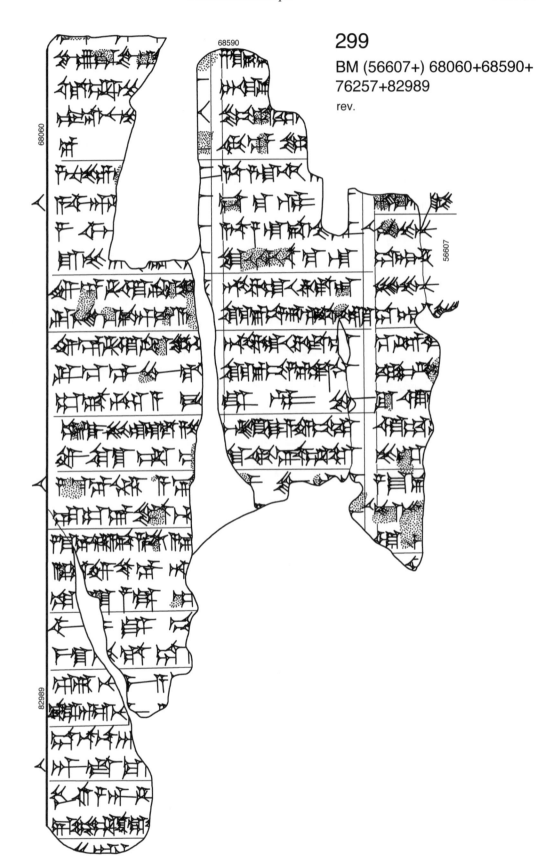

300
BM 33885
rev.

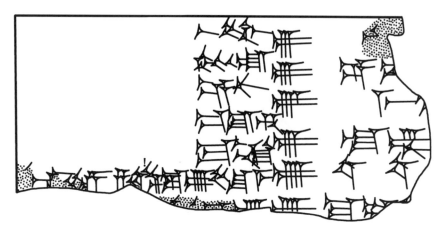

301
K 4551
obv.

302 K 7437

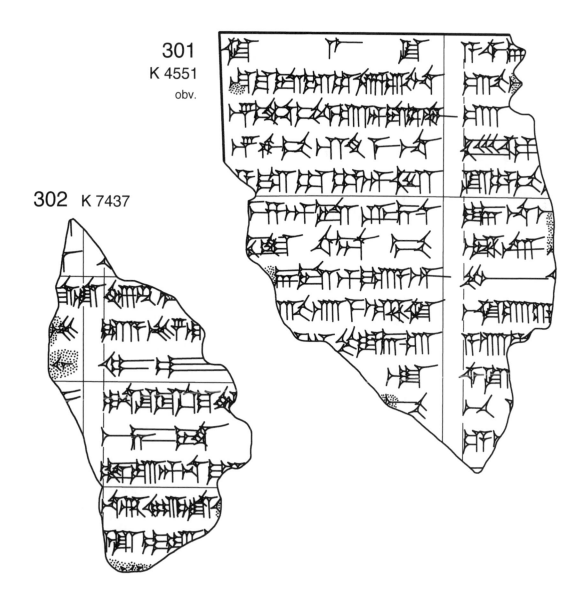

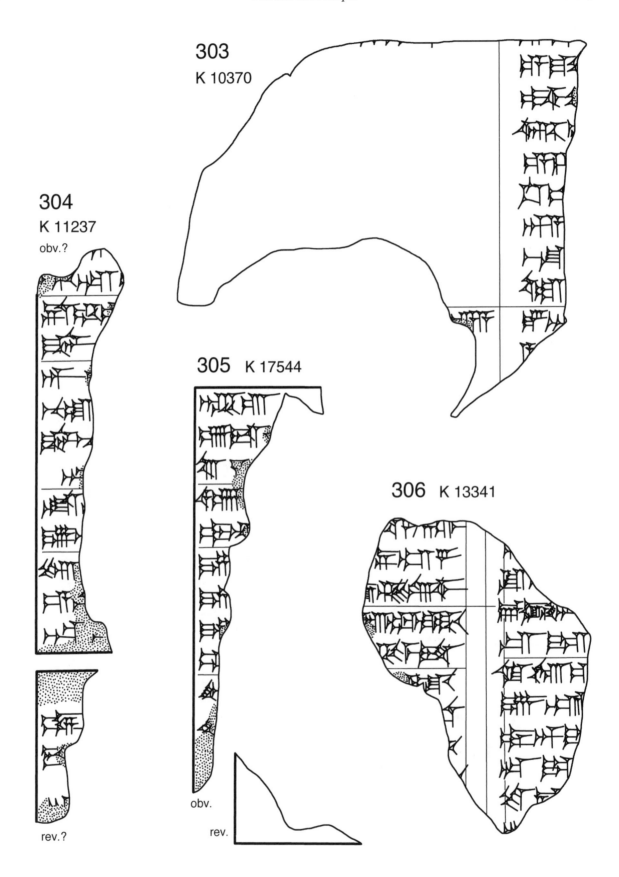

Plate 179

307
K 14178

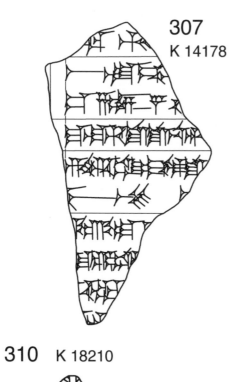

308
K 17540

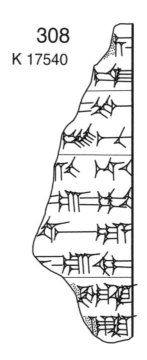

310   K 18210

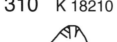

309   K 18116

311
K 21424

312
K 16804

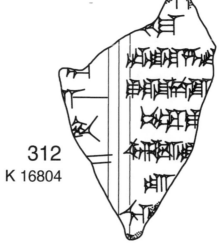

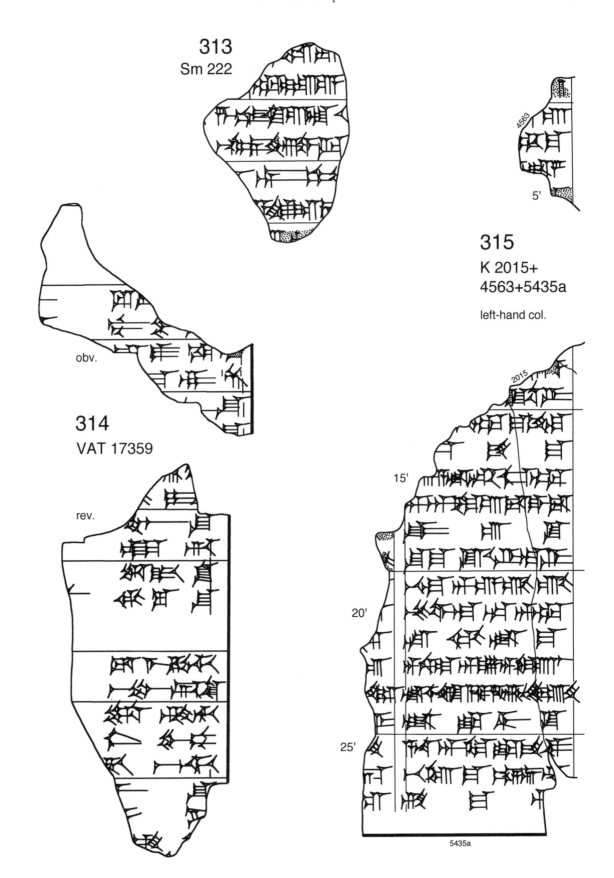

313
Sm 222

315
K 2015+
4563+5435a

left-hand col.

314
VAT 17359

obv.

rev.

5'

15'

20'

25'

5435a

Plate 181 *Proverbs and Precepts* 211

315
K 2015+
4563+5435a

right-hand col.

316 79-7-8, 209

317 K 10715

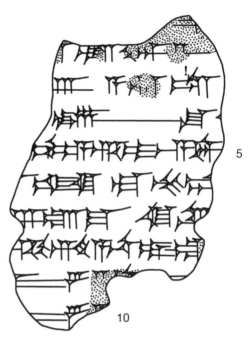

318 K 1578

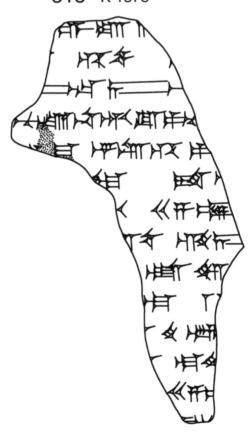

319 K 5252

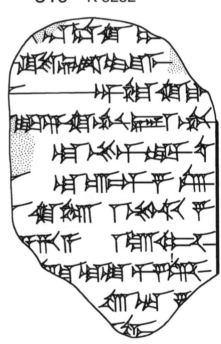

320
K 5911

321 K 9987

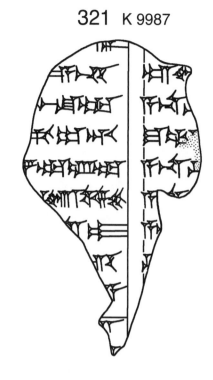

322 K 10912

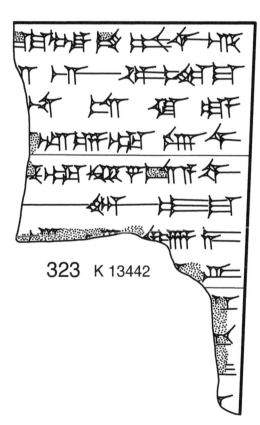

323 K 13442

324   K 11411

325   81-7-27, 106

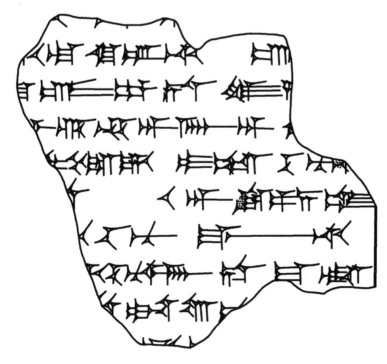

326   K 13859

328   Sm 1783

327   Rm 221

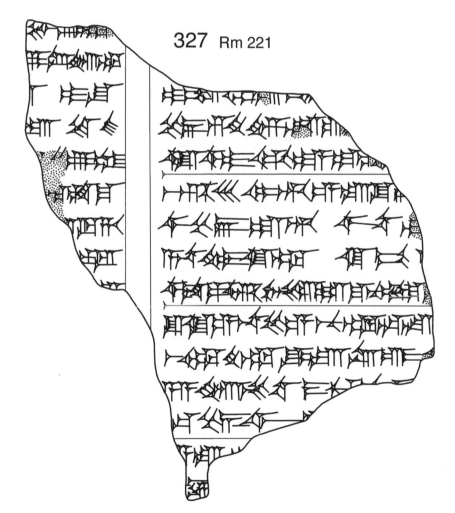

Unidentified Literary Compositions Plate 186

329 BM 33842

obv.

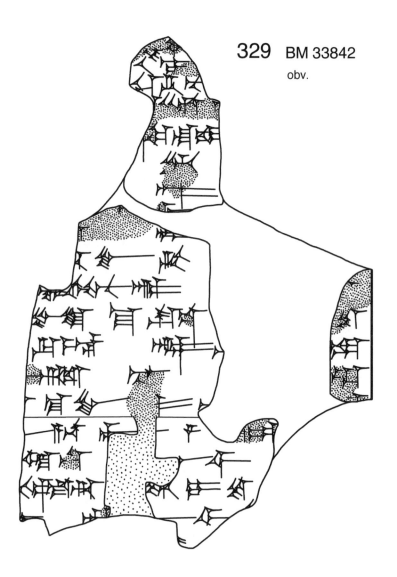

329   BM 33842

rev.